MW01412801

MICROSOFT WINDOWS PROGRAM DEVELOPMENT

Michael I. Hyman

MANAGEMENT INFORMATION SOURCE, INC.

COPYRIGHT

Copyright © 1988 by Michael I. Hyman
Published by Management Information Source, Inc.
1107 N.W. 14th Avenue
Portland, Oregon 97209
(503) 222-2399

Second Printing

ISBN 0-943518-34-2

Library of Congress Catalog Card Number:87-15379

All rights reserved. Reproduction or use, without express permission of editorial or pictorial content, in any manner is prohibited. No patent liability is assumed with respect to the use of the information contained herein. While every precaution has been taken in the preparation of this book, the publisher assumes no responsibility for errors or omissions. Neither is any liability assumed for damages resulting from the use of the information contained herein.

IBM PC and AT are trademarks of IBM Corporation

Microsoft Windows, Windows Software Development Toolkit, Assembler, and C are all trademarks of Microsoft Corporation

ACKNOWLEDGMENTS

I'd like to thank Bob Williams, Chris Williams, and Kim Thomas of MIS, Inc. for all their help with this project. Many thanks to Microsoft Corporation, in particular, Steve Ballmer, Nathan Mehrvold, and Dave Pritchard. Finally, I'd like to thank Richard and Roberta Hyman, Betsy Hyman, and Mirna Goldberger.

TABLE OF CONTENTS

Introduction vii
    What You Need..viii
    Companion Program Diskette...ix

Chapter 1: Introduction to the Windows Environment 1
    Why Program with Windows?...3
    Windows Really is Easy 3
    Approaching a Windows Program...4
    Style...6
    Further Differences..6
    The Overwhelming Similarity 7
    The Parts of a Windows Program 7
    Summary..8

Chapter 2: The Basic Outline of a Windows Program 9
    The Sections of a Windows Program...10
        WinMain..11
        The Initialization Routine 17
        The Message-Processing Routine 23
    A Program: TWO 24
        The Make File: TWO 26
        The Include File: TWO.H 26
        The Code: TWO.C 27
        The Module Definition: TWO.DEF 30
    Windows 2.0 Features 30
    Advanced Concepts: Variable Notations, Types, and Instances.........30
        The Module Definition File..32
        Instances 33
    Summary..34

Chapter 3: Using the Resource File: Adding Menus........................37
    Menus..38
    Choosing Menu Command Names..42
    Choosing Menu Command Names in Windows 2.0.....................................42
    Including the Menu in a Program...43
    Making Your Own Cursor..43
    Compiling Windows Programs with Resources...45
    A Program: THREE..47
        The Make File: THREE 48
        The Resource File: THREE.RC 49

  The Include File: THREE.H 49
  The Code: THREE.C 50
  The Module Definition File: THREE.DEF 53
 Advanced Concepts: Class 53
 Summary..54

Chapter 4: Input from Menus: Receiving Messages 55
 Getting Menu Commands..56
 Assigning Menu Item Numbers 57
 Changing the Cursor...58
 Using Global Variables 60
 Modifying Menu Items...61
 Making Your Own Icons 69
 A Program: FOUR1 70
  The Make File: FOUR1 72
  The Resource File: FOUR1.RC 73
  The Include File: FOUR1.H 74
  The Code: FOUR1.C 75
  The Module Definition File: FOUR1.DEF 81
 Accelerator Keys 81
 A Program: FOUR2 85
  The Make File: FOUR2 86
  The Resource File: FOUR2.RC 86
  The Include File: FOUR2.H 87
  The Code File: FOUR2.C 89
  The Module Definition File: FOUR2.DEF 95
 Summary..95

Chapter 5: Output: Text 97
 The Display Context 98
 The TextOut Function 99
 A Program: FIVE1 100
  The Make File: FIVE1 102
  The Resource File: FIVE1.RC 102
  The Include File: FIVE1.H 103
  The Code: FIVE1.C 103
  The Module Definition File: FIVE1.DEF 107
 Using and Modifying Fonts...108
 Updating the Cursor Position 112
 Text Metrics 113
 Accounting for Screen Size when Displaying Text...............................115
 Background and Text Color 116
 A Program: FIVE2 117

  The Make File: FIVE2 118
  The Resource File: FIVE2.RC 119
  The Include File: FIVE2.H 120
  The Code: FIVE2.C 121
  The Module Definition File: FIVE2.DEF 128
 Advanced Concepts: The DrawText Command................................129
 Summary 131

Chapter 6: System Messages 133
 Why Use Messages? 134
 The Messages 135
  The Window-related Messages..135
  Dialog Box Messages 137
  Mouse Messages 138
  Keyboard Messages 141
  Timer Messages 142
  Scroll Command Messages 142
  System Command Messages 144
  Other Messages 144
 A Program: SIX 145
  The Make File: SIX 146
  The Resource File: SIX.RC 147
  The Include File: SIX.H 147
  The Code: SIX.C 148
  The Module Definition File: SIX.DEF 155
 Summary 156

Chapter 7: Graphics 157
 An Introduction to GDI 158
 The Mapping Modes 159
   MM_TEXT...161
   MM_LOMETRIC 161
   MM_HIMETRIC 161
   MM_LOENGLISH 161
   MM_HIENGLISH 161
   MM_TWIPS 161
   MM_ISOTROPIC 162
   MM_ANISOTROPIC 162
 Window and Viewport..162
 Drawing Objects: Brushes, Pens, Colors..168
 The Graphics Commands 170
 Point and Line Commands 170
 Polygon, Curve, and Fill Commands..173

    Region Commands 177
    Some Examples of Using GDI: Clearing the Screen, Using
        the Mouse, and Changing the Clipping Area 182
    A Program: SEVEN 184
        The Make File: SEVEN 186
        The Resource File: SEVEN.RC 187
        The Include File: SEVEN.H 187
        The Code: SEVEN.C 189
        The Module Definition File 197
    Advanced Concepts: Metafiles 198
    Summary 200

Chapter 8: Dialog Boxes 203
    Why Use Dialog Boxes? 204
    Dialog Boxes are Windows 204
    The Dialog Box Input Features 206
    The Format of the .DLG File 208
    Adding Dialog Boxes to a Program 210
    A Program: EIGHT 220
        The Make File: EIGHT 222
        The Resource File: EIGHT.RC 222
        The Dialog Description File: EIGHT.DLG 223
        The Include File: EIGHT.H 223
        The Code: EIGHT.C 224
        The Module Definition File: EIGHT.DEF 231
    Summary 231

Chapter 9: System Resources 233
    Memory 234
    Memory, Linked Lists, and Pointers 239
    Using Disk Files 240
    Stylistic Considerations 246
    A Program: NINE 246
        The Make File: NINE 249
        The Resource File: NINE.RC 249
        The Dialog Description File: NINE.DLG 250
        The Include File: NINE.H 251
        The Disk File Access Include File: FILEIO.H 252
        The Code: NINE.C 252
        The Module Definition File: NINE.DEF 261
    Advanced Concepts: Using Assembly Language and Memory
        Models 261
        The Include File for C Programs: FILEIO.H 269

    The Disk Access Assembly Language Routines:
        FILEIO.ASM 269
    Changing the Memory Models 273
    Summary 275

Chapter 10: Miscellaneous Topics 277
    Message Boxes 278
    String Resource Tables 281
    Changeable Icons 282
    Scroll Bars 283
    Child Windows 293
    Using the Timer 297
    Programs with Multiple Instances 299
    Changing System Menus 299
    Program Cooperation 300
    Keyboard Style 303
    Debugging Hints 303
    A Program: TEN 304
        The Make File: TEN 305
        The Resource File: TEN.RC 306
        The Include File: TEN.H 307
        The Code: TEN.C 308
        The Module Definition File: TEN.DEF 320
    Advanced Concepts: Using the WIN.INI File and Printing 320
    Printing 324
    A Printing Example 327
    Advanced Printing Features 330
    Banding 331
    Summary 332

Chapter 11: The Clipboard 335
    Using the Clipboard 336
    Making Your Own Format 340
    Getting a List of Available Formats 341
    Formatting on Demand 342
    Stylistic Considerations 342
    A Program: ELEVEN 343
        The Make File: ELEVEN 345
        The Resource File: ELEVEN.RC 346
        The Include File: ELEVEN.H 347
        The Code: ELEVEN.C 348
        The Module Definition File: ELEVEN.DEF 364
    Summary 364

Chapter 12: Bit Maps and Advanced Printing 367
   What Are Bit Maps? 368
   Why Use Bit Maps? 368
   A Bit Map's Structure 369
   Displaying Bit Maps 370
   BitBlt and StretchBlt 371
   The Combine Style Options 375
   Making a Bit Map 377
   Creating a Bit Map from an Existing Image 378
   Tips on Successfully Using Bit Maps 379
   Copying a Bit Map Using the Clipboard 379
   Saving and Loading Bit Maps 382
   Additional Comments 383
   Printer Error Routines 383
   A Program: TWELVE 385
      The Make File: TWELVE 387
      The Resource File: TWELVE.RC 387
      The Dialog Description File: TWELVE.DLG 388
      The Include File: TWELVE.H 389
      The Code File: TWELVE.C 391
      The Module Definition File: TWELVE.DEF 420
   Summary 420

Bibliography 423
Index 425

INTRODUCTION

Welcome to the world of Windows programming. Windows is a powerful development environment—the wave of the future. It removes the drudgery of professional programming and provides a built-in, user-friendly interface. Programs are device-independent, multitasking, and easily transported to OS/2.

Windows has many great capabilities, but it is also complicated. The whole approach to programming, from simple input and output to the overall program structure, is quite different. And there are further precautions that must be taken because it is multitasking.

If you are familiar with general programming concepts and have a basic knowledge of C programming, this book will have you writing Windows programs in no time. For too long, Windows has been touted as a great development system but with a difficult learning curve. No more. Step by step, this book will show you the key concepts, features, and pitfalls of Windows programming. By the second chapter, you will have written a working Windows program; nine chapters later, you will be a pro.

This book is not an encyclopedia; it is a guide. You won't have to wade through thousands of details to figure out what is important and how to program. Instead, you'll learn the important concepts one by one and see them illustrated in working programs. Without wasting time and without nonsense, this book teaches what you, as a programmer, need to know about Windows.

You will first learn the basic concepts behind Windows programming and then develop a general Windows program outline. Next, how to use menus, how to display text, and how to input data will be discussed. You will learn about graphics, memory, and disk files and see how to use scroll bars, list boxes, child windows, the clipboard, and bit maps. In addition, advanced techniques, such as interfacing with Assembly Language, reading the WIN.INI file, and printing bit maps will be covered.

This book introduces topics in the order of necessity, starting with what is absolutely essential for creating a useful application and ending with what is the icing on the cake. Each chapter has at least one program—with complete code—illustrating the major concepts and showing how to integrate them. Some chapters have special sections on advanced concepts or on Windows 2.0. All chapters end with a brief chapter summary.

It is recommended that you read this book from start to finish and try out the programs and techniques each step of the way. Because topics are introduced in the order of their necessity, you won't have to finish the book before you can write your own, complete programs. But the more you read, the more polished and powerful those programs will be.

Don't worry if you feel a little lost along the way. Just read the chapter again and try out the sample program. Experiment a little. If you still don't understand, keep going, and come back later to sections you have trouble with.

What You Need

If you just want to learn about Windows programming, but not actually create your own programs, you will need the following:

Microsoft Windows 1.03 or 2.0
Windows Guide Diskette

If you plan to do your own Windows programming, you will then need the following:

Microsoft Windows 1.03 or 2.0
Microsoft Windows Development Toolkit
Microsoft C 4.0 (or later)

The *Windows Guide Diskette* is also recommended (see order form at then end of this book).

You can also use Microsoft Pascal or the Microsoft Macro Assembler.

Development will be quicker if you have a 1-megabyte RAM disk and a hard disk.

Companion Program Diskette

The *Windows Guide Diskette* is the program disk package that accompanies this book. The two-disk set contains the source code and the executable version of all of the programs contained in the text. In addition, it has the valuable Assembly Language files for disk access.

The companion diskette is recommend for several reasons. First, it will save you all the time spent typing in the programs. Instead of typing and checking for mistakes, you can try out the programs right away. Further, these programs provide a convenient outline for testing your own routines. You can quickly modify the programs to add new features, test other concepts, or develop applications, which will be a valuable resource while you are programming.

In the text, instructions on using the *Windows Guide Diskette* appear in boxes. If you are interested in using the companion diskette, please refer to the order form at the end of this book.

CHAPTER 1

INTRODUCTION TO THE WINDOWS ENVIRONMENT

1 Introduction to the Windows Environment

Windows provides a terrific computing environment. Because it is graphically oriented, you simply point and click the mouse to make selections. All programs have a similar format, and it is easy (if not intuitive) to use the menus; thus, the hassle and frustration of learning a different application's commands and formats are eliminated.

A key feature of Windows is that it is so easy to visualize what is going on. You see a list of files, and the files you are using are highlighted. You see a list of options or the results of your actions on the screen.

Windows is a *multitasking* system, which means it can run several programs at once. For example, you can simultaneously run a spreadsheet, a word processor, and a statistical package. With a click of the mouse, you can switch between them, which is very convenient. You also don't need to leave a program to format a disk, copy a file, make a few calculations, or even make a note. Windows removes the need for DOS menu programs and memory-resident utilities. You can "pop up" as many different programs as you want at any time.

Windows programs can also communicate with each other. You can copy data to the clipboard from one program and then read it in from another. For example, you can easily transfer data between a graphics package and your word processor.

Windows is *device-independent*, which means that as long as you have graphics capabilities, Windows programs will work with almost all system configurations.

Introduction to the Windows Environment 1

WHY PROGRAM WITH WINDOWS?

Windows is great for the user and great for the programmer. The Windows development environment is designed to let you quickly and easily create attractive, professional-looking, friendly programs. All the menuing and pop-up capabilities are built in. You don't need to poll the mouse position or keyboard state. Windows also takes care of full-screen editing features and adjusting the display for different sizes. Windows takes care of moving your applications, printing error messages, and much more. You must do very little to develop a sophisticated program. Further, Windows makes it much easier to give an intuitive look to your application's user-interface.

Windows' device-independence is another key feature for the developer. You don't need to tailor your programs for various input and output devices. You also don't need to create or license device drivers. Many graphics functions, such as line-drawing and region-filling, are provided.

If you are planning to develop software that includes windows, full-screen menus, or graphics, Windows is definitely the system to use. The only disadvantage of Windows is that it consumes system resources. Windows works much better on ATs than PCs; it occupies a great deal of memory and requires a hard drive. Windows also requires graphics capabilities. Most systems, and certainly those of the future, can support Windows.

WINDOWS REALLY IS EASY

A key point about Windows programming is that it is easy. Many people will laugh if you make this statement; for some time, Windows has been rumored to be a very difficult system to learn. All you must do to understand this rumor is examine the gargantuan manuals that come with the toolkit. Once you understand a few key concepts, however, Windows programming really is quite easy.

1 Introduction to the Windows Environment

APPROACHING A WINDOWS PROGRAM

Two important differences exist between Windows programs and most conventional programs: Windows programs are graphically oriented and event-driven. The graphical orientation has already been mentioned. The look and feel of the user interface is important; the notion of *event-driven* is built around these factors. Event-driven programs are built around processing events. *Events* are actions such as selecting a menu item or pressing a mouse button while drawing a picture.

Many conventional programs present you with a list of options. You select one of these options, and the program presents a different set of options. To get more data, the program asks a series of questions.

Windows programs usually present a wider variety of simultaneous options. In general, menus do not cascade down one after another; all inputs are full-screen. In a conventional program, when you enter information, the program changes state; it can go to a different set of subroutines or bring up a different set of possible actions. Windows programs are event receivers. The programs are sent messages (such as a mouse click on the screen); they process this single event, and then they stop. When another event comes along, the programs process it. While the programs wait for events, other programs run.

The difference is somewhat subtle. Use a few Windows programs to get a feel for the idea of event-driven programs. As a programmer, your program will have a routine called every time there is an event for your application. Your routine must receive this message and decide what to do with it. In a sense, a Windows program is an asynchronous message server.

Another important difference is that Windows takes care of all the input and output routines. You specify that you want menus and the other input devices, but Windows takes care of adjusting their placement and receiving the input. This assistance frees up time spent on complicated programming that would otherwise take you away from the main theme of your program.

Introduction to the Windows Environment 1

These three differences—the graphic orientation, the event-driven nature, and the built-in input and output functions—make approaching a Windows program a bit different. You know that your program will have a menu at the top of the screen and can have several other types of input devices. You must start by planning how the user will interact with the program.

This procedure is important. The emphasis during early development is to plan a system of menus and inputs that make the program easy to learn and operate. Concentrate on what commands are important and how they would best be organized. Fortunately, cosmetically altering the user interface during development is easy with Windows. Even major changes aren't too difficult.

Because Windows is a multitasking system, you don't need to build in utility features such as a shell command or file maintenance. You must, however, make sure that multiple copies of your program can run at the same time. For example, if your program uses a scratch file, you must make sure that if several copies of your program are running at once, they don't use the same scratch file.

With Windows, you can use the clipboard to transfer information between programs. You may want to think of ways that this strategy could enhance the utility of your applications.

In summary, start by planning the user interface. Place the major functions in a menu that is always available. Make a list of the commands on this menu and the type of actions they should trigger. Should they bring up a box that requests further information? Should they retrieve and display information? Should they change the format in which information is displayed? Once you have broken your program into such an outline, you are well on your way. As you read the next several chapters, you will see how to incorporate this approach into developing a Windows program. After you develop a few programs, this approach will become second nature.

STYLE

Your program will be easier to use if it conforms to certain stylistic considerations. If most Windows programs have a similar user interface, users will feel more comfortable working with them and won't have to learn a new approach for each program. While this book concentrates on the programming itself, it does make some stylistic recommendations. Microsoft supplies an interface style guide along with the Development Toolkit. Before you start developing commercial applications, read this guide.

FURTHER DIFFERENCES

There are further differences that result from Windows' graphic orientation and multitasking nature. First, you can't use **printf**s and **scanf**s; instead, you must use input and output functions that operate better when any number of programs could be running at the same time (on different parts of the screen) with windows of different sizes.

Secondly, because Windows is a multitasking system, it keeps several applications in memory at the same time. This action consumes RAM, virtual memory, and processing time; thus, the Windows environment is system-taxing. To optimize for this situation, Windows provides some compensating features. If several copies of a program are running at once, it only keeps one copy of the code. Some parts of programs are only kept in memory while they are being used. Resources (such as fonts) used by several programs are kept globally, so there is one copy for the system but not for each application. Further, to optimize free space, code and data can be moved around in memory during program operation, which changes the use of allocated memory. Finally, disk files can be accessed from any number of programs at any time. You must be careful not to clobber someone else's information, and you cannot assume that a certain disk is always in a drive.

Introduction to the Windows Environment

THE OVERWHELMING SIMILARITY

Despite these differences, writing a Windows program isn't much different than writing any other program. You must initially pay more attention to the interface. You also must include a special routine to receive messages from the Windows system (explained in the next chapter). Everything else—the language commands, the format of routines, the use of subroutines, structured programming, object modules, external routines, constants, and so forth—is exactly the same.

THE PARTS OF A WINDOWS PROGRAM

Four types of files make up a Windows program: the *code* files, the *module definition* file, the *resource* files, and the *make* file.

The *code* is the Windows program itself. It can be written in C, Pascal, or Assembly Language; this book uses C almost exclusively. Like any program in these languages, a Windows program can be composed of several source files individually compiled and linked together. The code in this book contains all routines for processing messages, creating displays, evaluating algorithms, and other tasks a program normally performs.

The *module definition* file tells Windows important information about the application. For example, the file tells if the program can be moved around in memory, how much space to allocate for local variables, and the name of the program. It also tells Windows the name of functions that the Windows system will call. Most of your Windows programs will use similar module definition files.

The *resource* file contains an outline of the menus and input boxes your program will use. By describing all the input features with a high level language, you can easily edit menus and add new features. Further, you don't need to recompile your program each time you modify a menu. The resource file also lists any special icons and cursors that the program might use. You'll find in Chapter 3 that resource files are quite easy to use.

1 Introduction to the Windows Environment

The *make file* is a conventional make file; it tells the computer what compilers and linkers to run in order to generate an executable program. The file also ensures that all of the files are up to date. Because compiling Windows programs is a bit more complicated than compiling conventional programs, it is strongly recommend that you use a make file for each of your Windows programs.

Every program in this book contains a listing of the code files, module definition file, resource files, and make file.

SUMMARY

- Windows makes it easy for users to learn and operate programs.

- Windows makes it easy for programmers to develop professional-looking, easy-to-use programs. Many input and output functions are built in.

- Windows is a multitasking, graphically oriented, event-driven, device-independent system.

- Windows makes it easy to transfer data between programs.

- When developing a Windows application, you must start by planning out the user interface.

- Because Windows is graphically oriented and multitasking, input and output processing is somewhat different than with conventional programs.

- There are four main parts to a Windows program: the code, the module definition file, the resource file, and the make file.

CHAPTER 2

THE BASIC OUTLINE OF A WINDOWS PROGRAM

2 The Basic Outline of a Windows Program

All Windows programs have three parts: an initialization section, a section to receive messages, and a section to process messages. In this chapter, you will develop the basic outline of a Windows program. It is an outline that you will use again and again, filling in details for each specific application.

THE SECTIONS OF A WINDOWS PROGRAM

In the previous chapter, you learned that Windows programs are based on messages. When the user clicks the mouse or selects a menu item, messages are sent to the Windows program. When several programs are operating at once, the messages are sent to the program in which the mouse cursor is located, i.e., the messages go to the proper program.

The whole idea of a Windows program is to receive these messages. Again, these messages can indicate that a certain item was selected from a menu, that a mouse button was pressed, or that a name was selected. The program then processes the messages. The basic outline of a Windows program is as follows:

- initialize
- receive the messages
- process the messages

These three steps correspond to the three basic routines all Windows programs must contain.

The first routine all Windows programs must have is **WinMain**. The routine is similar to **main** in a conventional program. **WinMain** is the procedure called when a Windows program is loaded; it starts by calling any initialization routines and then waits for and relays messages.

The next routine is the initialization routine. The routine is called by **WinMain** and tells the Windows system important information about the program. For example, it tells the title of the program and the type of cursor it uses.

The final routine is the message processor. When **WinMain** receives messages, it sends them via the Windows system to the message processor. The message processor decides what to do with the messages. For example, in Chapter 4, the message processor will receive commands from menus.

These three routines are the basis for any Windows program. Next, you will examine each in more detail. At the end of this chapter, you will see a Windows program that combines them all.

WinMain

WinMain is the start-up routine and message relayer. The routine's operation is very straightforward; it takes care of any initialization necessary, creates and displays a window for the application, and then receives and relays any messages.

You'll examine the kernel of a **WinMain** routine and then analyze each of its features in more detail. **WinMain** introduces several of the Windows commands. If you are slightly confused about the command parameters, don't worry; you won't need to change them until later.

For now, the following basic **WinMain** routine will be more than sufficient for your programs:

```
/*-----------------------------------------------------------
   This is the Start Up procedure and message relayer
-----------------------------------------------------------*/

int PASCAL
WinMain( hInstance, hPrevInstance, lpszCmdLine, cmdShow )
HANDLE   hInstance, hPrevInstance;
LPSTR    lpszCmdLine;
int      cmdShow;
{
```
   continued...

2 The Basic Outline of a Windows Program

```c
    HWND        hWnd;
    MSG         msg;

    /* If this is the first instance, register the window
       class
    */
    if (hPrevInstance == NULL)
        register_window( hInstance );

    /* don't need previous instance information */

    /* Create a tiled window */
    hWnd = CreateWindow( (LPSTR) "Chap2WIN",   /* class */
                (LPSTR) "Hello World",   /* title */
                WS_TILEDWINDOW,          /* style */
                0, 0, 0, 0,
                (HWND) NULL,             /* parent */
                (HMENU) NULL,            /* menu */
                (HANDLE) hInstance,      /* instance */
                (LPSTR) NULL );

    /* Now display it */
    ShowWindow( hWnd, cmdShow );
    UpdateWindow( hWnd );


    /* relay all messages to the message server */
    while (GetMessage( (LPMSG) &msg, NULL, 0, 0) ) {
        TranslateMessage( (LPMSG) &msg);
        DispatchMessage( (LPMSG) &msg);
    }

    exit(msg.wParam);
}
```

The Basic Outline of a Windows Program 2

To begin, note that the routine returns an integer and has the PASCAL keyword. The PASCAL keyword is a feature that allows a single program to contain modules written in different languages. The Windows system always calls procedures with the Pascal calling convention; thus, any procedures called by the Windows system—such as **WinMain** and the message processor—must be declared with the PASCAL keyword.

All routines called by the Windows system, except for **WinMain**, must be defined as FAR procedures. **WinMain** should not be declared as NEAR or FAR; it must be set to the default.[1]

WinMain is always called with the parameters hInstance, hPrevInstance, lpszCmdLine, and cmdShow. As mentioned, Windows is a multitasking system. If several copies of a program are running at the same time, each is called an *instance*. hInstance uniquely identifies the current instance. The program uses the parameter to create a unique window for the program. If several copies of the program are running, hPrevInstance points to an earlier copy; it is used if the application needs to retrieve information from a previous copy. You will see how this variable is used in Chapter 4. If this copy is the first copy of the program, hPrevInstance is NULL. lpszCmdLine is a far pointer to a string containing the command line arguments. cmdShow provides information to the routine that displays the window.

The first time that a particular program is loaded, it must register itself. Thus, the first thing **WinMain** does is register (i.e, initialize) the window by calling **register_window**. **register_window** is the second basic routine needed by every Windows program.

Next, **WinMain** creates a window for the application. A window is the display area used for input and output. All Windows programs need a window. The window is created using the **CreateWindow** function, and its parameters will be discussed shortly.

Next, **WinMain** displays the window, using the **ShowWindow** and **UpdateWindow** commands.

---

[1] For code models with more than one code segment—the medium, large, and huge—WinMain needs to be FAR. For the small and compact models, WinMain needs to be NEAR. The default setting is the proper one for all these models.

13

2 The Basic Outline of a Windows Program

Finally, **WinMain** has a loop to receive messages and pass them along to the message processor. This procedure is performed by the following code:

```
/* relay all messages to the message server */
while (GetMessage( (LPMSG) &msg, NULL, 0, 0) ) {
    TranslateMessage( (LPMSG) &msg);
    DispatchMessage( (LPMSG) &msg);
}
```

The message processor is the third routine needed by all Windows programs.

When the user ends the program, **WinMain** finishes with the **exit** command.

Now, examine the Windows commands in **WinMain** in more detail. Several data types are used by these commands; they will be briefly mentioned as the parameters are introduced and discussed in detail at the end of the chapter.

The only function in **WinMain** for which you'll need to change the parameters is **CreateWindow**. Its format is as follows:

```
HWND
CreateWindow( lpClass, lpTitle, style, xpos, ypos, width,
height, parent_window, menu, instance, params)
```

lpClass   is a far pointer to an ASCIIZ string containing the class name. You'll learn more about class in the section about initialization and in the next chapter. Basically, groups of Windows programs are broken up into classes. Each class uses the same cursor, icon, and several other features. If you want, you can make each of your programs have a different class name. What is important is that the class name you give **CreateWindow** is the same as the one that you use in **register__window**.

The Basic Outline of a Windows Program 2

Before looking at the next parameter, note that lpClass is a far pointer to a string. To make a far pointer to a string, cast a normal pointer to a LPSTR by prefixing it with (LPSTR). You can also type in a string within quotes and cast it with (LPSTR), as in the sample **WinMain**.

lpTitle is an LPSTR to the name of the program, which is the text that is displayed at the top of the program's window. In the program from this chapter, the title is "Hello World"; thus, when the program is run, the message "Hello World" appears at the top of the window.

style tells the type of the window. There are many possibilities. For now, use WS_TILED, which means make a normal, tiled window. Other options add scroll bars and other features to the window. The options are discussed more fully in Chapter 10.

xpos, **ypos**, **width**, and **height**

are shorts that request the size and location of the window. These parameters aren't used for tiled windows; thus, for all the applications in this book, you can set these values to zero.

parent_window

is a pointer to the parent window. Its type is HWND. In Chapter 10, you will see how to use this feature for child windows. For now, set this parameter to NULL.

menu is set if the window uses a special menu. For the programs in this book, you will always use the class menu; thus, all programs that you create with the same class will use the same menu. To use the class menu, set this parameter to NULL. Its type is HMENU.

instance identifies the current program. Set the parameter to the hInstance value that is passed to **WinMain**. Its type is HANDLE.

params passes a string to the window being created. You will not need it, so set it to NULL. Its type is LPSTR.

2 The Basic Outline of a Windows Program

CreateWindow returns a handle to the program's window. This handle is of the type HWND, and it is very important; it is used whenever you need to receive input, display output, or use most other Windows commands.

There are five other Windows commands in **WinMain**. You won't need to change their parameters for most of the Windows programs you write.

ShowWindow causes the window to be displayed. Its format is as follows:

```
ShowWindow( hWnd, command)
```

Set **hWnd** to the window handle returned from **CreateWindow**. Set **command** to the cmdShow parameter passed to **WinMain**.

UpdateWindow tells Windows that a window has been changed; thus, its appearance must be modified. Because the window was just popped up, it needs to be filled in, which is why **UpdateWindow** is called right after **ShowWindow**. Its format is as follows:

```
UpdateWindow( hWnd )
```

Set **hWnd** to the window handle returned from **CreateWindow**.

GetMessage, **TranslateMessage**, and **DispatchMessage** take care of receiving messages and sending them to the message processor.

GetMessage sees if there are any messages waiting for the program. Its format is as follows:

```
BOOL
GetMessage( lpmsg, hwnd, filtermin, filtermax )
```

lpmsg	is a pointer to an item with message structure. If there is a message, it will be returned in this structure.
hwnd	is a handle to the window. If it is NULL, it gets messages for the current window.

filtermin and **filtermax**

are WORDs that are used to filter out undesired messages. Set both of them to 0.

If there is a message, **GetMessage** returns a non-zero value. If the application receives the message to quit, **GetMessage** returns 0. If there aren't any messages, **GetMessage** lets Windows give processor time to other programs.

TranslateMessage converts keystrokes into character messages. Its format is as follows:

```
TranslateMessage( lpmsg )
```

lpmsg   is a long pointer to a message structure. Pass it the same structure passed to **GetMessage**.

DispatchMessage passes the message to the program's message processing procedure. Its format is as follows:

```
DispatchMessage( lpmsg )
```

lpmsg   is a long pointer to a message structure. Pass it the same structure passed to **GetMessage**.

The Initialization Routine

The initialization routine registers the program. This routine tells the program class name and what features to use for the class. In particular, it tells what cursor, icon, menu, background, style, and message processor to use by filling in a WNDCLASS data structure.

2 The Basic Outline of a Windows Program

In this book, the initialization routine is called **register_window**. The code is as follows:

```
/*-----------------------------------------------------------
   This procedure registers the window
-------------------------------------------------------------*/

int
register_window( hInstance )
HANDLE hInstance;
{
    PWNDCLASS      pClass;

    /* make space for the class structure */
    pClass = (PWNDCLASS) LocalAlloc(LPTR, sizeof(WNDCLASS));

    /* use an arrow for the cursor */
    pClass->hCursor = LoadCursor(NULL, (LPSTR) IDC_ARROW);

    /* use the standard application icon for the icon */
    pClass->hIcon = LoadIcon(NULL, (LPSTR) IDI_APPLICATION);

    /* no menu */
    pClass->lpszMenuName = (LPSTR) NULL;

    /* the class name */
    pClass->lpszClassName = (LPSTR) "Chap2WIN";

    /* make the background light gray */
    pClass->hbrBackground = GetStockObject(LTGRAY_BRUSH);

    /* set the instance */
    pClass->hInstance = hInstance;

    /* redraw window if its size changes */
    pClass->style = CS_HREDRAW | CS_VREDRAW;

    /* the procedure MsgServer() will handle all windows
       messages
    */
    pClass->lpfnWndProc = MsgServer;

    RegisterClass( (LPWNDCLASS) pClass);
    LocalFree( (HANDLE) pClass);
}
```

The Basic Outline of a Windows Program 2

As mentioned, **register_window** works by filling in a WNDCLASS data structure. The routine begins by making space for this structure with **LocalAlloc** and ends by freeing this space with **LocalFree**. **LocalAlloc** and **LocalFree** are equivalent to **malloc** and **free**. These routines are discussed in more detail in Chapter 9.

The WNDCLASS structure has the following elements:

hCursor a handle for the cursor to use for the class. If set to NULL, each application must set its own cursor.

hIcon a handle for the icon to use for the class. If set to NULL, each application must set its own icon.

lpszMenuName a far pointer to an ASCIIZ string containing the name of the menu to use for the class. If there is no menu, set it to NULL.

lpszClassName a far pointer to an ASCIIZ string containing the name of the class, which should be the same name used in the **CreateWindow** call.

hbrBackground a handle for the brush that will be used to paint the background of the window. Use this parameter to select the background color and texture of the window.

hInstance a handle to an instance of the class. Set it to the hInstance parameter passed to **WinMain**.

style a WORD describing some of the display characteristics of the window. Set it to CS_VREDRAW | CS_HREDRAW, which tells Windows to redraw the window if the size of the window changes.

lpfnWndProc a FAR function pointer to the procedure that will process the messages received by **WinMain**. The **DispatchMessage** function, reviewed in the section on **WinMain**, sends all messages to this function. In this book, the message processing routine is always called **MsgServer**. If you name your message processing routine something else, put that name here.

2 The Basic Outline of a Windows Program

Once you have filled in this data structure, register it with the **RegisterClass** command. Its format is as follows:

```
RegisterClass( pClass )
```

pClass is a pointer to a WNDCLASS structure.

Windows has several built in icons, cursors, and background brushes you can use for your application. Access these features with the **LoadCursor**, **LoadIcon**, and **GetStockObject** commands.

Choose the cursor your application will use by setting the hCursor parameter to a cursor loaded with **LoadCursor**. **LoadCursor** has the following format:

```
hCursor
LoadCursor( hInstance, lpCursorName )
```

hInstance is set to NULL to use built-in cursors. To use your own cursor, as shown in Chapter 3, set this parameter to the hInstance parameter passed to **WinMain**.

lpCursorName is one of the following:

IDC_ARROW	diagonal arrow cursor
IDC_IBEAM	I-shaped cursor used with text
IDC_WAIT	hourglass
IDC_UPARROW	upward-pointing arrow
IDC_CROSS	crosshair
IDC_SIZE	small box in the corner of a larger box. Used by Windows when sizing a window.
IDC_ICON	thick-framed box. Used by Windows when pulling an icon.

To load a cursor you have made, as shown in Chapter 3, set this value to a far pointer to the ASCIIZ name of the cursor.

The Basic Outline of a Windows Program 2

The sample program from this chapter uses **LoadCursor** to load the standard arrow cursor. You might like to experiment by changing the cursor.

Choosing the icon your application will use is quite similar to choosing the cursor. Set the hIcon parameter to a value returned by **LoadIcon**. **LoadIcon**'s format is as follows:

```
hIcon
LoadIcon( hInstance, lpIconName )
```

hInstance is set to NULL to use the built-in icons. To use your own icon, as shown in Chapter 4, set this parameter to the hInstance parameter passed to **WinMain**.

lpIconName is one of the following:

  IDI_APPLICATION

  Application icon. A hollow square.

  IDI_HAND

  A hand. Typically used for warning messages.

  IDI_QUESTION

  A question mark. Typically used in prompt messages.

  IDI_EXCLAMATION

  An exclamation mark. Typically used in warning messages.

  IDI_ASTERISK

  An asterisk. Typically used in information messages.

2 The Basic Outline of a Windows Program

If you are loading an icon you have made, as shown in Chapter 4, set this parameter to a far pointer to an ASCIIZ string containing the icon name.

Whenever the window needs to be repainted (e.g., when it is first loaded or when its size changes), it is painted with a background brush, just as the background of a painting is colored by a brush. You can select the color of the window's background by setting hbrBackground to a value returned by **GetStockObject**. The format of **GetStockObject** is as follows:

```
hBrush
GetStockObject( object )
```

object is one of the following:

- WHITE_BRUSH
- LTGRAY_BRUSH
- GRAY_BRUSH
- DKGRAY_BRUSH
- BLACK_BRUSH
- HOLLOW_BRUSH

The meaning of each of these brush types is self-explanatory. Most Windows applications use the WHITE_BRUSH as the background brush.[2]

You can see that the **register_window** routine provides much flexibility in designing a window's appearance. After you run the program from this chapter, experiment by changing its cursor, icon, and background brush.

---

[2] GetStockObject can be used to retrieve pens and fonts as well as brushes.

The Basic Outline of a Windows Program 2

The Message-Processing Routine

The message-processing routine receives and processes messages passed to it by **WinMain**. Chapters 4 and 6 discuss the various messages, which range from menu selections to requests to terminate the program.

Because the routine is called by the Windows system, it must be declared with the FAR and PASCAL keywords, and it should also return a long value. Set the return value to zero if the message is successfully handled. In all the programs in this book, the message server is called **MsgServer**.

Note that the lpfnWndProc parameter in **register_window** is set to the name of this procedure.

The message server procedure is essentially a big switch statement that contains a list of commands to enact for the various messages it wants to process. To see a quick example of this procedure, look at the **MsgServer** routine in Chapter 6.

Though there may be several messages that you want to process, there will be many more you don't care about. Windows supplies a procedure that performs default operations on these messages; it will handle most operations that you need—moving the window, changing it to an icon, showing and selecting menu items, ending the program, and so forth. This default message processor is called **DefWindowProc**. Use it for all messages you don't plan to process yourself. The format is as follows:

```
long
DefWindowProc( hWnd, message, wParam, lParam )
```

The parameters passed to this routine are those passed to the message server routine, as will be seen in a moment.[3]

You won't be processing messages until Chapter 4. Until then, use **DefWindowProc** for all the messages sent to **MsgServer**.

---

[3] Microsoft provides a listing of the code for DefWindowsProc on disk #7 of the toolkit.

2 The Basic Outline of a Windows Program

Following is a sample **MsgServer**. Note its parameters, which are passed to the routine by the Windows system. Also, note that the routine is declared as a long FAR PASCAL procedure:

```
/*-----------------------------------------------------
    This procedure receives the messages from Windows and
    decides how to process them.
  -----------------------------------------------------*/
long FAR PASCAL
MsgServer( hWnd, message, wParam, lParam )
HWND        hWnd;
unsigned    message;
WORD        wParam;
LONG        lParam;
{
    /* just use the defaults */
    return( DefWindowProc(hWnd, message, wParam, lParam) );
}
```

A PROGRAM: TWO

The following program puts together the three essential parts of a Windows program. It creates a fully functional window that prints the message "Hello World" on its title bar (see Figure 2.1). You can bring up as many copies of the program at once as you would like, and you can run it along with other programs. You can turn the program into an icon or move it around the screen.

Note that the program is composed of the three essential routines: the start-up routine and message relayer, **WinMain**; the initialization routine, **register_window**; and the message processor, **MsgServer**. The program may seem long and complex to simply print a title, but remember that it is a basic framework into which many sophisticated features can easily be added.

The program #includes a file named "windows.h." All your Windows programs must #include this file; it contains the typedefs, constants, and external declarations necessary for Windows programs.

The Basic Outline of a Windows Program 2

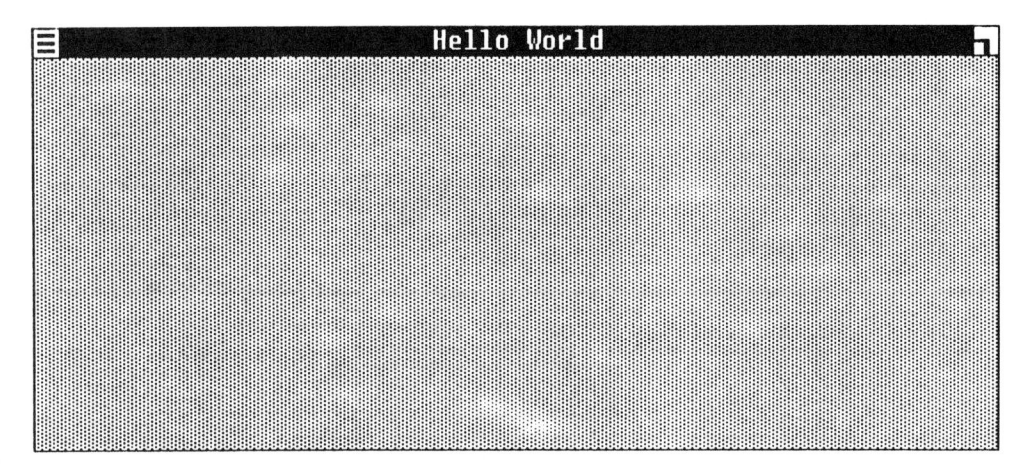

[Window screenshot titled "Hello World"]

Figure 2.1   The program TWO.

Enter the code and compile it. Note that you must type in the module definition file as well. There is no resource file because the program doesn't use any resources. Note the listing of the make file. It is strongly recommended that you use make files. If you don't use make files, be sure to set the compiler options with the flags listed. Such steps are necessary for compiling Windows programs.

You will note that the make file assumes that all of the TWO files are in the current working directory. It is suggested that you keep all of your source program files in one directory and switch to that directory before compiling. Use PATH and SET statements so the computer can find the various compiler, linker, library, and include files.

If possible, copy all the compiler programs, link4, rc, make, the various libraries, and your source code to a RAM disk, which will greatly speed compilation time.

2 The Basic Outline of a Windows Program

```
/--------------------------------------------------\
|                                                  |
| The code for this program is found in the        |
| TWO directory of the Windows Guide               |
| diskette.  The make file is called TWO.  The     |
| include file is TWO.H.  The code is TWO.C.       |
| The module definition file is TWO.DEF.  The      |
| executable version is TWO.EXE.                   |
|                                                  |
\--------------------------------------------------/
```

The Make File: TWO

```
#
#   Make file for Chapter 2
#


cc=cl -d -c -AS -Gsw -Os -Zpe

.c.obj:
    $(cc) $*.c


two.obj: two.c  two.h

two.exe: two.obj two.def
    link4 two, /align:16, NUL, slibw, two.def
```

The Include File: TWO.H

```
/***********************************************************
    Contains typedefs, constants, and external declarations
    for Chapter 2
***********************************************************/


extern int PASCAL WinMain();
extern int register_window();
extern long FAR PASCAL MsgServer();
```

The Basic Outline of a Windows Program 2

The Code: TWO.C

```
/************************************************************
      File:      two.c
      Program:   two

      This is the first windows program.  It brings up a window
      with a title.  You can bring up as many copies as you want
      and resize them.

      This is the basic outline of a Windows program.
************************************************************/

#include "windows.h"
#include "two.h"

/*----------------------------------------------------------
  This is the Start Up procedure and message relayer
----------------------------------------------------------*/

int PASCAL
WinMain( hInstance, hPrevInstance, lpszCmdLine, cmdShow )
HANDLE    hInstance, hPrevInstance;
LPSTR     lpszCmdLine;
int       cmdShow;
{
    HWND      hWnd;
    MSG       msg;

    /* If this is the first instance, register the window
       class
    */
    if (hPrevInstance == NULL)
        register_window( hInstance );

    /* don't need previous instance information */

    /* Create a tiled window */
    hWnd = CreateWindow( (LPSTR) "Chap2WIN",   /* class */
                 (LPSTR) "Hello World",   /* title */
                 WS_TILEDWINDOW,          /* style */
                 0, 0, 0, 0,
```

continued...

2 The Basic Outline of a Windows Program

...from previous page

```
                    (HWND) NULL,            /* parent */
                    (HMENU) NULL,           /* menu */
                    (HANDLE) hInstance,     /* instance */
                    (LPSTR) NULL );

    /* Now display it */
    ShowWindow( hWnd, cmdShow );
    UpdateWindow( hWnd );


    /* relay all messages to the message server */
    while (GetMessage( (LPMSG) &msg, NULL, 0, 0) ) {
        TranslateMessage( (LPMSG) &msg);
        DispatchMessage( (LPMSG) &msg);
    }

    exit(msg.wParam);
}




/*-------------------------------------------------------
   This procedure registers the window
---------------------------------------------------------*/

int
register_window( hInstance )
HANDLE hInstance;
{
    PWNDCLASS       pClass;

    /* make space for the class structure */
    pClass = (PWNDCLASS) LocalAlloc(LPTR, sizeof(WNDCLASS));

    /* use an arrow for the cursor */
    pClass->hCursor = LoadCursor(NULL, (LPSTR) IDC_ARROW);

    /* use the standard application icon for the icon */
    pClass->hIcon = LoadIcon(NULL, (LPSTR) IDI_APPLICATION);
```

continued...

The Basic Outline of a Windows Program 2

...from previous page

```
    /* no menu */
    pClass->lpszMenuName = (LPSTR) NULL;

    /* the class name */
    pClass->lpszClassName = (LPSTR) "Chap2WIN";

    /* make the background light gray */
    pClass->hbrBackground = GetStockObject(LTGRAY_BRUSH);

    /* set the instance */
    pClass->hInstance = hInstance;

    /* redraw window if its size changes */
    pClass->style = CS_HREDRAW | CS_VREDRAW;

    /* the procedure MsgServer() will handle all windows
       messages
    */
    pClass->lpfnWndProc = MsgServer;

    RegisterClass( (LPWNDCLASS) pClass);
    LocalFree( (HANDLE) pClass);
}




/*-----------------------------------------------------------
  This procedure receives the messages from Windows and
  decides how to process them.
  ----------------------------------------------------------*/

long FAR PASCAL
MsgServer( hWnd, message, wParam, lParam )
HWND     hWnd;
unsigned message;
WORD     wParam;
LONG     lParam;
{
    /* just use the defaults */
    return( DefWindowProc(hWnd, message, wParam, lParam) );
}
```

2 The Basic Outline of a Windows Program

The Module Definition: TWO.DEF

```
NAME       Two
DESCRIPTION    'Second Window Program'
STUB       'winstub.exe'
CODE       MOVEABLE
DATA       MOVEABLE MULTIPLE
HEAPSIZE   4096
STACKSIZE  4096
EXPORTS
           MsgServer @1
```

WINDOWS 2.0 FEATURES

Windows 2.0 does not use tiled windows; rather, it uses overlapping windows. Instead of using the constant WM_TILED in the CreateWindow call, use the constant WM_OVERLAPPEDWINDOW. You can still use the WS_TILED parameter; it will be treated as if you used WM_OVERLAPPEDWINDOW.

Because the windows overlap, you can request an initial size, using the **xpos**, **ypos**, **width**, and **height** parameters. Refer to Chapter 10 for more information on how to use these parameters. If you set the parameters to 0, Windows will choose an initial size and position for you. This selection should be sufficient for most of your needs.

ADVANCED CONCEPTS: VARIABLE NOTATIONS, TYPES, AND INSTANCES

There are several types unique to Windows programs. Microsoft uses a set of variable prefixes to indicate the variable type. The types you will come across most frequently include the following:

The Basic Outline of a Windows Program 2

General Types

BYTE	an unsigned 8-bit integer
WORD	an unsigned 16-bit integer
BOOL	a boolean, 16-bit value
FAR	a far or long pointer
NEAR	a short or near pointer
LPSTR	a long pointer to a char

Graphics Types

HANDLE	a general, 16-bit pointer
HCURSOR	a handle for a cursor
HICON	a handle for an icon
HMENU	a handle for a menu
HPEN	a handle for a pen
HFONT	a handle for a font
HBRUSH	a handle for a brush
HBITMAP	a handle for a bit map
HRGN	a handle for a region
RECT	a structure describing a rectangle
LPRECT	a long pointer to a rectangle structure
RGB	a long integer containing a color r, g, and b value
METAFILEPICT	a metafile structure

System Types

HWND	a handle to a window
WNDCLASS	a window class structure
PWNDCLASS	a pointer to a window class
MSG	a message structure
LPMSG	a long pointer to a message
HDC	a handle to a display context
GLOBALHANDLE	a handle for global memory
LOCALHANDLE	a handle for local memory
OFSTRUCT	a structure for opening files

2 The Basic Outline of a Windows Program

Font Types

LOGFONT	a structure defining font characteristics
LPLOGFONT	a long pointer to a font structure
TEXTMETRIC	a structure listing characteristics of a physical font
LPTEXTMETRIC	a long pointer to a text metric structure

Variable Prefixes

b	indicates a BOOL
h	indicates a handle
l	indicates a LONG
lp	indicates a long pointer
lpsz	indicates an LPSTR
w	indicates a WORD

The Module Definition File

There are several important parameters in the module definition file. The **NAME** parameter defines the name of the program, and it should be the same name as the executable program. For example, if a program is called TWO.EXE, the module definition file should have the following line:

```
NAME    Two
```

The **DESCRIPTION** parameter is a text message (enclosed in single quotes) that describes the file. This message is embedded in the program.

The **STUB** command specifies a program to append to the Windows program to check if Windows is running. You can use **winstub.exe**, which comes with the Software Developer's Toolkit. **winstub.exe** prints an error message if you try to run a Windows program when Windows isn't running.

Windows can optimize memory by moving around program code and data segments. The **CODE** parameter tells whether the code segment can be moved or not. Specify MOVEABLE. The **DATA** parameter tells if the data segment can be used. Specify MOVEABLE MULTIPLE. The MULTIPLE option indicates that each instance of a program will have its own copy of the data.

HEAPSIZE defines the minimum amount of local memory available. Memory use is discussed in Chapter 8. You can use any number between 0 and 64K.

STACKSIZE determines the minimum size of the stack. Use at least 4096 bytes. If your application has many nested function calls with passed parameters, you might want to specify a larger amount.

The **SEGMENT** statement is used by programs with several different code or data segments. None of the programs in this book uses the **SEGMENT** command. Each segment is a code or data module that can be separately loaded, which is useful for large programs. Code or data is loaded only as it is needed, which saves memory. Follow the **SEGMENT** command with the name of the segment, such as _CODE, and then the segment options. Use MOVEABLE DISCARDABLE.

The **EXPORTS** command lists the names of procedures in the program that the Windows system will call directly.

Instances

Because Windows is a multitasking system, several programs can run at once. In fact, several copies of the same program can run at once. Each copy of the same program is called an *instance*. When there are several instances of a program, the program's code is loaded once, and a separate data section is loaded for each instance.

The **WinMain** procedure checks if the program is the first instance. If so, it calls the **register_window** procedure. This procedure contains commands that run only for the first instance of a program.

2 The Basic Outline of a Windows Program

In later chapters, you will see how programs create *resources*, such as fonts. Instances save time and memory by using an earlier instance's resources, which is also disussed in later chapters. Commands to retrieve earlier instance data are executed for all instances except the first.

There are also actions, such as the initialization of variables, that should be undertaken by all instances.

SUMMARY

- There are three essential routines for a Windows program: the initialization routine, the message relayer, and the message processor.

- The initialization routine sets up the class structure and any other structures necessary, which includes selecting the cursor, icon, and background brush.

- The message relayer receives the messages and passes them on to the message processor.

- The message processor receives the messages and decides how to act on them. It can use **DefWindowProc** for most messages.

- When a program is run, **WinMain** is called. **WinMain** calls the initialization routine. **WinMain** also receives and relays messages.

- Procedures that the Windows system calls must be cast as FAR PASCAL procedures, except for **WinMain**. **WinMain** is cast as PASCAL.

- If you don't use any resources, you don't need a resource file.

- There are special options for the compiler to compile Windows programs. Use a make file.

The Basic Outline of a Windows Program 2

- Windows uses some special types. There are prefix conventions for indicating variable type.

- Several copies of the same program can be run at once. Each copy is called an *instance*.

CHAPTER 3

USING THE RESOURCE FILE: ADDING MENUS

3 Using the Resource File: Adding Menus

In this chapter, you will learn how to use the resource file, add menus to programs, and create your own cursors.

MENUS

Menus are the medium through which users interact with a Windows program. Menus appear at the top of a window and present a list of command options. The user selects a menu command by clicking a mouse on that entry. A more specific list of command options pops up when the menu item is selected.

If you are not familiar with menus, run a few Windows programs, such as Paint or Write, to see what menus are all about.

Menus are added to a Windows program through the resource file by using a menu description language. You list the commands a menu contains in the order you want them to appear. You can also describe a set of commands to pop up when a particular item is selected.

Because menus are described in the resource file, they can be edited easily. You don't need to change lines of code or recompile your program. Instead, you just run the program through the *resource compiler* (*RC*), which adds resources to a program. This feature will be discussed with the make file at the end of this chapter.

Create the resource file as you would any other text file. Give it a file extension of .RC. Start the resource file with a comment indicating what program the file is for. Enclose comments with /* and */, just as in C programs. Then, **#include** any files containing constant definitions. For example, you could start your resource file with the following:

```
/***********************************************************
      Resource file for Chapter 3
***********************************************************/


#include "windows.h"
#include "three.h"
```

Using the Resource File: Adding Menus 3

If an include file is not located in the root directory or in a directory specified by the INCLUDE environment variable, you must specify its complete path location. Indicate subdirectories by \\, not \.

There are five commands to describe menus: MENU, MENUITEM, POPUP, BEGIN, and END. Use the MENU command when you begin the description of a menu. Its format is as follows:

```
menuname MENU
```

where *menuname* is any string without spaces. For example, you could use

```
three    MENU
```

The BEGIN and END commands define where a menu begins and ends. They are just like **begin** and **end** in Pascal or { and } in C.

MENUITEM defines the text for one of the items in the menu. Place a list of MENUITEM commands within the BEGIN and END commands for a menu. The order in which they appear in the list is the order in which they will appear on the menu. The format of the MENUITEM command is as follows:

```
MENUITEM "text",  number
```

text can be any ASCII string you want displayed in the menu. Note that the text must be enclosed within double quotation marks. **number** is a number associated with the menu item. You will see how to use **number** in Chapter 4. Until then, just fill in any number greater than 100.

3 Using the Resource File: Adding Menus

The following is an example of a menu description:

```
three     MENU
BEGIN
     MENUITEM  "File",              100
     MENUITEM  "Place a Bet",       200
     MENUITEM  "Deal the Cards",    300
END
```

This menu will have three items appearing across the top of the window: "File," "Place a Bet," and "Deal the Cards." Note that the text for menu commands can have several words in it. Also, note the use of BEGIN and END. The spacing is optional, but it makes the resource file easier to read.

If you want a menu item to pop up a further series of commands, use the POPUP command. POPUP has the following format:

```
POPUP "text"
```

where **text** is any ASCII text enclosed within double quotes. Follow the POPUP command by BEGIN and END commands. Place a list of MENUITEM commands, describing the list to pop up, within these BEGIN and ENDs. Following is an example:

```
three     MENU
BEGIN
     POPUP      "File"
     BEGIN
          MENUITEM  "Open...",          100
          MENUITEM  "Save",             110
     END
     POPUP      "Place a Bet"
     BEGIN
          MENUITEM  "Up the Ante",      200
          MENUITEM  "Borrow Money",     201
          MENUITEM  "Bet it All",       202
     END
     MENUITEM   "Deal the Cards",       300
END
```

Using the Resource File: Adding Menus

When the user selects the text associated with the POPUP item, the menu described within the BEGIN and END commands will pop up on the screen in a vertical list. You cannot nest POPUPs.

There are several options you can use to modify the appearance of a menu item. Place these options after the number associated with the item. The options are as follows:

- CHECKED   Places a check next to the menu item.

- GRAYED   Grays the menu text. The item cannot be selected.

- INACTIVE   The menu item cannot be selected.

- MENUBREAK   This item, and all items following it, starts a new row.

If you want to use several of these options, place them after each other, separated by commas. Do not use INACTIVE and GRAYED together.

With menu items in a pop-up menu, MENUBREAK begins a new column starting with the item having the MENUBREAK option. You can also use the MENUBARBREAK option with pop-up menu items. This option starts a new column and separates it with a bar. Adding a \a to pop-up text causes remaining text to be right-justified; adding a \t inserts a tab.

One further way of separating menu items is to use the MENUITEM SEPARATOR command, which places a dividing bar between two menu items. You can use it in normal and pop-up menus:

```
MENUITEM  "Create",    100
MENUITEM  SEPARATOR
MENUITEM  "Delete",    200
```

3 Using the Resource File: Adding Menus

You now know all the commands to design menus. Design a few. Following is the menu used in this chapter's program:

```
three MENU
BEGIN
    MENUITEM  "Hi",         100
    POPUP     "A PopUp"
    BEGIN
        MENUITEM  "Hi Mom",     200
        MENUITEM  "Hi Dad",     201
        MENUITEM  "Hi Mirna",   202, CHECKED
        MENUITEM  "Hi Betsy",   203, GRAYED
    END
    POPUP     "Two Cols"
    BEGIN
        MENUITEM  "Column 1",    300
        MENUITEM  "Next Line",   301
        MENUITEM  "Next Column", 302, MENUBARBREAK
    END
END
```

CHOOSING MENU COMMAND NAMES

For Windows 1.03, you can select menu items from the keyboard by simultaneously pressing the Alt key and the first letter of a menu item; thus, you might not want to have two commands with the same first letter in the same menu. Windows 2.0 provides more flexibility.

CHOOSING MENU COMMAND NAMES IN WINDOWS 2.0

With Windows 2.0, you can choose which letter in a menu item is used to select that item from the keyboard. This letter will be underlined on the screen. Insert a **&** in the MENUITEM text before the letter you want used. If you don't select a letter, the first letter will be used.

For example, suppose you have a menu option called Derivative and a menu option called Density. You could use Alt-D to select derivative and Alt-N to select density by including the following:

```
MENUITEM    "Derivative", 1007
MENUITEM    "De&nsity",   1023
```

INCLUDING THE MENU IN A PROGRAM

You include a menu in a program by defining it as the class menu. To do so, in **register_window,** set the lpszMenuName field in the WNDCLASS structure to the name of the menu. For example, the previous menu is called "three." To declare it as the menu for a program, place the following line in **register_window**:

```
/* use the menu "three" for this window. */
pClass->lpszMenuName = (LPSTR) "three";
```

Look for this line in the listing of THREE.C, which appears at the end of this chapter. Remember that in Chapter 2, the lpszMenuName parameter was set to NULL. When it is passed a menu name, that menu is used for the window.

MAKING YOUR OWN CURSOR

The program from Chapter 2 used one of the built-in Windows cursors. You can easily make and use your own cursor instead.

To make a cursor, use the ICONEDIT program that comes with the Windows Toolkit. Complete documentation for this program is listed in the "Programmer's Utility Guide" section of the Toolkit manuals.

Start up Windows, and load the ICONEDIT program. Select the Mode menu, and change the mode to Cursor. Draw the cursor you want to use in the large gray box on the screen. You can select colors with the Color menu. When you are finished, save the cursor, using the File menu.

3 Using the Resource File: Adding Menus

A cursor called MIKE.CUR is used for the remaining programs in this book. It is a picture of a face. You can make your own cursor or copy MIKE.CUR from the *Windows Guide Diskette*. Name your cursor whatever you like, but be sure to change the resource and make files appropriately.

To use the cursor you have designed in a Windows program, define the cursor in the resource file with the CURSOR command. Its format is as follows:

```
cursor_name    CURSOR    file_name
```

cursor_name is any name you choose that doesn't contain spaces. **file_name** is the name of the disk file containing the cursor. Use the name of the file that you created with ICONEDIT. For example, suppose the cursor is called "face" and is stored in the file "mike.cur." You could place the following line in the resource file:

```
face       CURSOR    mike.cur
```

Note that you do not use quotation marks for the cursor name, and you do not need to use quotation marks for the file name. If the file is not in the current working directory, you must specify a full path name.

Declare this cursor as the class cursor in **register_window**. Use **LoadCursor** to load the cursor. Pass it the instance handle and the name of the cursor, as defined in the resource file. Set the pClass->hCursor parameter to the value **LoadCursor** returns. For example, to load the face cursor, you would place the following line in **register_window**:

```
/* use the face cursor for the window's cursor */
pClass->hCursor = LoadCursor( hInstance, (LPSTR) "face");
```

Using the Resource File: Adding Menus 3

Note that the name passed to **LoadCursor** is the **cursor_name** parameter from the CURSOR statement, not the file name. You may want to look over the **register_window** procedure from the program in this chapter.

COMPILING WINDOWS PROGRAMS WITH RESOURCES

If your program uses resources, your make file must contain lines to process the resources. First, add a line to compile the resources to a file with a .RES extension. This file is dependent on the .RC file and any files that the .RC file references. For example, if the .RC file mentions a cursor file, the .RES file is dependent on the cursor file.

Compile the resources with the following line:

```
rc -r file.rc
```

where **file.rc** is the name of the resource file. This process creates a file called "file.res."

Then, add the resources to your executable code by placing the following line after the link4 statement:

```
rc file.res
```

Following is the make file for this chapter's program. Note the addition of the lines for compiling resources.

3 Using the Resource File: Adding Menus

```
#
#   Make file for Chapter 3
#

cc = cl -d -c -AS -Gsw -Os -Zpe

.c.obj:
    $(cc) $*.c


three.obj: three.c   three.h


#
# compile resources.  Note that three.res needs to be updated
# if three.rc, mike.cur, or three.h change
#

three.res: three.rc mike.cur three.h
    rc -r three.rc


#
# note that three.exe needs to change if three.res changes
# note the use of rc after the link
#

three.exe: three.obj three.res three.def
    link4 three,/align:16,NUL,slibw, three.def
    rc three.res
```

This make file assumes that the code, module definition file, resource file, include file, and cursor file are all in the working directory. If you set your system up differently, change your make file appropriately. It is suggested that you keep all of your source and resource files for a particular program in one directory. Switch to that directory before compiling. Use SET and PATH statements so that the computer can find make, link4, rc, the libraries, and the compiler programs.

Using the Resource File: Adding Menus **3**

A PROGRAM: THREE

Following is a program, THREE, that ties together the features discussed in this chapter. It has a menu with several items, including a pop-up, checked items, and grayed items, and it uses its own cursor (see Figure 3.1).

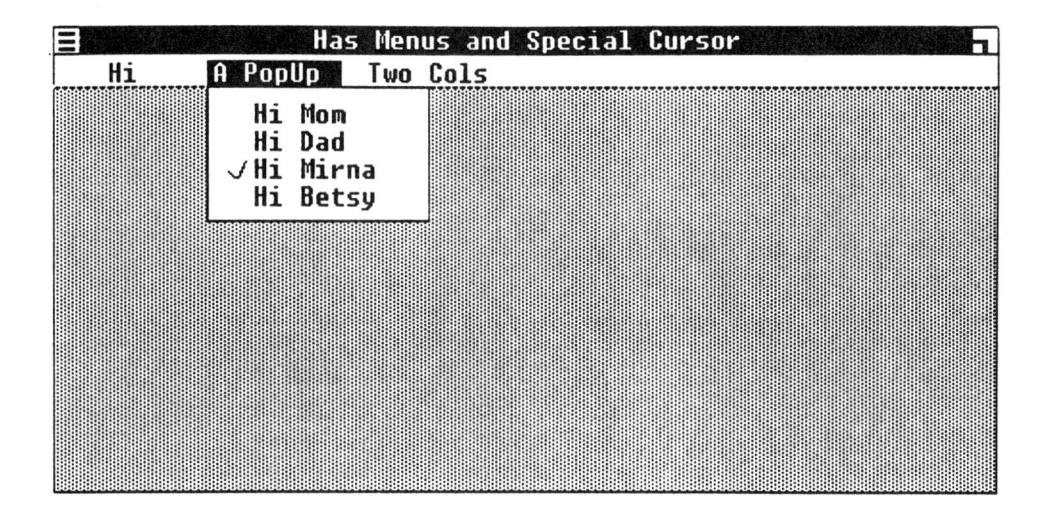

Figure 3.1 The program THREE with a pop-up menu.

Note the resource file and how **register_window** has been changed to incorporate a menu and a different cursor.

Run this program along with another application. Note how the cursor changes once you enter THREE's window. Select items from THREE's menu. Note how the pop-up menus work. Make THREE's window very small (by adjusting the size of the other application so that THREE doesn't have much room). Make THREE small vertically and horizontally. Perhaps create several cursors and change THREE.RC to use them.

47

3 Using the Resource File: Adding Menus

The listing for THREE is as follows:

```
/------------------------------------------\
|                                          |
| MIKE.CUR is in the root directory of the |
| Windows Guide diskette.  The rest of the |
| programs are in the THREE directory.  The|
| make file is THREE.  The include file is |
| THREE.H.  The code is in THREE.C.  The   |
| module definition file is THREE.DEF, and |
| the resource file is THREE.RC.  The      |
| executable version is THREE.EXE.  Copy   |
| MIKE.CUR to the working directory before |
| you compile the program.                 |
|                                          |
\------------------------------------------/
```

The Make File: THREE

```
#
#  Make file for Chapter 3
#

cc = cl -d -c -AS -Gsw -Os -Zpe

.c.obj:
    $(cc) $*.c



three.obj: three.c  three.h

three.res: three.rc mike.cur three.h
    rc -r three.rc


three.exe: three.obj three.res three.def
    link4 three,/align:16,NUL,slibw, three.def
    rc three.res
```

The Resource File: THREE.RC

```
/**************************************************************
    Resource file for Chapter 3
**************************************************************/



#include "windows.h"
#include "three.h"

face        CURSOR      "mike.cur"

three MENU
BEGIN
    MENUITEM    "Hi",       100
    POPUP       "A PopUp"
    BEGIN
        MENUITEM    "Hi Mom",       200
        MENUITEM    "Hi Dad",       201
        MENUITEM    "Hi Mirna",     202, CHECKED
        MENUITEM    "Hi Betsy",     203, GRAYED
    END
    POPUP       "Two Cols"
    BEGIN
        MENUITEM    "Column 1",     300
        MENUITEM    "Next Line",    301
        MENUITEM    "Next Column",  302, MENUBARBREAK
    END
END
```

The Include File: THREE.H

```
/**************************************************************
    Contains typedefs, constants, and external declarations
    for Chapter 3
**************************************************************/


extern int PASCAL WinMain();
extern int register_window();
extern long FAR PASCAL MsgServer();
```

3 Using the Resource File: Adding Menus

The Code: THREE.C

```c
/************************************************************
    File:      three.c
    Program:   three

    This is the Windows program for Chapter 3.  It creates a
    window with a title bar and a menu.  It also uses a user
    created cursor.
************************************************************/



#include "windows.h"
#include "three.h"




/*---------------------------------------------------------
    This is the Start Up procedure and message relayer
---------------------------------------------------------*/

int PASCAL
WinMain( hInstance, hPrevInstance, lpszCmdLine, cmdShow )
HANDLE    hInstance, hPrevInstance;
LPSTR     lpszCmdLine;
int       cmdShow;
{
    HWND      hWnd;
    MSG       msg;

    /* If this is the first instance, register the
       window class
    */
    if (hPrevInstance == NULL)
        register_window(hInstance);

    /* don't need previous instance information */
```

continued...

...from previous page

```
    /* Create a tiled window */
    hWnd = CreateWindow( (LPSTR) "Chap3WIN",    /* class */
                /* title */
                (LPSTR) "Has Menus and Special Cursor",
                WS_TILEDWINDOW,          /* style */
                0, 0, 0, 0,
                (HWND) NULL,             /* parent */
                (HMENU) NULL,            /* use class menu */
                (HANDLE) hInstance,      /* instance */
                (LPSTR) NULL );

    /* now display it */
    ShowWindow(hWnd,cmdShow);
    UpdateWindow(hWnd);


    /* relay all messages to the message server */
    while (GetMessage( (LPMSG) &msg, NULL, 0, 0) ) {
        TranslateMessage( (LPMSG) &msg);
        DispatchMessage( (LPMSG) &msg);
    }

    exit(msg.wParam);
}




/*-----------------------------------------------------------
   This procedure registers the window
-------------------------------------------------------------*/

int
register_window(hInstance)
HANDLE hInstance;
{
    PWNDCLASS      pClass;

    pClass = (PWNDCLASS) LocalAlloc(LPTR, sizeof(WNDCLASS));

    /* Use your own cursor, as defined in three.rc */
    pClass->hCursor = LoadCursor(hInstance, (LPSTR) "face");
```

continued...

3 Using the Resource File: Adding Menus

...from previous page

```
        pClass->hIcon = LoadIcon(NULL, (LPSTR) IDI_APPLICATION);

        /* Use the menu "three", as defined in three.rc */
        pClass->lpszMenuName = (LPSTR) "three";

        pClass->lpszClassName = (LPSTR) "Chap3WIN";
        pClass->hbrBackground = GetStockObject(LTGRAY_BRUSH);
        pClass->hInstance = hInstance;
        pClass->style = CS_HREDRAW | CS_VREDRAW;
        pClass->lpfnWndProc = MsgServer;

        RegisterClass( (LPWNDCLASS) pClass);
        LocalFree( (HANDLE) pClass);
}




/*-----------------------------------------------------------
   This procedure receives the messages from Windows and
   decides how to process them.
  -----------------------------------------------------------*/
long FAR PASCAL
MsgServer( hWnd, message, wParam, lParam )
HWND        hWnd;
unsigned    message;
WORD        wParam;
LONG        lParam;
{
    /* just use the defaults */
    return( DefWindowProc(hWnd,message,wParam,lParam) );
}
```

The Module Definition File: THREE.DEF

```
NAME       Three
DESCRIPTION   'Third Window Program'
STUB       'winstub.exe'
CODE       MOVEABLE
DATA       MOVEABLE MULTIPLE
HEAPSIZE 4096
STACKSIZE 4096
EXPORTS
           MsgServer @1
```

ADVANCED CONCEPTS: CLASS

When a program starts, it creates a window using the **CreateWindow** command. This command specifies the *class* to use for the window. The **register_window** routine gives details about the class if the program is the first instance.

The class defines the cursor, menu, icon, background color, and other features for every program in that class. If, as occurs in the next chapter, a program changes part of the class structure, that change takes effect for all programs in that class. For example, the program FOUR1 changes the class cursor. If there are several copies of FOUR1 running at the same time, as soon as one of the copies changes the class cursor, the cursor will change for every copy of FOUR1.

Similarly, if a new program loads that uses the same class, and changes the class parameters, the latest parameters will hold for all programs in that class.

Class provides a convenient way of grouping programs with similar display features. If you want to, you can use a different class for each program. If, however, you can make several different programs with the same class, you will save system memory because Windows will not need to keep information on as many classes.

3 Using the Resource File: Adding Menus

SUMMARY

- Describe menus in the *resource file*. The resource file is a normal text file with the extension .RC.

- Use **#include** to include constant definitions and /* */ to add comments to a resource file.

- *Menus* are described by the MENU, MENUITEM, POPUP, BEGIN, and END commands. Each item in a menu has text and a number associated with it.

- *Pop-up* items cause a further list of commands to be displayed.

- You can modify the appearance of a menu with the CHECKED, GRAYED, INACTIVE, MENUBREAK, and MENUBARBREAK commands. You can add a separator with the MENUITEM SEPARATOR command.

- Menus are added to a Windows program by setting the lpszMenuName parameter of WNDCLASS in the **register_window** procedure.

- You can design your own cursor with the ICONEDIT utility.

- To add a cursor to a program, define it in the resource file with the CURSOR command. Then, set the hCursor parameter of WNDCLASS in the **register_window** procedure by using the **LoadCursor** function.

- *Classes* group programs with similar display characteristics. Changes to the class affect all programs in that class.

CHAPTER 4

INPUT FROM MENUS: RECEIVING MESSAGES

4 Input from Menus: Receiving Messages

In the last chapter, you learned how to add a menu to a Windows program. In this chapter, you will see how to process commands from menus. You will also learn how to change a program's cursor, change a class's cursor, use global variables, modify menu items, create your own icon, get information from previous instances, and use an accelerator table.

GETTING MENU COMMANDS

When a user selects a menu item by pointing and clicking the mouse, a message is sent to the **WinMain** procedure. **WinMain**, in turn, passes it to **MsgServer**. This message has two parts. The first identifies it as a command from a menu. The second indicates the menu item.

Remember that the MENUITEM command, which is used in the resource file to describe a menu, has two parts: the text and a number. This number is used to identify the menu item selected.

Specifically, when a menu item is selected, **MsgServer** is passed the value **WM_COMMAND** in the parameter **message** and the menu item number in the parameter **wParam**.

So, to process a menu command, check for the WM_COMMAND message in **MsgServer**. If it is found, pass the wParam value to a procedure that processes menu commands. Be sure also to pass the hWnd parameter. You could use the following routine:

```
/*-------------------------------------------------------------
    This procedure receives the messages from Windows and
    decides how to process them.  Commands from the menu
    come in with a WM_COMMAND message, and the command
    number in wParam.
-------------------------------------------------------------*/
long FAR PASCAL
MsgServer( hWnd, message, wParam, lParam )
HWND      hWnd;
unsigned  message;
WORD      wParam;
LONG      lParam;
{
```
continued...

Input from Menus: Receiving Messages 4

...from previous page

```
    /* if it is a menu command, process it */
    if (message == WM_COMMAND)
        return( process_menu_cmds(hWnd,wParam) );

    /* else just use the defaults */
    return( DefWindowProc(hWnd,message,wParam,lParam) );
}
```

The procedure that processes menu commands needs to check for the various menu commands and act on them. If it is successful, it should return a LONG 0.

ASSIGNING MENU ITEM NUMBERS

In the program THREE, menu items were labeled with numbers somewhat arbitrarily. Now that you will be processing these numbers, you need a better system. Use constants for all of your menu numbers. Define these constants in an include file that is loaded in the resource and code files. It will be much easier to refer to these constants when creating the menu description and when writing routines to process the menu commands.

Start all your menu message constants with the prefix IDM_. Have each column start a new hundreds place, and have all of the items within a pop-up have the same hundreds place. Don't assign any values less than 100.

For example, you could use the following constants and menu description:

4 Input from Menus: Receiving Messages

```
#define  IDM_FILE            100
#define  IDM_EDIT_CHECK      200
#define  IDM_EDIT_GRAY       210
#define  IDM_EDIT_CHANGE     220


four1 MENU
BEGIN
    MENUITEM   "File",         IDM_FILE
    POPUP      "Edit Menu"
    BEGIN
        MENUITEM   "Check",    IDM_EDIT_CHECK
        MENUITEM   "Gray",     IDM_EDIT_GRAY
        MENUITEM   "Change",   IDM_EDIT_CHANGE
    END
END
```

CHANGING THE CURSOR

In the last chapter, you selected a cursor for the class by setting the class's hCursor parameter in **register_window**. This procedure is fine if you never want the cursor to change. You might, however, want to change the cursor while a program is running. For example, you could switch to the hourglass cursor during extensive calculations, or use the I-beam cursor for text operations.

To change the cursor, the class cursor must be set to NULL; otherwise, whenever the mouse moves, the class cursor is displayed; any other cursor will never be seen.

If the class cursor is NULL, you can use the **SetCursor** command to select the cursor. Its format is as follows:

```
HCURSOR
SetCursor( hCursor )
```

hCursor is a handle to the cursor to be used. The function returns a handle to the previous cursor.

For example, if you wanted to switch to the hourglass cursor, you could use the following command:

```
SetCursor( LoadCursor( NULL, IDC_WAIT ) );
```

To switch to the face cursor, you could use the following command:

```
SetCursor( LoadCursor( hInstance, (LPSTR) "face" ) );
```

There is one drawback to selecting the cursor using this method. If the user moves the cursor outside of the application, the cursor will change. For example, if the user moves to the icon area, the cursor will change to the icon cursor, which is fine. But when the user moves the cursor back into your program, the cursor won't change. The last cursor (the icon cursor, for example) will be the one displayed.

To get around this problem, you can change the class cursor. Every time the cursor moves into your application, it will be set to the class cursor. Use the **SetClassWord** command. Its format is as follows:

```
WORD
SetClassWord( hWnd, nIndex, wNewWord )
```

hWnd   is a handle to the window. You should use the hWnd that is passed as a parameter to **MsgServer**. If you use this command in a routine other than **MsgServer**, make sure that **MsgServer** passes its hWnd parameter.

nIndex   tells what class item to set. It can be one of the following:

         GCW_HBRBACKGROUND
         GCW_HCURSOR
         GCW_HICON
         GCW_HMODULE   (for setting hInstance)
         GCW_STYLE

         Use GCW_CURSOR to set the cursor.

4 Input from Menus: Receiving Messages

wNewWord   is a handle for the new item. If you are setting the cursor, it should be a handle to the cursor, typecast as a WORD.

The return value is a handle to the previous item.

If you wanted to select the hourglass as the class cursor, for example, you could do the following:

```
/* select the hourglass cursor, and define it as the
   class cursor.
*/
hCursor = LoadCursor( NULL, IDC_WAIT );
SetClassWord(hWnd, GCW_HCURSOR, (WORD) hCursor);
```

The disadvantage of using this method is that it changes the cursor for all applications in the class. Thus, if one of the programs switches to the hourglass cursor, all applications of that class will switch to the hourglass cursor. You can see a demonstration of this process when you run FOUR1 or FOUR2.

Note that you can use **SetClassWord** to change many of the class's features.

USING GLOBAL VARIABLES

Now that you can process menu commands, your programs will become more complex, and you will find you need global variables. You probably try to avoid global variables in conventional programs and instead rely on passing parameters. Remember, however, that Windows programs don't change state. All commands start in **WinMain** and flow to **MsgServer**; thus, you really can't have a set of local variables storing important information that is passed through procedure parameters.[1] Instead, you will need to keep state information in global variables. State information gives you status details, such as whether a word processor is in insert or typeover mode or whether a drawing program is drawing lines or filled circles.

---

[1] You could, however, use static variables.

For example, if you had a menu option to select whether text was italicized or not, you would set up a global Boolean variable called **italics_glbl**. If the user selected the italics option, you would set this variable to TRUE. If the user chose not to have italics, you would set this variable to FALSE.

Define global variables just as you would in any other C program. Programs are easier to read if you indicate global variables with a prefix or suffix. For example, you could end all global variables with **_glbl**. It is stylistically better if you place all global variables right after any **#include**s or **#define**s at the beginning of the main code module. It is suggested that you place the **WinMain** procedure right after the global variables. Remember that if you are using several code modules, you will need to declare the global variables as external if other modules are to use them. You can see an example of external declarations in the file FOUR1.H.

If you need to initialize global variables, do so after the **UpdateWindow** call in **WinMain**. You can see an example of this step in the file FOUR1.C.

MODIFYING MENU ITEMS

Menu items display a list of commands from which the user chooses. Sometimes you need to alter the menu choices. For example, you may want to prevent the user from editing an object if there are no objects to edit. You do so by disabling the edit command. Or you might want to place a check mark next to a menu item. You could do so to indicate which type size was selected. You also might like to add new menu commands or change the wording of existing ones while a program is running.

This section will show you how to modify menu items. It is an important technique you will use many times throughout this book and in your own programs.

Before you edit a menu, you need to get a pointer to the menu structure with the **GetMenu** command. Its format is as follows:

```
HMENU
GetMenu( hWnd )
```

4 Input from Menus: Receiving Messages

hWnd is a handle for the program's window. The return value is a pointer to the menu.

Once you have this handle, you can change any of the items in the menu. If you want to place or remove a check mark from a menu item, use the **CheckMenuItem** command. Its format is as follows:

```
BOOL
CheckMenuItem( hMenu, MenuItem, wCheck )
```

hMenu   is a handle for the menu. Get this value using **GetMenu**.

MenuItem   is the number associated with the menu item. Use the same number that is returned when the item is selected. Remember, menu items are described in the resource file by the command **MENUITEM "text", number**. Set MenuItem to **number**.

wCheck   is a combination of the following commands, combined with the bitwise OR (|) operator:

    MF__CHECKED   checks the item

    MF__UNCHECKED   removes a check from the item

    MF__BYCOMMAND MenuItem is the number associated with the menu item.

You can use MF__BYPOSITION instead of MF__BYCOMMAND, which lets you describe the menu item to alter by its position in the menu. If you use this method, set MenuItem to the position of the object in the menu, where the first object is numbered zero.

It is suggested that you always use the MF__BYCOMMAND option; thus, to check a menu item, set wCheck to MF__CHECKED | MF__BYCOMMAND. To uncheck an item, set wCheck to MF__UNCHECKED | MF__BYCOMMAND.

The return value is the previous state of the menu item. It is either MF_CHECKED or MF_UNCHECKED.

Although you can call **CheckMenuItem** to see if an item is checked or not, you should instead keep the status of the item in a global variable. For example, suppose you had a menu command to select italics. Selecting this command would toggle italics mode, which you can accomplish by setting up a global Boolean variable to store the state of italics. Set it to TRUE when italics are active, and FALSE when they are not. Whenever the italics command is selected, toggle the variable's state. You could use the following code fragment:

```
switch (menu_command) {

case IDM_ITALICS:
    if (italics_glbl == TRUE) {
        CheckMenuItem( hMenu, IDM_ITALICS, MF_UNCHECKED |
            MF_BYCOMMAND );
        italics_glbl = FALSE;
    }
    else {
        CheckMenuItem( hMenu, IDM_ITALICS, MF_CHECKED |
            MF_BYCOMMAND );
        italics_glbl = TRUE;
    }

}
```

The main body of your program would examine the variable italics_glbl to determine whether to italicize or not.

This fragment operates on a menu command and is intended as part of the **process_menu_cmds** procedure. Note that the value identifying the menu command is the same value used to identify the item to italicize, which is quite convenient.

Suppose that a menu contained a list of mutually exclusive choices, such as text size. For example, suppose that you could choose either 10-, 12-, or 15-pitch text. You could use menu checks to indicate the currently selected item.

4 Input from Menus: Receiving Messages

If you wanted to, you could include three Booleans indicating whether or not each pitch was selected. A much better way would be to have a variable storing the pitch selection command. Preferably, the low order digits of this command would indicate the pitch. For example, you could include

```
#define IDM_PITCH_10    110
#define IDM_PITCH_12    112
#define IDM_PITCH_15    115
#define IDM_PITCH       100
```

as the values for the menu commands. Then, the menu processing section could be as follows:

```
switch (menu_command) {

case IDM_PITCH_10:
case IDM_PITCH_12:
case IDM_PITCH_15:
    CheckMenuItem( hMenu, pitch_glbl, MF_UNCHECKED |
        MF_BYCOMMAND);
    CheckMenuItem( hMenu, menu_command, MF_CHECKED |
        MF_BYCOMMAND);
    pitch_glbl = menu_command;

}
```

To determine the pitch, you would subtract IDM__PITCH from pitch__glbl.

Note the simplicity of this routine. Instead of having three similar sets of routines to process the three possible commands, you only need one simple, efficient routine. This routine works because pitch__glbl not only indicates the pitch but also identifies the menu command for selecting the pitch; thus, it can be used to remove the check from the previous selection. As menu__command identifies the newly selected item, it can be used to place a check next to the new pitch value.

Input from Menus: Receiving Messages 4

If you have a list of mutually exclusive commands, try to use the format just described. It will save space and make your code more legible. Note, however, that you cannot use this format for all mutually exclusive lists.

Sometimes, instead of checking a menu item, you want to disable it. For example, suppose you didn't want to allow the user to italicize text. You could ignore all requests to do so. A better approach is not to let the user even select italics. That way, it is clear that the option is not available, rather than that the program is broken. Prevent the user from selecting an item by graying it with the **EnableMenuItem** command. Its format is as follows:

EnableMenuItem(hMenu, MenuItem, wEnable)

hMenu is a handle to the menu. Obtain this value with **GetMenu**.

MenuItem is the number associated with the menu item, which is the same as for **CheckMenuItem**.

wEnable is one of the following:

MF__GRAYED	grays and disables the item
MF__DISABLED	disables but does not gray the item
MF__ENABLED	enables the item

Combine this command with MF__BYPOSITION or MF__BYCOMMAND.

It is suggested that you do not use MF__DISABLED or MF__BYPOSITION; thus, to disable an item, use MF__GRAYED | MF__BYCOMMAND. To enable an item, use MF__ENABLED | MF__BYCOMMAND.

When an item is disabled, there is no way to select that item. The actions from some other command must enable the item before it can be selected.

4 Input from Menus: Receiving Messages

You can also insert, delete, or alter items in a menu, which allows you to add new commands or change old ones because of some choice the user made.

To change, add, or delete menu items, use the **ChangeMenu** command. Its format is as follows:

ChangeMenu(hMenu, MenuItem, lpNewItem, wNewMenuItem, wChange)

hMenu   is a handle to the menu.

MenuItem   is the number associated with the item to change. If you are inserting a new command, the command will be inserted before the item identified by MenuItem. If you want to append a new command, set MenuItem to NULL.

lpNewItem   is a pointer to the new menu item. If you are changing the text for a given menu item, or inserting or appending a new menu item, set this pointer to a long pointer to the ASCIIZ text for the new item. For example, you could set it to (LPSTR) "A New Choice." If you are adding a pop-up menu, set this pointer to a handle to the pop-up menu. You will see how to make pop-up menus shortly. If you want to add a horizontal separator to the menu, set this pointer to NULL. If the new item is a bit map, set this pointer to a handle to the bit map.

wNewMenuItem is the number to identify the new menu item. This number is the value that will be returned when the item is selected. Set this number to MenuItem if you are not inserting or appending a new menu item. If you are adding a pop-up menu, set this number to the handle of the pop-up menu.

wChange is one of the following. Choices can be ORed together where appropriate:

MF__CHANGE	changes the specified item
MF__INSERT	inserts a new item
MF__APPEND	adds the new item to the end of the list
MF__DELETE	removes the menu item
MF__ENABLED	enables the item
MF__GRAYED	grays and disables the item
MF__DISABLED	disables but doesn't gray the item
MF__CHECKED	checks the item
MF__UNCHECKED	unchecks the item
MF__MENUBREAK	starts the item on a new line or column
MF__MENUBARBREAK	starts the item on a new line or column; separates new columns by a bar
MF__SEPARATOR	separates pop-up items by a horizontal bar
MF__STRING	the new item is a text string
MF__POPUP	the new item is a pop-up menu
MF__BITMAP	the new item is a bit map
MF__BYCOMMAND	MenuItem identifies the number associated with the menu item
MF__BYPOSITION	MenuItem identifies the position of the menu item

Pop-up menus can only be added to top-level menu commands. If you change a top-level menu item, call **DrawMenuBar** so that the menu display will be updated. **DrawMenuBar** has the following format:

```
DrawMenuBar( hWnd )
```

hWnd is a handle for the window.

4 Input from Menus: Receiving Messages

Before you change the text for a menu item, you may want to copy the current text with the **GetMenuString** function. Its format is as follows:

```
int
GetMenuString( hMenu, MenuItem, lpString, Count, wFlag )
```

hMenu　　　is a handle for the menu.

MenuItem　　is the number for the menu item.

lpString　　is a long pointer to a buffer to which the menu text will be copied.

Count　　　is the maximum number of characters to copy, which must not be greater than the size of the lpString buffer.

wFlag　　　is either MF__BYCOMMAND or MF__BYPOSITION.

The function returns the number of characters copied.

If you want to add a pop-up menu to the current menu, you first need to create the pop-up. Create a new menu with the **CreateMenu** command. Its format is as follows:

```
HMENU
CreateMenu()
```

The value returned is a handle to a new menu structure.

Use **ChangeMenu** to add items to a new menu. To add the menu as a pop-up, pass the handle as the lpNewItem parameter for **ChangeMenu**, and select the other parameters appropriately.

You can also completely replace the main menu. Create a new menu with **CreateMenu** and **ChangeMenu**, just as you did to add a pop-up. Then, call **SetMenu**. Its format is as follows:

SetMenu(hWnd, hMenu)

hWnd   is a handle to the window.

hMenu   is a handle to the new menu. Set it to NULL if you want to remove the menu bar.

The new menu will now be the system menu. **Note:** this command will not change the class menu, only the menu for the current window. If you want to restore the original menu, make sure that you save a handle to it using **GetMenu**. This handle should be stored as a global variable.[2]

MAKING YOUR OWN ICONS

The programs from Chapters 2 and 3 used the same icon, which could be confusing if both were in the iconic state at the same time. You should develop a unique icon for each program you create.

You create a new icon with ICONEDIT. The steps are the same as for creating a new cursor, only select Icon mode rather than Cursor mode. Then, add an **ICON** statement to your resource file. Its format is as follows:

icon_name   ICON   icon_file

Note that the format is quite similar to the CURSOR format. **icon__name** is the name programs use for the icon. **icon__file** is the name of the file you created with ICONEDIT.

---

[2] By changing menus, you can create the cascading menu structure typical of many conventional programs. Make sure that commands from different menus don't use the same menu item identifier values.

4 Input from Menus: Receiving Messages

All remaining programs in this book have their own icons. These icons have an extension of .ICO. For example, the icon for the program FOUR1 is called FOUR1.ICO. It is referenced in the file FOUR1.RC:

```
four1          ICON          four1.ico
```

Set a program's icon in the **register_window** procedure. Instead of loading a built-in icon, load your own. For example, you could use the following:

```
/* load the special icon for FOUR1 */
pClass->hIcon = LoadIcon( hInstance, (LPSTR) "four1" );
```

A PROGRAM: FOUR1

So far, this chapter has shown you how to

- get commands from menus
- change the cursor
- use global variables
- modify menu items
- change menus
- use unique icons

Now, look at a program that uses many of these techniques. It has two pop-up menus. The first pop-up lets the user select the cursor. The first six choices change the program cursor; the last two change the class cursor. The second pop-up demonstrates the menu editing techniques. It lets the user toggle the check mark on an item, gray a selection, and alter the text of an item. The program uses a special icon (see Figure 4.1).

Input from Menus: Receiving Messages 4

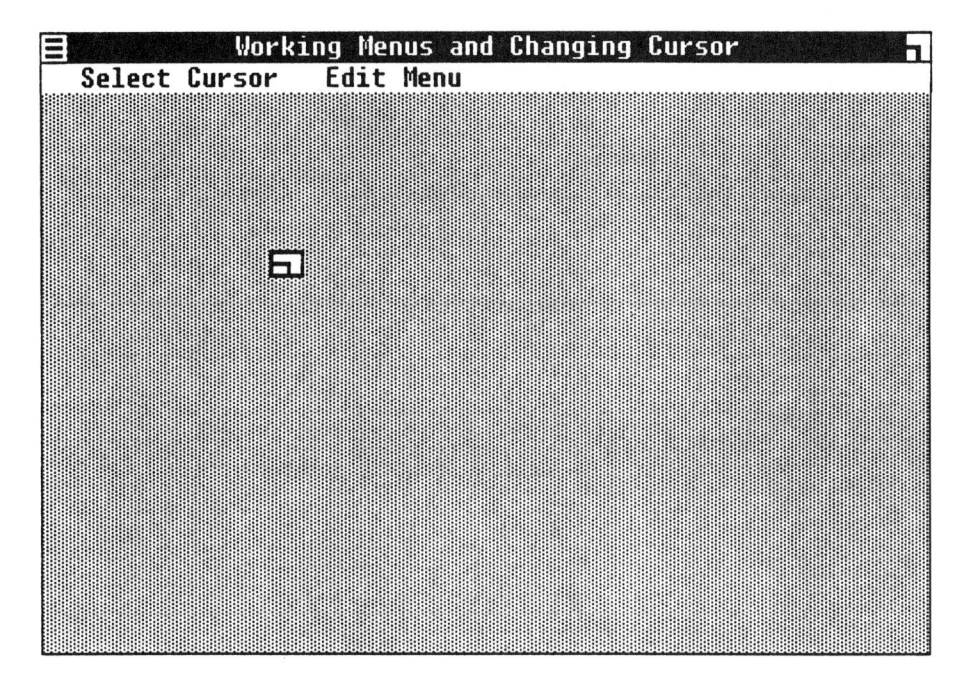

Figure 4.1   The program FOUR1.

There are a few points you should examine when you look over the program. First, note the use of constants in the resource file and the code. Also, note the use of ICON in the resource file.

Note the declaration and initialization of global variables. Also, see how hCursor and hIcon are set in **register_window**. The class cursor is set to NULL, and a program cursor is set in **register_window**.

Notice how **MsgServer** checks for the WM_COMMAND message and relays the particular command to a routine called **process_menu_cmds**. **process_menu_cmds** is a big switch statement. Note the use of **SetCursor**, **SetClassWord**, **GetMenu**, and the menu editing commands.

Load a few copies when you test the program. See what happens when you change the program cursor. See what happens when you change the class cursor. Note that when you edit the menu from one program, it has no effect on the menu in another program.

4 Input from Menus: Receiving Messages

```
/--------------------------------------------\
|                                            |
| The code for this program is found in the  |
| FOUR1 directory.  The make file is FOUR1.  |
| The resource file is FOUR1.RC.  The        |
| include file is FOUR1.H.  The code is      |
| FOUR1.C.  The module definition file is    |
| FOUR1.DEF.  The icon is FOUR1.ICO.  The    |
| cursor, MIKE.CUR, is located in the root   |
| directory.  FOUR1.EXE is the executable    |
| file.                                      |
|                                            |
\--------------------------------------------/
```

The Make File: FOUR1

```
#
#  Make file for the first program in Chapter 4
#

cc=cl -d -c -AS -Gsw -Os -Zpe

.c.obj:
    $(cc) $*.c


four1.obj: four1.c  four1.h

four1.res: four1.rc four1.h four1.ico
    rc -r four1.rc

four1.exe: four1.obj four1.res four1.def
    link4 four1, /align:16, NUL, slibw, four1.def
    rc four1.res
```

Input from Menus: Receiving Messages 4

The Resource File: FOUR1.RC

```
/************************************************************
    Resource file for the first program in Chapter 4.
    No accelerator table.
************************************************************/


#include "windows.h"
#include "four1.h"



face      CURSOR    mike.cur
four1     ICON      four1.ico

four1 MENU
BEGIN
    POPUP       "Select Cursor"
    BEGIN
        MENUITEM    "Arrow",          IDM_CURSOR_ARROW
        MENUITEM    "I-Beam",         IDM_CURSOR_IBEAM
        MENUITEM    "Size Box",       IDM_CURSOR_SIZE
        MENUITEM    "Icon Cursor",    IDM_CURSOR_ICON
        MENUITEM    "Cross",          IDM_CURSOR_CROSS,
                                      MENUBARBREAK
        MENUITEM    "My Cursor",      IDM_CURSOR_MINE
        MENUITEM    "Hourglass",      IDM_CURSOR_WAIT
        MENUITEM    "Up Arrow",       IDM_CURSOR_UPARROW
    END
    POPUP       "Edit Menu"
    BEGIN
        MENUITEM    "Check",          IDM_EDIT_CHECK
        MENUITEM    "Gray",           IDM_EDIT_GRAY
        MENUITEM    "Change",         IDM_EDIT_CHANGE
    END
END
```

4 Input from Menus: Receiving Messages

The Include File: FOUR1.H

```
/************************************************************
     Include file for FOUR1.  Contains typedefs, constants,
     and external declarations.
************************************************************/


extern int PASCAL WinMain();
extern int register_window();
extern long FAR PASCAL MsgServer();
extern long process_menu_cmds();


int       checked_glbl;
HANDLE    instance_glbl;


/* Constants for the menu choices */

#define   IDM_CURSOR_ARROW      100
#define   IDM_CURSOR_IBEAM      110
#define   IDM_CURSOR_SIZE       120
#define   IDM_CURSOR_ICON       130
#define   IDM_CURSOR_CROSS      140
#define   IDM_CURSOR_MINE       150
#define   IDM_CURSOR_WAIT       160
#define   IDM_CURSOR_UPARROW    170


#define   IDM_EDIT_CHECK        200
#define   IDM_EDIT_GRAY         210
#define   IDM_EDIT_CHANGE       220
```

Input from Menus: Receiving Messages 4

The Code: FOUR1.C

```
/************************************************************
     File:      four1.c
     Program:   four1

     This is the first program from Chapter 4.  The menus
     are operational.  One menu selects the cursor.  The
     other menu illustrates menu editing features.  It also
     illustrates the use of global variables.

     In addition, this program uses its own icon.

     The cursor selection demonstrates how class parameters
     affect the Window in a more permanent way.
*************************************************************/


#include "windows.h"
#include "four1.h"


/*----------------------------------------------------------
  global variables
------------------------------------------------------*/

int        checked_glbl;
HANDLE     instance_glbl;



/*----------------------------------------------------------
    This is the Start Up procedure and message relayer
------------------------------------------------------*/

int PASCAL
WinMain(hInstance, hPrevInstance, lpszCmdLine, cmdShow)
HANDLE     hInstance, hPrevInstance;
LPSTR      lpszCmdLine;
int        cmdShow;
```

continued...

4 Input from Menus: Receiving Messages

...from previous page

```
{
    HWND      hWnd;
    MSG       msg;
    /* If this is the first instance, register the
       window class
    */
    if (!hPrevInstance)
        register_window(hInstance);

    /* don't need previous instance information */

    /* Create a tiled window */
    hWnd = CreateWindow( (LPSTR) "Chap41WIN",     /* class */
             (LPSTR) "Working Menus and Changing Cursor",
             WS_TILEDWINDOW,          /* style */
             0, 0, 0, 0,
             (HWND) NULL,             /* parent */
             (HMENU) NULL,            /* use class menu */
             (HANDLE) hInstance,      /* instance */
             (LPSTR) NULL );

    /* Now display it */
    ShowWindow(hWnd,cmdShow);
    UpdateWindow(hWnd);

    /* initialize global variables */
    checked_glbl = FALSE;
    instance_glbl = hInstance;

    /* relay all messages to the message server */
    while (GetMessage( (LPMSG) &msg, NULL, 0, 0) ) {
        TranslateMessage( (LPMSG) &msg);
        DispatchMessage( (LPMSG) &msg);
    }

    exit(msg.wParam);
}
```

continued...

Input from Menus: Receiving Messages 4

...from previous page

```
/*-----------------------------------------------------
    This procedure registers the window.  Because we will
    change cursors in the application, we need to register
    the cursor as NULL and then immediately set it.  The
    routine also loads the user created icon.
-------------------------------------------------------*/

int
register_window( hInstance )
HANDLE   hInstance;
{
    PWNDCLASS      pClass;

    pClass = (PWNDCLASS) LocalAlloc(LPTR, sizeof(WNDCLASS));

    /* register the cursor as NULL so that the application can
       change it
    */
    pClass->hCursor = (HCURSOR) NULL;

    /* load a special icon, defined in four1.rc */
    pClass->hIcon = LoadIcon( hInstance, (LPSTR) "four1");

    pClass->lpszMenuName = (LPSTR) "four1";
    pClass->lpszClassName = (LPSTR) "Chap41WIN";
    pClass->hbrBackground = GetStockObject(LTGRAY_BRUSH);
    pClass->hInstance = hInstance;
    pClass->style = CS_HREDRAW | CS_VREDRAW;
    pClass->lpfnWndProc = MsgServer;

    RegisterClass( (LPWNDCLASS) pClass);
    LocalFree( (HANDLE) pClass);

    /* Set the initial cursor.  Use the standard arrow */
    SetCursor(LoadCursor(NULL, (LPSTR) IDC_ARROW));
}
```

continued...

4 Input from Menus: Receiving Messages

...from previous page

```
/*-----------------------------------------------------------
    This procedure receives the messages from Windows and
    decides how to process them.  Commands from the menu
    come in with a WM_COMMAND message, and the command
    number in wParam.
-----------------------------------------------------------*/
long FAR PASCAL
MsgServer( hWnd, message, wParam, lParam )
HWND      hWnd;
unsigned  message;
WORD      wParam;
LONG      lParam;
{
    /* if it is a menu command, process it */
    if (message == WM_COMMAND)
        return( process_menu_cmds(hWnd,wParam) );
    /* else just use the defaults */
    return( DefWindowProc(hWnd,message,wParam,lParam) );
}




/*-----------------------------------------------------------
    This routine processes commands from the menu.  It
    returns a 0 if everything was OK.

    Note that the command values are those specified in
    the menu definition of four1.rc.
-----------------------------------------------------------*/
long
process_menu_cmds( hWnd, command )
HWND      hWnd;
WORD      command;
{
    HMENU     hMenu;
    HCURSOR   hCursor;
    char      new_string[10];
```

continued...

...from previous page

```c
    /* get the handle for the menu */
    hMenu = GetMenu(hWnd);

    /* now process the commands */
    switch (command) {
    case IDM_CURSOR_ARROW:
        /* select the arrow cursor */
        SetCursor( LoadCursor(NULL,IDC_ARROW) );
        break;
    case IDM_CURSOR_IBEAM:
        /* select the I-Beam cursor */
        SetCursor( LoadCursor(NULL,IDC_IBEAM) );
        break;
    case IDM_CURSOR_CROSS:
        /* select the cross cursor */
        SetCursor( LoadCursor(NULL,IDC_CROSS) );
        break;
    case IDM_CURSOR_SIZE:
        /* select the size box cursor */
        SetCursor( LoadCursor(NULL,IDC_SIZE) );
        break;
    case IDM_CURSOR_ICON:
        /* select the icon selection cursor */
        SetCursor( LoadCursor(NULL,IDC_ICON) );
        break;
    case IDM_CURSOR_MINE:
        /* select the user defined cursor.  Note the use
           of instance_glbl
        */
        SetCursor(LoadCursor( instance_glbl,
            (LPSTR) "face"));
        break;
    case IDM_CURSOR_WAIT:
        /* select the hourglass cursor, and define it as
           the class cursor.
        */
        hCursor = LoadCursor( NULL, IDC_WAIT );
        SetClassWord(hWnd, GCW_HCURSOR, (WORD) hCursor);
        break;
```

continued...

...from previous page

```
    case IDM_CURSOR_UPARROW:
        /* select the up arrow cursor, and define it as the
           class cursor.
        */
        hCursor = LoadCursor( NULL, IDC_UPARROW );
        SetClassWord(hWnd, GCW_HCURSOR, (WORD) hCursor);
        break;

    /* these cases process edit changes.  Note that
       command = the command number for the particular
       menu item
    */
    case IDM_EDIT_CHECK:
        /* check or uncheck the text in the menu for
            IDM_EDIT_CHECK
        */
        if (checked_glbl == TRUE) {
            CheckMenuItem( hMenu, command, MF_UNCHECKED |
                MF_BYCOMMAND);
            checked_glbl = FALSE;
        }
        else {
            CheckMenuItem( hMenu, command, MF_CHECKED |
                MF_BYCOMMAND);
            checked_glbl = TRUE;
        }
        break;
    case IDM_EDIT_GRAY:
        /* gray the menu item */
        EnableMenuItem( hMenu, command, MF_GRAYED |
            MF_BYCOMMAND);
        break;
    case IDM_EDIT_CHANGE:
        /* change an entry in the menu list.  In particular,
           we will change the word "Change" to "Alter" or
           vice versa.  It would be simpler to keep a
           Boolean of whether the string was "Change" or
           "Alter".  Instead, we will illustrate
           GetMenuString.
```

continued...

Input from Menus: Receiving Messages 4

...from previous page

```
            */
            GetMenuString( hMenu, command, (LPSTR) new_string,
                8, MF_BYCOMMAND);
            if (strcmp(new_string,"Change") == 0)
                strcpy(new_string, "Alter\0");
            else
                strcpy(new_string, "Change\0");
            /* now change it */
            ChangeMenu(hMenu, command, (LPSTR) new_string,
                command, MF_STRING | MF_BYCOMMAND | MF_CHANGE);
            break;
    }
    return(0L);
}
```

The Module Definition File: FOUR1.DEF

```
NAME        Four1
DESCRIPTION 'Fourth Window Program'
STUB        'winstub.exe'
CODE        MOVEABLE
DATA        MOVEABLE MULTIPLE
HEAPSIZE 4096
STACKSIZE 4096
EXPORTS
            MsgServer @1
```

ACCELERATOR KEYS

Accelerator keys allow you to use single keystrokes to replace menu commands. For example, you could use Control-S to save a file instead of moving the cursor to the File command then down to the Save command. Accelerator keys make it easier for an advanced user to manipulate a program.

4 Input from Menus: Receiving Messages

Accelerator keys are defined in the resource file, using the **ACCELERATORS** command. Its format is as follows:

```
table_name      ACCELERATORS
BEGIN
     key,       menu_command
        .
        .
        .
END
```

table_name is any single-word ASCII text. Make a list of the accelerators between the BEGIN and END commands. **key** is the key to use for the accelerator. Enclose it within double quotation marks. Use ^ to indicate a control key. **menu_command** is the value that will be sent when the accelerator key is pressed.[3]

For example, if you wanted to use Control-S to save a file, you could use the following:

```
four2     ACCELERATORS
BEGIN
     "^S",     IDM_FILE_SAVE
END
```

When a user presses an accelerator key, Windows translates it to the message it represents—the **menu_command**. This message is sent to **MsgServer** just as if the command were selected from the menu; thus, your program is completely unaware that an accelerator key was used. All it knows is that the particular command was selected, which is a great feature.

To use accelerators, you must load the accelerator table when the window is initialized. Do so in **register_window**. After you have registered the class, use the **LoadAccelerators** command. Its format is as follows:

---

[3] There are some more advanced features for describing accelerator keys. Refer to the "File Formats" section in the Windows Toolkit *Programmer's Reference Guide*.

82

Input from Menus: Receiving Messages 4

```
HANDLE
LoadAccelerators( hInstance, lpTableName )
```

hInstance   is the hInstance parameter passed to **WinMain**.

lpTableName   is a long pointer to an ASCIIZ string containing the name of the accelerator table. For example, this string could be (LPSTR) "four2."

The value returned is a handle to the accelerator table. Store it in a global variable.

Remember that **register_window** is called only for the first instance of a program. If the program isn't the first instance, you still need to load the accelerator table. There is no reason to take up memory with a new copy of the table because another program that is running already has the table.

Thus, if the program isn't the first instance, it should get a pointer to an earlier instance's accelerator table. This procedure is accomplished with the command **GetInstanceData**. Its format is as follows:

```
int
GetInstanceData( hOldInstance, pVariable, VarLength )
```

hOldInstance   is the hPrevInstance parameter passed to **WinMain**.

pVariable   is a near pointer to the variable you want to fill with previous information.

VarLength   is the amount of information you want to copy. Typically, pass it the size of the variable you are copying.

The return value is the number of bytes actually copied.

4 Input from Menus: Receiving Messages

For example, if you want to get a pointer to an earlier instance's accelerator table, you could use the following:

```
/* load the accelerator table from a previous instance */
GetInstanceData( hPrevInstance, (PSTR) &hAccelTable_glbl,
      sizeof( hAccelTable_glbl ) );
```

Place this statement in **WinMain**. Call it if there was a previous instance. You can look at the **WinMain** procedure in FOUR2.C for an example.

There is one further change you need to make to use accelerator tables. Change to the following the loop that dispatches messages:

```
/* relay all messages to the message server.  Any key
   commands that are accelerator keys are translated
   into messages and dispatched as if they were selected
   from one of the menus
*/
while (GetMessage( (LPMSG) &msg, NULL, 0, 0) ) {
    /* translate accelerator keys */
    if (TranslateAccelerator( hWnd, hAccelTable_glbl,
        (LPMSG)&msg) == 0) {
         TranslateMessage( (LPMSG) &msg);
         DispatchMessage( (LPMSG) &msg);
    }
}
```

The command **TranslateAccelerator** checks if any accelerator keys have been pressed. If so, it translates and dispatches them. If not, it returns a non-zero value, and the if statement drops through. The command's format is as follows:

```
BOOL
TranslateAccelerator( hWnd, hAccelTable, lpMsg )
```

hWnd is a handle to the window.

hAccelTable is the handle for the accelerator table. Get this value from a previous instance or from **LoadAccelerators**.

lpMsg is a long pointer to a message structure.

The return value is zero if no accelerators were translated.

When you use an accelerator table, you should indicate the accelerator keys in the program's menu. For example, you could change the text for a save command to "Save ^S" or "Save\a^S". You can see an example of this command in the file FOUR2.RC.

A PROGRAM: FOUR2

FOUR2 adds accelerator keys to the program FOUR1. Note the changes to the resource file and to **WinMain**. In particular, note how **WinMain** retrieves information from the previous instance. Also, look at the changed message relayer loop. Examine **register_window** to see how the accelerator table is loaded. **MsgServer** and **process_menu_cmds** do not change at all.

```
/------------------------------------------------\
|                                                |
| The files for this program are in the FOUR2    |
| directory.  The make file is FOUR2.  FOUR2.RC  |
| is the resource file.  FOUR2.H is the include  |
| file.  FOUR2.C is the code, and FOUR2.DEF is   |
| the module definition file.  The icon is       |
| FOUR2.ICO.  The cursor, MIKE.CUR, is in the    |
| root directory.  The executable version is     |
| FOUR2.EXE.                                     |
|                                                |
\------------------------------------------------/
```

4 Input from Menus: Receiving Messages

The Make File: FOUR2

```
#
# Make file for the second program in Chapter 4
#

cc=cl -d -c -AS -Gsw -Os -Zpe

.c.obj:
     $(cc) $*.c



four2.obj: four2.c  four2.h

four2.res: four2.rc four2.h four2.ico mike.cur
    rc -r four2.rc

four2.exe: four2.obj four2.res four2.def
    link4 four2, /align:16, NUL, slibw, four2.def
    rc four2.res
```

The Resource File: FOUR2.RC

```
/***********************************************************
    Resource file for the second program in Chapter 4.
    Includes an accelerator table.
***********************************************************/

#include "windows.h"
#include "four2.h"


face       CURSOR     mike.cur
four2      ICON       four2.ico
```

continued...

...from previous page

```
four2       ACCELERATORS
BEGIN
    "^A",       IDM_CURSOR_ARROW
    "^I",       IDM_CURSOR_IBEAM
END


four2 MENU
BEGIN
    POPUP       "Select Cursor"
    BEGIN
        MENUITEM    "Arrow\t^A",    IDM_CURSOR_ARROW
        MENUITEM    "I-Beam\t^I",   IDM_CURSOR_IBEAM
        MENUITEM    "Size Box",     IDM_CURSOR_SIZE
        MENUITEM    "Icon Cursor",  IDM_CURSOR_ICON
        MENUITEM    "Cross",        IDM_CURSOR_CROSS,
                                        MENUBARBREAK
        MENUITEM    "My Cursor",    IDM_CURSOR_MINE
        MENUITEM    "Hourglass",    IDM_CURSOR_WAIT
        MENUITEM    "Up Arrow",     IDM_CURSOR_UPARROW
    END
    POPUP       "Edit Menu"
    BEGIN
        MENUITEM    "Check",        IDM_EDIT_CHECK
        MENUITEM    "Gray",         IDM_EDIT_GRAY
        MENUITEM    "Change",       IDM_EDIT_CHANGE
    END
END
```

The Include File: FOUR2.H

```
/************************************************************
    Include file for FOUR2.  Contains typedefs, constants,
    and external declarations.
************************************************************/
```

continued...

4 Input from Menus: Receiving Messages

...from previous page

```
extern int PASCAL WinMain();
extern int register_window();
extern long FAR PASCAL MsgServer();
extern long process_menu_cmds();


extern int     checked_glbl;
extern HANDLE  hInstance_glbl;
extern HANDLE  hAccelTable_glbl;


/* ID def's for the icon select menu */

#define   IDM_CURSOR_ARROW      100
#define   IDM_CURSOR_IBEAM      110
#define   IDM_CURSOR_SIZE       120
#define   IDM_CURSOR_ICON       130
#define   IDM_CURSOR_CROSS      140
#define   IDM_CURSOR_MINE       150
#define   IDM_CURSOR_WAIT       160
#define   IDM_CURSOR_UPARROW    170


#define   IDM_EDIT_CHECK        200
#define   IDM_EDIT_GRAY         210
#define   IDM_EDIT_CHANGE       220
```

Input from Menus: Receiving Messages 4

The Code File: FOUR2.C

```c
/**************************************************************
    File:      four2.c
    Program:   four2

    This is the second program from Chapter 4.  It is the
    same as the first program, except that it includes an
    accelerator table.  Note how this table is read in when
    the class is registered if it is the first instance of
    a program in this class.  If it is not the first
    instance, the table is retrieved from a previous
    instance.

***************************************************************/



#include "windows.h"
#include "four2.h"




/*-----------------------------------------------------------
   global variables
-------------------------------------------------------------*/

int       checked_glbl;
HANDLE    hInstance_glbl;
HANDLE    hAccelTable_glbl;




/*-----------------------------------------------------------
   This is the Start Up procedure and message relayer
-------------------------------------------------------------*/

int PASCAL
WinMain(hInstance, hPrevInstance, lpszCmdLine, cmdShow)
HANDLE    hInstance, hPrevInstance;
LPSTR     lpszCmdLine;
int       cmdShow;
```

continued...

4 Input from Menus: Receiving Messages

...from previous page

```
{
    HWND        hWnd;
    MSG         msg;
    if (!hPrevInstance)
        /* If this is the first instance, register the
           window class
        */
        register_window(hInstance);
    else
        /* load the accelerator table from a previous
           instance
        */
        GetInstanceData(hPrevInstance, (PSTR)
            &hAccelTable_glbl, sizeof( hAccelTable_glbl) );


    /* Create a tiled window */
    hWnd = CreateWindow( (LPSTR) "Chap42WIN",    /* class */
            /* title */
            (LPSTR) "Uses Accelerator Table",
            WS_TILEDWINDOW,             /* style */
            0, 0, 0, 0,
            (HWND) NULL,                /* parent */
            (HMENU) NULL,               /* use class menu */
            (HANDLE) hInstance,         /* instance */
            (LPSTR) NULL );

    /* Now display it */
    ShowWindow(hWnd,cmdShow);
    UpdateWindow(hWnd);

    /* initialize global variables */
    checked_glbl = FALSE;
    hInstance_glbl = hInstance;

    /* relay all messages to the message server.  Any key
       commands that are accelerator keys are translated
       into messages and dispatched as if they were selected
       from one of the menus
```

continued...

...from previous page

```
    */
    while (GetMessage( (LPMSG) &msg, NULL, 0, 0) ) {
        /* translate accelerator keys */
        if (TranslateAccelerator( hWnd, hAccelTable_glbl,
            (LPMSG)&msg) == 0) {
               TranslateMessage( (LPMSG) &msg);
               DispatchMessage( (LPMSG) &msg);
        }
    }

    exit(msg.wParam);
}




/*-----------------------------------------------------------
  This procedure registers the window.  It sets the cursor
  to NULL so that it can be changed during program
  operation.  It loads a user made icon.

  It also loads the accelerator table.
  -----------------------------------------------------------*/
int
register_window( hInstance )
HANDLE   hInstance;
{
    PWNDCLASS      pClass;

    pClass = (PWNDCLASS) LocalAlloc(LPTR, sizeof(WNDCLASS));
    pClass->hCursor = (HCURSOR) NULL;
    pClass->hIcon = LoadIcon(hInstance, (LPSTR) "four2");
    pClass->lpszMenuName = (LPSTR) "four2";
    pClass->lpszClassName = (LPSTR) "Chap42WIN";
    pClass->hbrBackground = GetStockObject(LTGRAY_BRUSH);
    pClass->hInstance = hInstance;
    pClass->style = CS_HREDRAW | CS_VREDRAW;
    pClass->lpfnWndProc = MsgServer;

    RegisterClass( (LPWNDCLASS) pClass);
    LocalFree( (HANDLE) pClass);
```

continued...

4 Input from Menus: Receiving Messages

...from previous page

```
    SetCursor(LoadCursor(NULL, (LPSTR) IDC_ARROW));

    /* load in the accelerator table */
    hAccelTable_glbl = LoadAccelerators(hInstance,
        (LPSTR) "four2");
}
```

```
/*-------------------------------------------------------
    This procedure receives the messages from Windows and
    decides what to do with them.
--------------------------------------------------------*/
long FAR PASCAL
MsgServer( hWnd, message, wParam, lParam)
HWND      hWnd;
unsigned  message;
WORD      wParam;
LONG      lParam;
{
    /* if it is a menu command, process it */
    if (message == WM_COMMAND)
        return( process_menu_cmds(hWnd, wParam) );

    /* else just use the defaults */
    return(DefWindowProc(hWnd,message,wParam,lParam));
}
```

```
/*-------------------------------------------------------
    This routine processes commands from the menu.  It
    returns a 0 if everything was OK.

    Note that it is completely ignorant of the presence
    of accelerators. There is no need to specially check
    for them.
--------------------------------------------------------*/
```

continued...

...from previous page

```
long
process_menu_cmds( hWnd, command )
HWND      hWnd;
WORD      command;
{
    HMENU       hMenu;
    HCURSOR     hCursor;
    char        new_string[10];

    /* get the handle for the menu */
    hMenu = GetMenu(hWnd);

    /* now process the commands */
    switch (command) {
    case IDM_CURSOR_ARROW:
        SetCursor(LoadCursor( NULL, IDC_ARROW ));
        break;
    case IDM_CURSOR_IBEAM:
        SetCursor(LoadCursor( NULL, IDC_IBEAM ));
        break;
    case IDM_CURSOR_CROSS:
        SetCursor(LoadCursor( NULL, IDC_CROSS ));
        break;
    case IDM_CURSOR_SIZE:
        SetCursor(LoadCursor( NULL, IDC_SIZE ));
        break;
    case IDM_CURSOR_ICON:
        SetCursor(LoadCursor( NULL, IDC_ICON ));
        break;
    case IDM_CURSOR_MINE:
        SetCursor(LoadCursor( hInstance_glbl,
            (LPSTR) "face"));
        break;
    case IDM_CURSOR_WAIT:
        hCursor = LoadCursor( NULL, IDC_WAIT );
        SetClassWord(hWnd, GCW_HCURSOR, (WORD) hCursor);
        break;
    case IDM_CURSOR_UPARROW:
        hCursor = LoadCursor( NULL, IDC_UPARROW );
        SetClassWord(hWnd, GCW_HCURSOR, (WORD) hCursor);
        break;
```

continued...

4 Input from Menus: Receiving Messages

...from previous page

```
        /* these cases process edit changes.  Note that
           command = the command number for the particular
           menu item
        */
        case IDM_EDIT_CHECK:
            if (checked_glbl == TRUE) {
                CheckMenuItem( hMenu, command, MF_UNCHECKED |
                    MF_BYCOMMAND);
                checked_glbl = FALSE;
            }
            else {
                CheckMenuItem( hMenu, command, MF_CHECKED |
                    MF_BYCOMMAND);
                checked_glbl = TRUE;
            }
            break;
        case IDM_EDIT_GRAY:
            EnableMenuItem( hMenu, command, MF_GRAYED |
                MF_BYCOMMAND);
            break;
        case IDM_EDIT_CHANGE:
            GetMenuString( hMenu, command, (LPSTR) new_string,
                8, MF_BYCOMMAND);
            if (strcmp(new_string,"Change") == 0)
                strcpy(new_string, "Alter\0");
            else
                strcpy(new_string, "Change\0");
            ChangeMenu(hMenu, command, (LPSTR) new_string,
                command, MF_STRING | MF_BYCOMMAND | MF_CHANGE);
            break;
    }
    return(0L);

}
```

The Module Definition File: FOUR2.DEF

```
NAME        Four2
DESCRIPTION     'Fourth Window Program'
STUB        'winstub.exe'
CODE        MOVEABLE
DATA        MOVEABLE MULTIPLE
HEAPSIZE 4096
STACKSIZE 4096
EXPORTS
            MsgServer @1
```

SUMMARY

- When a menu item is selected, **MsgServer** receives the value WM_COMMAND in the message parameter and the menu item number in wParam. Pass the menu item number to a procedure that handles menu commands.

- Use constants for the menu item numbers. Use a different hundreds place for items in different columns. Don't use numbers less than 100.

- You can change the cursor during program operation. To do so, the class cursor must be NULL. You can also change the class cursor.

- Use global variables as you would in a conventional program. You will probably need to use global variables more often than you are used to. End global variables with the suffix _glbl.

- You can check, disable, and alter menu items. You can also add and delete items, or create completely new menus.

- Icons are created with ICONEDIT and registered with the resource file command ICON. Make a unique icon for each of your applications.

- Accelerator keys provide the user with a shortcut for entering commands.

4 Input from Menus: Receiving Messages

- You can retrieve information from earlier instances using **GetInstanceData**. You can use this command to get handles to resources, such as an accelerator table, or to see how variables were set in an earlier instance.

CHAPTER 5

OUTPUT: TEXT

5 Output: Text

In this chapter, you will learn how to print information on the screen. First, the display context and the **TextOut** function will be described. Then, you will learn how to modify fonts, the text color, and the background color. You will also learn about **DrawText**.

THE DISPLAY CONTEXT

Before you send any output to the screen, whether it is to print text or draw pictures, you must first get a *display context*. The display context is a structure that contains information about the display window and graphics options. Windows uses the display context when it interprets output commands.

When you process a user's command that requires output, start by getting the display context using **GetDC**. Then, perform your display routine. When you are finished processing the user's command, release the display context using **ReleaseDC**. You must release the display context before you exit **MsgServer**. If you don't, the system could crash.

GetDC's format is as follows:

```
HDC
GetDC( hWnd )
```

hWnd is a handle for the window. The return value is a handle to the display context.

ReleaseDC's format is as follows:

```
ReleaseDC( hWnd, hDC )
```

hWnd is a handle to the window, and **hDC** is a handle for the display context.

THE TEXTOUT FUNCTION

In conventional programs, you mostly use **printf** for output. **TextOut** is the rough equivalent in Windows. Like **printf**, it prints to the screen. But there are some major differences. First, **TextOut** is graphics-based and will work in any size window at any place on the screen. It also can use any size font, as you will see at the end of this chapter. As is suited for Windows, **TextOut** clips, rather than wraps, lines that extend beyond the edge of the screen.

Unlike **printf**, **TextOut** can only print strings. In fact, it will only print a single string at a time. Further, **TextOut** doesn't update a cursor location. You need to explicitly state where the text should appear and keep track of the location for further text.

Maintain two global variables to track the text's x and y locations. The upper left corner of the screen is (0,0). To print a line of text starting in the upper left corner, set the x and y text cursors to 0. The x value increases to the right, and the y value increases going down. Assume for now that each character is 12 units high and 8 units wide; thus, if you want to start a line of text on a new line, add 12 to the text y cursor and set the x text cursor to 0.

Following is the format of **TextOut**:

TextOut(hDC, xloc, yloc, lpString, Count)

hDC	is the handle for the display context. This handle is the value returned by **GetDC**.
xloc	is the x location for the text.
yloc	is the y location for the text.
lpString	is a long pointer to the text to be printed.
Count	is the number of characters to print. Typically, pass it **strlen**(lpString).

5 Output: Text

Note that **TextOut** only prints strings. If you want to print a mixture of text and numbers, you must do all of the formatting yourself, using conversion routines, **strcpy**, **strcat**, and **strlen**. If you are using **strcpy** or **strcat**, make sure that the character array in which you are placing the string is long enough. It does not hurt to leave extra room at the end. If you overwrite the array, you will crash the system.

You can use **sprintf**, **ecvt**, **fcvt**, **gcvt**, **itoa**, **ltoa**, and **ultoa** to convert numbers to strings. These functions are part of the C library.

As an example of using **TextOut**, the following will print "Hello World" in the upper left corner of the window:

```
hDC = GetDC( hWnd );
TextOut( hDC, 0, 0, (LPSTR) "Hello World", 11 );
ReleaseDC( hWnd, hDC);
```

You can see further examples of **TextOut** in the programs FIVE1 and FIVE2. For an example of converting numbers to text, you can look in the programs SEVEN (Chapter 7) and NINE (Chapter 9).

A PROGRAM: FIVE1

Following is a program that displays text on the screen. When the menu item Print Time is selected, the program prints the current time and advances to the next line. As you can see, printing text is simple (see Figure 5.1).

Note the use of the display context and **TextOut** in **process__menu__cmds**. In particular, see how **strlen** is used with **TextOut**. The routines to get the current time and date and convert it to a string are part of the standard C library.

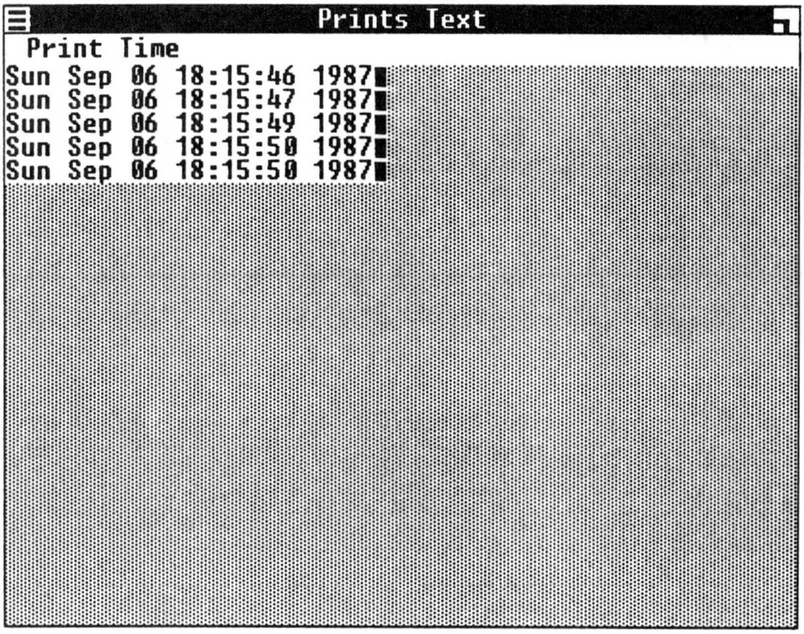

Output: Text 5

```
┌─────────────────────────────────────────┐
│ ≡              Prints Text            ⌐ │
│ Print Time                              │
│ Sun Sep 06 18:15:46 1987▌               │
│ Sun Sep 06 18:15:47 1987▌               │
│ Sun Sep 06 18:15:49 1987▌               │
│ Sun Sep 06 18:15:50 1987▌               │
│ Sun Sep 06 18:15:50 1987▌               │
│                                         │
│                                         │
└─────────────────────────────────────────┘
```

Figure 5.1   The program FIVE1.

```
/-----------------------------------------\
|                                         |
| The files for this program are located in |
| the FIVE1 directory.  The make file is  |
| FIVE1.  The resource file is FIVE1.RC.  |
| The include file is FIVE1.H.  FIVE1.C is |
| the code.  FIVE1.ICO is the icon.  The  |
| module definition is FIVE1.DEF.  The    |
| cursor, MIKE.CUR, is in the root        |
| directory.  MIKE.EXE is the executable. |
|                                         |
\-----------------------------------------/
```

5 Output: Text

The Make File: FIVE1

```
#
#   Make file for the first program of Chapter 5
#

cc=cl -d -c -AS -Gsw -Os -Zpe

.c.obj:
    $(cc) $*.c


five1.obj: five1.c  five1.h

five1.res: five1.rc five1.h five1.ico mike.cur
    rc -r five1.rc

five1.exe: five1.obj five1.res five1.def
    link4 five1, /align:16, NUL, slibw, five1.def
    rc five1.res
```

The Resource File: FIVE1.RC

```
/************************************************************
    Resource file for five1
************************************************************/


#include "windows.h"
#include "five1.h"


face        CURSOR      mike.cur
five1       ICON        five1.ico

five1 MENU
BEGIN
    MENUITEM   "Print Time", IDM_PRINT
END
```

The Include File: FIVE1.H

```c
/**********************************************************
    Include file for FIVE1.  Contains typedefs, constants,
    and external declarations.
**********************************************************/


extern int PASCAL WinMain();
extern int register_window();
extern long FAR PASCAL MsgServer();
extern long process_menu_cmds();


extern int     cur_text_y_glbl;


/* Constants for the menu choices */

#define  IDM_PRINT      100
```

The Code: FIVE1.C

```c
/**********************************************************
    File:     five1.c
    Program:  five1

    This is the first program from Chapter 5.  It
    demonstrates how to print text.  Note that you are
    responsible for maintaining a text "cursor" that
    indicates where to print next.
**********************************************************/


#include "windows.h"
#include "string.h"
#include "time.h"
#include "stdio.h"
#include "five1.h"
```

continued...

5 Output: Text

...from previous page

```
/*---------------------------------------------------
   global variables
---------------------------------------------------*/

int      cur_text_y_glbl;




/*---------------------------------------------------
   This is the Start Up procedure and message relayer
---------------------------------------------------*/
int PASCAL
WinMain(hInstance, hPrevInstance, lpszCmdLine, cmdShow)
HANDLE    hInstance, hPrevInstance;
LPSTR     lpszCmdLine;
int       cmdShow;
{
    HWND     hWnd;
    MSG      msg;

    /* If this is the first instance, register the
       window class
    */
    if (!hPrevInstance)
        register_window(hInstance);

    /* don't need previous instance information */

    /* Create a tiled window */
    hWnd = CreateWindow( (LPSTR) "Chap51WIN",    /* class */
             (LPSTR) "Prints Text",   /* title */
             WS_TILEDWINDOW,          /* style */
             0, 0, 0, 0,
             (HWND) NULL,             /* parent */
             (HMENU) NULL,            /* use class menu */
             (HANDLE) hInstance,      /* instance */
             (LPSTR) NULL );
```

continued...

...from previous page

```
    /* Now display it */
    ShowWindow(hWnd,cmdShow);
    UpdateWindow(hWnd);

    /* initialize global variables */
    cur_text_y_glbl = 0;

    /* relay all messages to the message server */
    while (GetMessage( (LPMSG) &msg, NULL, 0, 0) ) {
        TranslateMessage( (LPMSG) &msg);
        DispatchMessage( (LPMSG) &msg);
    }

    exit(msg.wParam);
}




/*-------------------------------------------------------
   This procedure registers the window.
---------------------------------------------------------*/

int
register_window( hInstance )
HANDLE   hInstance;
{
    PWNDCLASS       pClass;

    pClass = (PWNDCLASS) LocalAlloc(LPTR, sizeof(WNDCLASS));
    pClass->hCursor = LoadCursor(hInstance, (LPSTR) "face");
    pClass->hIcon = LoadIcon(hInstance, (LPSTR) "five1");
    pClass->lpszMenuName = (LPSTR) "five1";
    pClass->lpszClassName = (LPSTR) "Chap51WIN";
    pClass->hbrBackground = GetStockObject(LTGRAY_BRUSH);
    pClass->hInstance = hInstance;
    pClass->style = CS_HREDRAW | CS_VREDRAW;
    pClass->lpfnWndProc = MsgServer;

    RegisterClass( (LPWNDCLASS) pClass);
    LocalFree( (HANDLE) pClass);
}
```

continued...

5 Output: Text

...from previous page

```c
/*-----------------------------------------------------
    This procedure receives the messages from Windows and
    decides how to process them.
-------------------------------------------------------*/
long FAR PASCAL
MsgServer( hWnd, message, wParam, lParam)
HWND      hWnd;
unsigned  message;
WORD      wParam;
LONG      lParam;
{
    /* if it is a menu command, process it */
    if (message == WM_COMMAND)
        return( process_menu_cmds(hWnd, wParam) );

    /* else just use the defaults */
    return(DefWindowProc(hWnd,message,wParam,lParam));
}



/*-----------------------------------------------------
    This routine processes commands from the menu.  If the
    command is PRINT, it gets the time, converts it to an
    ASCII string, gets the display context, and then prints
    the time.  It then advances the cursor and releases the
    display context.
-------------------------------------------------------*/
long
process_menu_cmds( hWnd, command )
HWND      hWnd;
WORD      command;
{
    HDC       hDC;
    char      *time_string;
    long      ltime;
```

continued...

...from previous page

```
    /* now process the commands */
    switch (command) {
    case IDM_PRINT:
        /* print a string */
        time(&ltime);
        time_string = asctime( localtime( &ltime ) );

        /* get display context */
        hDC = GetDC(hWnd);

        /* print the string, starting at the left side of
           the screen, and cur_text_y_glbl dots down.
        */
        TextOut(hDC, 0, cur_text_y_glbl,
            (LPSTR) time_string, strlen(time_string));

        /* release the display context */
        ReleaseDC(hWnd, hDC);

        /* update the cursor */
        cur_text_y_glbl += 12;
        break;
    }
    return(0L);

}
```

The Module Definition File: FIVE1.DEF

```
NAME      Five1
DESCRIPTION   'Fifth Window Program'
STUB      'winstub.exe'
CODE      MOVEABLE
DATA      MOVEABLE MULTIPLE
HEAPSIZE 4096
STACKSIZE 4096
EXPORTS
          MsgServer @1
```

5 Output: Text

USING AND MODIFYING FONTS

With Windows you have a great deal of flexibility over the size and appearance of text. There are several built-in fonts that you can alter in a wide number of ways.

The first program, FIVE1, used the default font. To use a different font you must first describe the font, create it, and select it. At any time, you can change any of the font's characteristics. For example, you can start a sentence with 30-unit-high italicized letters, and print the rest of the sentence with 8-unit-high underlined characters.

You describe a font with the LOGFONT structure. You pass a pointer to this structure to the **CreateFontIndirect** command. Windows will use your requested characteristics to modify one of its built-in fonts. After you have grabbed the display context, you select the font with the **SelectObject** command.

The LOGFONT structure has the following parameters:

lfHeight   is the height of characters, measured in device units (one unit equals one dot). If lfHeight is zero, a default value is used.

lfWidth   is the average width of characters. If zero, Windows will choose a width that goes well with the height.

lfEscapement is the counterclockwise angle in tenths of degrees between the line formed by the first and last characters on a line and the x axis. Normally, this angle is zero.

lfOrientation is the counterclockwise angle in tenths of degrees between the base of the character and the x axis. Usually, this angle is zero.

lfWeight   indicates the thickness of the characters, which is measured in terms of inked pixels per 1000, and can be any number between 0 and 1000. Typically, 400 is used for normal text and 700 for bold text.

lfItalic   is set to TRUE for italicized text, FALSE for normal text.

lfUnderline	is set to TRUE for underlined text, FALSE for normal text.
lfStrikeOut	is set to TRUE for a strikeout font, FALSE for a normal font.
lfCharSet	specifies the character set. Can be ANSI_CHARSET or OEM_CHARSET. You can find a listing of the ANSI_CHARSET on page 432 of the Windows Toolkit *Programmer's Reference Manual*.
lfOutPrecision	must be set to OUT_DEFAULT_PRECIS.
lfClipPrecision	must be set to CLIP_DEFAULT_PRECIS.
lfQuality	controls how closely the requested font characteristics will be matched to an existing physical font. It can be one of the following:

        PROOF_QUALITY   the quality of characters is more important than the actual attributes. The size might be different than that requested.

        DRAFT_QUALITY   more sizes of fonts are available because the attributes are more important than with PROOF_QUALITY.

        DEFAULT_QUALITY   the size will be matched because the closeness to an existing font is not important.

For screen display, you should be quite safe with DEFAULT_QUALITY. With DEFAULT_QUALITY, Windows will mathematically alter an existing font to create the requested font. With PROOF_QUALITY, Windows only uses an existing font.

5 Output: Text

lfPitchAndFamily

>Selects the pitch and the style of text. OR together one from

>DEFAULT_PITCH
>FIXED_PITCH
>VARIABLE_PITCH

>and one from

>FF_DONTCARE
>FF_ROMAN
>FF_SWISS
>FF_MODERN
>FF_SCRIPT
>FF_DECORATIVE

lfFaceName set this value to NULL. If you were to create your own font with the FONTEDIT utility, you could set this value to an ASCIIZ string of the font's name, as defined in the resource file.

You can see an example of setting up a LOGFONT structure in the routine **init_font** in FIVE2.C.

Once you have set up the structure, pass it to **CreateFontIndirect**. Its format is as follows:

```
HFONT
CreateFontIndirect( lpLogFont)
```

lpLogFont is a long pointer to a LOGFONT structure with the font's desired characteristics. The return value is a handle for the font.

To use a font, select it with the **SelectObject** command. Its format is as follows:

```
HANDLE
SelectObject( hDC, hObject )
```

hDC   is a handle for the display context.

hObject   is a handle for the object to be selected. If you are selecting a font, set it to the font handle returned by **CreateFontIndirect**.

You can also use **SelectObject** to select a pen, brush, bit map, or region. **SelectObject** returns a handle to the previous item. If you are selecting a font, it returns a handle to the previous font.

When you are finished using a font, you should delete it, which will save memory. Use the **DeleteObject** command. Its format is as follows:

```
DeleteObject( hObject )
```

hObject is a handle to the object to be deleted. To delete a font, pass it the handle of the font to be deleted. **DeleteObject** can also delete pens, brushes, bit maps, and regions.

If a program changes font characteristics on the fly, make sure that the font is up to date before printing. You can do so by creating the new font every time its parameters change or every time a message that causes text output is received. Or you can set a flag when the characteristics change and examine this flag before outputting. Try to minimize the number of times a new font is created.

To save memory, delete fonts once you are finished using them. For example, if you store the font handle in a global variable, use **DeleteObject** on the handle before assigning it a new value. If you create a font every time the display context is called, delete the font after releasing the display context.

You need to select the font each time you get the display context. Windows will not remember what font was last used. You do not need to recreate the font each time you get the display context.

5 Output: Text

UPDATING THE CURSOR POSITION

There are two ways to update the text cursor position. The first way is to add the average or maximum character width to the x text cursor for every character printed and to add the character height to the y text cursor for every line printed. FIVE1 and FIVE2 use this method, with one exception: they don't use an x text cursor because each printout of the time and date starts on a new line.

To add the height and character width, you need to find the values using the **GetTextMetrics** command. You will see how to do so shortly. This method is a little clumsy because it relies on the average or maximum, instead of actual, character width.

Another way to update the text cursors is to determine the length of the text you are about to print. You can determine this information with the **GetTextExtent** command. It returns the height and width of a string. Its format is as follows:

```
LONG
GetTextExtent( hDC, lpString, Count)
```

hDC is a handle to the display context.

lpString is a long pointer to a string.

Count is the number of characters in the string to examine. Typically, this number is set to **strlen**(lpString).

The high word of the return value is the height; the low word is the width. You can extract these values using the HIWORD and LOWORD macros. These macros take a long value and return the high and low words respectively.

TEXT METRICS

When you request a font, Windows matches it as closely as possible. Depending on the font's attributes and the lfQuality value, the actual font may or may not match the size you requested. To get the exact characteristics of the font, look at the text metrics, using the following command:

GetTextMetrics(hDC, lpMetrics)

hDC is a handle for the display context.

lpMetrics is a long pointer to a TEXTMETRIC structure in which the information will be stored.

The TEXTMETRIC structure contains the following:

tmHeight height of characters

tmAscent height of the portion of characters that is above the baseline

tmDescent height of portion of characters that is below the baseline

tmInternalLeading

amount of leading within character block

tmExternalLeading

amount of leading between rows

tmAveCharWidth

the average width of characters

tmMaxCharWidth

the maximum width of characters

5 Output: Text

tmWeight font weight

tmItalic non-zero if italicized

tmUnderlined non-zero if underlined

tmStruckOut non-zero if a strikeout font

tmFirstChar value of the first character in the font

tmLastChar value of the last character in the font

tmDefaultCHar value of character used to represent characters not in the font

tmBreakChar value of character used for word breaks for text justification

tmPitchAndFamily

low-order bit is set if the font is variable pitch. (tmPitchAndFamily & 0xf0) is the font. Font values are the same as for the LOGFONT structure.

tmCharSet character set

tmOverhand amount of extra width that might be added when creating bold and italic fonts.

tmDigitizedAspectX

used with tmDigitizedAspectY to give the aspect ratio of the device for which the font was designed.

tmDigitizedAspectY

used with tmDigitizedAspectX to give the aspect ratio of the device for which the font was designed.

The parameters you will use most are tmHeight, tmExternalLeading, tmAveCharWidth, and tmMaxCharWidth. If you are maintaining a text cursor, increment the x text cursor by tmMaxCharWidth for each character and the y text cursor by tmHeight + tmExternalLeading for each row.

You may never need to examine the text metrics.

ACCOUNTING FOR SCREEN SIZE WHEN DISPLAYING TEXT

The size of a program's window depends on the size of the display screen and the placement of any other applications that are running. With **TextOut**, text that would go beyond the program's window is clipped; thus, if the program's window is small, much of the text you display could be clipped. There are two ways to get around this problem. First, you can add a scroll bar to the window, which allows you to change what portion of the "page" is displayed in the window. Chapter 10 covers scroll bars. The second method is to change the size of the font so that more characters fit onto the screen. If the window is small, make the characters small. If the window is big, make the characters big.

To determine the size of the screen, use the **GetClientRect** command. Its format is as follows:

```
GetClientRect( hWnd, lpRect )
```

hWnd   is a handle for the window.

lpRect   is a long pointer to a structure of type RECT.

RECT structures have four fields: left, right, bottom, and top. The width of the display area is lpRect-right - lpRect-left. The height of the display area is lpRect-bottom - lpRect-top. Note that the height is determined by subtracting the top from the bottom because the screen coordinates increase going down.

Once you have the screen height and width, you can adjust character size, within reason, to fit more characters on the screen.

5 Output: Text

BACKGROUND AND TEXT COLOR

In FIVE1, text was black and the text background was white. You can change these colors easily.

In Windows, colors are described by RGB values. An RGB value is a combination of red, green, and blue intensities. Each intensity ranges from 0 (not present) to 255 (fully present). For example, bright red would have R = 255, G = 0, B = 0. White would be R = 255, G = 255, B = 255. Very dark gray would be R = 10, G = 10, B = 10.

By combining the red, green, and blue values, you can make 16 million colors. Because most display boards can't display 16 million colors at once, Windows chooses the closest available color to that requested.

Windows uses the RGB type to describe colors. It is a long integer formed by red_value + green_value * 256 + blue_value * 256 * 256.

To set the text color, use

```
RGB
SetTextColor( hDC, Color )
```

hDC is a handle to the display context, and **Color** is an RGB color. The function returns the previous text color.

To set the background color, use

```
RGB
SetBkColor( hDC, Color )
```

hDC is a handle to the display context, and **Color** is an RGB color. The function returns the previous background color.

To find what the text color is, use

```
RGB
GetTextColor( hDC )
```

hDC is a handle to the display context. The return value is the text color.

You can use this function to determine the actual RGB value for the text color. It will differ from the requested value if Windows' palette needed to find a different, but close, color for the text. For example, suppose you requested deep gold text, but the closest color was yellow. **GetTextColor** will return the RGB value for yellow.

A similar function is **GetBkColor**. Its format is as follows:

```
RGB
GetBkColor( hDC )
```

where **hDC** is a handle to the display context, and the return value is the RGB background color.

As with **GetTextColor**, you can use this function to determine the color actually used. For example, the program FIVE2 sets the background color to a low intensity green (64*256). On some computers the closest color is black (0), which is the value that **GetBkColor** returns.

A PROGRAM: FIVE2

Like FIVE1, FIVE2 prints the time. But FIVE2 also lets the user modify the font. For simplicity of demonstration, this program only modifies the font size. You might like to change FIVE2 so that the user can modify many other font characteristics. FIVE2 also sets the background and text colors.

5 Output: Text

FIVE2 sets up the initial font characteristics in the procedure **init_font**. The LOGFONT information is stored in a global variable, LogFont_glbl. The menu commands for selecting font size modify this structure. Font size is a mutually exclusive choice. Examine how **process_menu_cmds** handles the IDM_SIZE_10, IDM_SIZE_15, and IDM_SIZE_30 commands.

create_font deletes the old font, then creates and selects the new font. **create_font** also selects the background and text colors. Note that before **create_font** creates a new font, it examines a flag that is set in **process_menu_cmds** when the font characteristics change.

For a change in pace, **register_window** sets the background color to white.

```
/----------------------------------------------\
|                                              |
| The files for this program are in the FIVE2  |
| directory.  The make file is FIVE2.  FIVE2.RC|
| is the resource file.  FIVE2.H is the include|
| file.  FIVE2.C is the code.  FIVE2.DEF is the|
| module definition.  FIVE2.ICO is the icon.   |
| The cursor, MIKE.CUR, is in the root directory.|
| FIVE2.EXE is the executable.                 |
|                                              |
\----------------------------------------------/
```

The Make File: FIVE2

```
#
#  Make file for the second program in Chapter 5
#

cc=cl -d -c -AS -Gsw -Os -Zpe

.c.obj:
    $(cc) $*.c
```

continued...

...from previous page

```
five2.obj: five2.c  five2.h

five2.res: five2.rc five2.h five2.ico mike.cur
    rc -r five2.rc


five2.exe: five2.obj five2.res five2.def
    link4 five2, /align:16,NUL, slibw, five2.def
    rc five2.res
```

The Resource File: FIVE2.RC

```
/*
    Resource file for FIVE2
*/


#include "windows.h"
#include "five2.h"


face        CURSOR      mike.cur
five2       ICON        five2.ico

five2       MENU
BEGIN
    MENUITEM    "Print Time", IDM_PRINT
    POPUP       "Size"
    BEGIN
        MENUITEM    "10",   IDM_SIZE_10,    CHECKED
        MENUITEM    "15",   IDM_SIZE_15
        MENUITEM    "30",   IDM_SIZE_30
    END
END
```

5 Output: Text

The Include File: FIVE2.H

```
/************************************************************
    Include file for the second program in Chapter 5.
    Includes typedefs, constants, and external declarations.
************************************************************/


extern int PASCAL WinMain();
extern int register_window();
extern long FAR PASCAL MsgServer();
extern long process_menu_cmds();
extern init_font();
extern create_font();


extern int       text_size_glbl;
extern int       cur_text_y_glbl;
extern LOGFONT   LogFont_glbl;
extern HANDLE    hFont_glbl;
extern int       font_changed_glbl;


/* constant definitions for menus */

#define  IDM_PRINT      100
#define  IDM_SIZE       200
#define  IDM_SIZE_10    210
#define  IDM_SIZE_15    215
#define  IDM_SIZE_30    230
```

The Code: FIVE2.C

```
/************************************************************
    File:       five2.c
    Program:    five2

    This is the second program from Chapter 5.  It
    illustrates how to modify fonts.  In particular, it
    changes the font size, the text color, and the text
    background color.
************************************************************/


#include "windows.h"
#include "string.h"
#include "time.h"
#include "stdio.h"
#include "five2.h"



/*-----------------------------------------------------------
    global variables
-----------------------------------------------------------*/

int         cur_text_y_glbl;
int         text_size_glbl;
LOGFONT     LogFont_glbl;
HANDLE      hFont_glbl;
int         font_changed_glbl;
```

continued...

5 Output: Text

...from previous page

```
/*---------------------------------------------------
    This is the Start Up procedure and message relayer
-----------------------------------------------------*/
int PASCAL
WinMain(hInstance, hPrevInstance, lpszCmdLine, cmdShow)
HANDLE    hInstance, hPrevInstance;
LPSTR     lpszCmdLine;
int       cmdShow;
{
    HWND      hWnd;
    MSG       msg;

    /* If this is the first instance, register the
       window class
    */
    if (!hPrevInstance)
        register_window(hInstance);

    /* set up the description of the font */
    init_font();


    /* Create a tiled window */
    hWnd = CreateWindow( (LPSTR) "Chap52WIN",    /* class */
              (LPSTR) "Modifies the Font",    /* title */
              WS_TILEDWINDOW,         /* style */
              0, 0, 0, 0,
              (HWND) NULL,            /* parent */
              (HMENU) NULL,           /* use class menu */
              (HANDLE) hInstance,     /* instance */
              (LPSTR) NULL );

    /* now display it */
    ShowWindow(hWnd,cmdShow);
    UpdateWindow(hWnd);
```

continued...

...from previous page

```
    /* initialize global variables */
    cur_text_y_glbl = 0;
    text_size_glbl = 10;
    hFont_glbl = NULL;
    font_changed_glbl = TRUE;


    /* relay all messages to the message server */
    while (GetMessage( (LPMSG) &msg, NULL, 0, 0) ) {
        TranslateMessage( (LPMSG) &msg);
        DispatchMessage( (LPMSG) &msg);
    }

    exit(msg.wParam);
}




/*-------------------------------------------------------------
    This procedure registers the window.  Note that for
    variety the background is white instead of light gray.
  -------------------------------------------------------------*/
int
register_window( hInstance )
HANDLE    hInstance;
{
    PWNDCLASS      pClass;

    pClass = (PWNDCLASS) LocalAlloc(LPTR, sizeof(WNDCLASS));
    pClass->hCursor = LoadCursor(hInstance, (LPSTR) "face");
    pClass->hIcon = LoadIcon(hInstance, (LPSTR) "five2");
    pClass->lpszMenuName = (LPSTR) "five2";
    pClass->lpszClassName = (LPSTR) "Chap52WIN";
    pClass->hbrBackground = GetStockObject(WHITE_BRUSH);
    pClass->hInstance = hInstance;
    pClass->style = CS_HREDRAW | CS_VREDRAW;
    pClass->lpfnWndProc = MsgServer;

    RegisterClass( (LPWNDCLASS) pClass);
    LocalFree( (HANDLE) pClass);
}
```
continued...

5 Output: Text

...from previous page

```
/*------------------------------------------------------------
    This procedure receives the messages and decides what
    to do with them.
-------------------------------------------------------------*/
long FAR PASCAL
MsgServer( hWnd, message, wParam, lParam )
HWND        hWnd;
unsigned    message;
WORD        wParam;
LONG        lParam;
{
    /* if it is a menu command, process it */
    if (message == WM_COMMAND)
        return( process_menu_cmds(hWnd, wParam) );

    /* else just use the defaults */
    return(DefWindowProc(hWnd,message,wParam,lParam));
}




/*------------------------------------------------------------
   This routine processes commands from the menu
-------------------------------------------------------------*/
long
process_menu_cmds( hWnd, command )
HWND        hWnd;
WORD        command;
{
    HMENU       hMenu;
    HDC         hDC;
    char        *time_string;
    long        ltime;


    /* get the handle for the menu */
    hMenu = GetMenu(hWnd);
```

continued...

...from previous page

```
    /* now process the commands */
    switch (command) {

    case IDM_PRINT:
        /* print the time  */
        time(&ltime);
        time_string = asctime( localtime( &ltime ) );

        /* get the display context */
        hDC = GetDC(hWnd);

        /* We need to load the updated font each time */
        create_font(hDC);

        /* now print the string */
        TextOut(hDC, 0, cur_text_y_glbl,
            (LPSTR) time_string, strlen(time_string));

        /* release the display context and update the
            cursor position
        */
        ReleaseDC(hWnd, hDC);
        cur_text_y_glbl += text_size_glbl;
        break;
    case IDM_SIZE_10:
    case IDM_SIZE_15:
    case IDM_SIZE_30:
        /* command is to change the font size.  First, get
            rid of the old menu check mark
        */
        CheckMenuItem(hMenu, text_size_glbl + IDM_SIZE,
            MF_UNCHECKED | MF_BYCOMMAND);
```

continued...

5 Output: Text

...from previous page

```
            /* now put a check mark by the newly selected
               size
            */
            CheckMenuItem(hMenu, command, MF_CHECKED |
               MF_BYCOMMAND);

            /* update the size information */
            text_size_glbl = command - IDM_SIZE;
            LogFont_glbl.lfHeight = text_size_glbl;

            /* indicate that the size has changed */
            font_changed_glbl = TRUE;
            break;
     }

     return(0L);
}




/*-----------------------------------------------------------
   This routine sets up the characteristics for the font.
   Note that the font data structure and pointer are put
   as global variables
-----------------------------------------------------------*/

init_font()
{
     /* initialize font values */
     LogFont_glbl.lfHeight = 10;       /* character height
                                              of 10 */
     LogFont_glbl.lfWidth = 0;         /* let Windows select
                                            best width */
     LogFont_glbl.lfEscapement = 0;    /* orient along
                                            horizontal */
     LogFont_glbl.lfOrientation = 0;   /* orient along
                                            horizontal */
     LogFont_glbl.lfWeight = 400;      /* uses normal
                                            weight */
     continued...
```

...from previous page

```
    LogFont_glbl.lfItalic = 0;      /* no italics */
    LogFont_glbl.lfUnderline = 0;   /* no underline */
    LogFont_glbl.lfStrikeOut = 0;   /* no strike out */
    LogFont_glbl.lfCharSet = ANSI_CHARSET;   /* use the
                                                ANSI char
                                                set */
    LogFont_glbl.lfOutPrecision = OUT_DEFAULT_PRECIS;
    LogFont_glbl.lfClipPrecision = CLIP_DEFAULT_PRECIS;

    /* give Windows freedom to match characteristics */
    LogFont_glbl.lfQuality = DEFAULT_QUALITY;

    /* use a Roman font */
    LogFont_glbl.lfPitchAndFamily = DEFAULT_PITCH |
        FF_ROMAN;
    LogFont_glbl.lfFaceName[0] = (BYTE) NULL;
}



/*-----------------------------------------------------------
    This procedure creates and selects the font.  Note that
    the font is created only if its characteristics have
    changed.  If the characteristics haven't changed, the
    previous font is valid and only needs to be selected.
-------------------------------------------------------------*/

create_font( hDC )
HDC     hDC;
{
    /* See if a new font needs to be created */
    if (font_changed_glbl == TRUE) {
        /* delete the old font */
        DeleteObject( hFont_glbl );
```

continued...

5 Output: Text

...from previous page

```
        /* create the font from its description */
        hFont_glbl = CreateFontIndirect( (LPLOGFONT)
           &LogFont_glbl);

        font_changed_glbl = FALSE;
   }

   /* select new font */
   SelectObject(hDC, hFont_glbl);

   /* set text color to red */
   SetTextColor(hDC, (LONG) 255);

   /* make background whatever is closest to dark green */
   SetBkColor(hDC, (LONG) 256*64);
}
```

The Module Definition File: FIVE2.DEF

```
NAME      Five2
DESCRIPTION   'Fifth Window Program'
STUB      'winstub.exe'
CODE      MOVEABLE
DATA      MOVEABLE MULTIPLE
HEAPSIZE 4096
STACKSIZE 4096
EXPORTS
          MsgServer @1
```

ADVANCED CONCEPTS: THE DRAWTEXT COMMAND

Windows has an additional command for outputting text, **DrawText**. **DrawText** is much more powerful than **TextOut** because it also formats the text. For example, you can use **DrawText** to wrap words instead of clip words or to justify text.

Like **TextOut**, **DrawText** prints a single string. But instead of passing **DrawText** a starting screen location, you pass it a rectangle in which to draw the text. For example, you could use **GetClientRect** to tell **DrawText** to use the whole window for displaying text. The program in Chapter 10 uses this technique. Any text going outside of the rectangle is clipped.

Following is **DrawText**'s format:

```
DrawText( hDC, lpString, Count, lpRect, wFormat)
```

hDC   is a handle for the display context.

lpString   is a long pointer to the string to display.

Count   is the number of characters to display. Typically, set this number to **strlen**(lpString). If Count is -1, **DrawText** assumes lpString is ASCIIZ and prints until the string's end.

lpRect   is a long pointer to a RECT structure defining the area in which to print the text.

wFormat   is a combination of the following:

         DT_LEFT   left-justify the text

         DT_CENTER   center the text

         DT_RIGHT   right-justify the text

DT_WORDBREAK	start a new line if a word would go beyond the rectangular boundary. Wrap the word to this new line.
DT_SINGLELINE	print the whole string on a single line, which is what **TextOut** does.
DT_TOP	top-justify text. Can only be used with DT_SINGLELINE.
DT_BOTTOM	bottom-justify text. Can only be used with DT_SINGLELINE.
DT_VCENTER	vertically center text. Can only be used with DT_SINGLELINE.
DT_EXPANDTABS	expand tab characters
DT_TABSTOP	set tab stops every *n* characters. Specify *n* by setting the high order byte of wFormat to *n*. The default is 8.
DT_NOCLIP	don't clip text going outside of the rectangle
DT_EXTERNALLEADING	include external leading in the height of a line of text. Usually not used.

Output: Text 5

SUMMARY

- Before displaying text, you need to get the display context with **GetDC**. You must release the display context, using **ReleaseDC**, when you are finished processing a menu command.

- **TextOut** displays text. Lines are clipped to the window's boundary. You must maintain your own text cursors.

- There is great flexibility in modifying fonts. Describe the font with the LOGFONT structure; create it with **CreateFontIndirect**.

- Delete fonts when you are finished using them.

- You can find out how much space it will take to display a string by using the **GetTextExtent** command.

- **GetClientRect** returns the boundaries of a program's display window.

- Text metrics describe the actual parameters for a font.

- You can change the text and background colors.

- **DrawText** is a powerful command for displaying text.

CHAPTER 6

SYSTEM MESSAGES

6 System Messages

Chapter 3 showed you how selecting a menu item sent a message to **MsgServer**. Windows also sends messages when the mouse is moved, mouse buttons are clicked, keys are pressed, or windows are moved. In addition, Windows sends many other messages. This chapter discusses the important messages and how and why to use them.

WHY USE MESSAGES?

Programs receive all information about their environment through *system messages*. For example, when a key is pressed, a message is sent. When a program window is moved, a message is sent. So far, you have been using **DefWindowProc** to process these messages. But there are many times a program needs to be aware of and process system messages. In fact, there are certain system messages all programs should process. And any program using the mouse for graphics input needs to process system messages.

There are several different types of system messages. Those related to the window include messages sent when a window is moved, sized, opened, or closed, and those messages are useful for keeping the display up to date. They are also used for controlling system resources.

Following is a quick exercise demonstrating the need to process window-related messages. Run two copies of FIVE2. Press "Print Time" several times for each copy. Then, resize one of the windows. The screens for both FIVE2 copies will clear. Print the time again. The new time message will appear in the screen location below the last time message printed. By processing window-related messages, you could reset the text cursor location each time the screen was cleared. Or you could redisplay the text. In Chapter 7, you will redraw a graphics image whenever the window is moved.

When you use global memory and system timers, the window-related messages will be even more important.

Other messages are strictly related to input. These include messages sent when keys are pressed or the mouse is moved.

There are also messages from system timers, scroll bars, and special features such as dialog and list boxes.

THE MESSAGES

The following sections will cover the most important system messages and provide some suggestions on how to use them. Use **DefWindowProc** for messages you don't need to pay special attention to. For messages you trap, you may want to first call **DefWindowProc**, then add some additional lines. Or you can add additional lines and then call **DefWindowProc**. For many messages, you don't need to call **DefWindowProc** at all. There is a listing of **DefWindowProc** on the Windows Development Toolkit disks.

As with WM_COMMAND, all messages are sent in the message parameter of **MsgServer**. Any mention of wParam or lParam refers to **MsgServer**'s parameter of that name.

Window-related Messages

WM_PAINT

This message is sent whenever a window needs updating. It is sent after a window's size has changed, when a window is moved, or after a call to **UpdateWindow** or **InvalidateRect**. It is also sent when a window is made iconic or active and is sent to an icon when the icon is moved.

The default action is to clear the screen. Trap this message to keep the display up to date after moving or sizing. For example, instead of having the screen clear after a move, you could redraw the screen.

The remaining programs in this book trap WM_PAINT.

WM_CLOSE

This message is sent when there is a request to close a window. The default is to call **DestroyWindow**. You can trap this message to prompt the user before closing an application. For example, you could check if the user wants to save a file before quitting. To prevent closure, return without calling **DestroyWindow**. Do not call **DefWindowProc** if you trap this message.

6 System Messages

WM_QUERYENDSESSION

This message is sent when the user selects the **End Session** command. You can trap it to ask users if they want the session to end. Return a zero if a user does not want to stop. Do not call **DefWindowProc** if you trap this message.

WM_DESTROY

This message is sent just before a window is destroyed. Trap it if you are using system resources such as the timer or global memory. Free those resources when this message is received.

WM_INITMENU

This message is sent when a user clicks on a menu item. You can use it to enable or disable items in a pop-up menu. For example, you can use it to enable or disable the Paste option in a clipboard menu.

WM_ACTIVATE

This message is sent when a window becomes active or inactive. wParam is 0 if the window becomes inactive; wParam is 2 if the window becomes active because of a mouse click; and wParam is 1 if the window becomes active through some other means.

You can use this message to perform special tasks when a window becomes active. For example, you can set the cursor whenever the window becomes active.

WM_CREATE

This message is sent when a window is created. You can trap it to perform system initialization.

WM_SIZE

This message is sent whenever the size of a window changes. wParam is set to one of the following:

SIZEICONIC	The window was made iconic.
SIZEFULLSCREEN	The window was zoomed.
SIZENORMAL	The window has been resized, but not because of a zoom or becoming iconic.
SIZEZOOMSHOW	Some other window became unzoomed.
SIZEZOOMHIDE	Some other window is zooming.

The high word of lParam contains the new height; the low word contains the new width.

WM_ERASEBKGND

This message is sent when the window's background needs to be erased. If you set the hbrBackground parameter of the window's class to NULL, then you must trap this message and do your own background erasing; otherwise, you can probably ignore it, and just trap WM_PAINT to keep the window up to date.

Dialog Box Messages

WM_INITDIALOG

This message is sent just before a dialog box is displayed. Refer to Chapter 8 to learn about dialog boxes. Trap this message if there are any list boxes or other features in a dialog box that need to be initialized.

6 System Messages

Mouse Messages

Whenever the mouse is moved or a mouse button is clicked, a message is sent. The mouse messages pass the position of the mouse in lParam. The x coordinate is in the low-order word, and the y coordinate is in the high-order word. You can extract these values with HIWORD and LOWORD.

You can also convert these values to a POINT structure. POINT is a data structure containing an integer value for x and y coordinates. For example, if the variable **pt** is a POINT, **pt.x** contains the x coordinate, and **pt.y** contains the y coordinate. To convert a long into a POINT, use the MAKEPOINT macro. Its format is as follows:

```
POINT
MAKEPOINT( lParam )
```

lParam is a long containing the x and y coordinates.

The mouse always returns the position in device coordinates, which is the default coordinate system and was discussed in the last chapter. The upper left corner of the screen is (0,0). Coordinates increase going down and to the right. You will learn more about the coordinate systems in Chapter 7.

You do not need to call **DefWindowProc** if you trap these messages.

Normally, mouse messages are sent only when the mouse is moved in the program's window. If you want messages sent whenever the mouse is moved regardless of the window it is in, use the **SetCapture** command. Its format is as follows:

```
SetCapture( hWnd )
```

hWnd is a handle to the window. Keep the capture held only as long as necessary. Release it with the following command:

```
ReleaseCapture()
```

WM_MOUSEMOVE

This message is sent whenever the mouse is moved. wParam is a combination of the following bit values:

MK_LBUTTON	set if left button is down
MK_RBUTTON	set if right button is down
MK_MBUTTON	set if middle button is down
MK_SHIFT	set if shift key is down
MK_CONTROL	set if control key is down

You can check for any of these values using the AND function. For example, (wParam & MK_RBUTTON) will be non-zero if the right button is down.

lParam contains the position of the mouse.

WM_LBUTTONDOWN

This message is sent when the user presses the left mouse button. It is not sent while the user holds down the button. The program SIX traps this message.

wParam is a combination of the following bit values:

MK_RBUTTON	set if right button is down
MK_MBUTTON	set if middle button is down
MK_SHIFT	set if shift key is down
MK_CONTROL	set if control key is down

lParam contains the mouse position.

6 System Messages

WM_RBUTTONDOWN

This message is sent when the user presses the right mouse button. It is not sent while the user holds down the button. wParam is a combination of the following:

MK_LBUTTON	set if left button is down
MK_MBUTTON	set if middle button is down
MK_SHIFT	set if shift key is down
MK_CONTROL	set if control key is down

lParam contains the mouse position.

WM_MBUTTONDOWN

This message is sent when the user presses the middle mouse button. It is not sent while the user holds down the button. wParam is a combination of the following:

MK_LBUTTON	set if left button is down
MK_RBUTTON	set if right button is down
MK_SHIFT	set if shift key is down
MK_CONTROL	set if control key is down

lParam contains the mouse position.

WM_LBUTTONUP

This message is sent when the user releases the left mouse button. Its parameters are the same as for WM_LBUTTONDOWN.

WM_RBUTTONUP

This message is sent when the user releases the right mouse button. Its parameters are the same as for WM_RBUTTONDOWN.

WM_MBUTTONUP

This message is sent when the user releases the middle mouse button. Its parameters are the same as for WM_MBUTTONDOWN.

WM_LBUTTONDBLCLK

This message is sent when the user double clicks the left mouse button. Its parameters are the same as for WM_LBUTTONDOWN. This message is sent only if the class has the CS_DBLCLKS style option. When double clicking occurs, down, up, double-click, and up messages are sent.

WM_RBUTTONDBLCLK

This message is sent when the user double clicks the right mouse button. Its parameters are the same as for WM_RBUTTONDOWN. This message is sent only if the class has the CS_DBLCLKS style option. When double clicking occurs, down, up, double-click, and up messages are sent.

WM_MBUTTONDBLCLK

This message is sent when the user double clicks the middle mouse button. Its parameters are the same as for WM_MBUTTONDOWN. This message is sent only if the class has the CS_DBLCLKS style option. When double clicking occurs, down, up, double-click, and up messages are sent.

Keyboard Messages

Keyboard messages are sent to the active window. You can read keyboard messages if you want to receive input character by character. If you want to read in a string of text, use a dialog box, as discussed in Chapter 8. You do not need to call **DefWindowProc** if you trap WM_CHAR.

6 System Messages

WM_CHAR

This message is sent when the user presses a key. If the user holds down the key, this message is sent each time the key repeats. wParam contains the ASCII value of the key.

WM_SYSCHAR

This message is sent when the user holds down the ALT key and simultaneously presses another key. wParam contains the ASCII key code of the key being pressed.

Timer Messages

The user can set a timer that elapses after a certain number of milliseconds. Chapter 10 discusses the timer. You can use a timer to run a process, such as a clock, in the background. The following two messages relate to timers. You do not need to call **DefWindowProc** if you trap these messages.

WM_TIMER

This message is sent when a timer expires. wParam contains the timer ID.

WM_TIMECHANGE

This message is sent when the system time is changed. Trap this message if your routine depends on the system time. For example, if you set an alarm to go off after a certain amount of time has elapsed, a change in the system time could invalidate the alarm.

Scroll Command Messages

You will learn about scroll bars in Chapter 10. The following two messages relate to scroll bars and will be discussed in more detail in Chapter 10. You do not need to call **DefWindowProc** if you trap these messages.

WM_VSCROLL

This message occurs when a window's vertical scroll bar is used. **wParam** contains a code indicating the type of scroll bar activity. It can be as follows:

SB_LINEUP	scroll one line up
SB_LINEDOWN	scroll one line down
SB_PAGEUP	scroll one page up
SB_PAGEDOWN	scroll one page down
SB_THUMBPOSITION	move the thumb to **LOWORD(lParam)**
SB_THUMBTRACK	the user is dragging the thumb. Its current position is **LOWORD(lParam)**.
SB_TOP	move to the top of the scroll bar
SB_BOTTOM	move to the bottom of the scroll bar

WM_HSCROLL

This message occurs when a window's horizontal scroll bar is used. wParam contains a code indicating the type of scroll bar activity. It can be as follows:

SB_LINEUP	scroll one line left
SB_LINEDOWN	scroll one line right
SB_PAGEUP	scroll one page left
SB_PAGEDOWN	scroll one page right

SB_THUMBPOSITION

    move the thumb to **LOWORD**(lParam)

SB_THUMBTRACK   the user is dragging the thumb. Its current position is **LOWORD**(lParam).

SB_TOP   move to the far left of the scroll bar

SB_BOTTOM   move to the far right of the scroll bar

System Command Messages

WM_SYSCOMMAND

This message is sent whenever the user selects an item from the system menu (the striped box in the upper left corner of the window). Trap this message if you have added commands to the system menu. In general, you should not alter the function of the system menu commands provided by Windows. You must call **DefWindowProc** if you trap this message. If you add commands to the system menu, do not send these commands to **DefWindowProc**.

(wParam & 0xFFF0) contains the menu id of the system command. It can be as follows:

SC_SIZE
SC_MOVE
SC_ICON
SC_ZOOM
SC_CLOSE

Other Messages

There are many other messages in addition to the ones discussed in this chapter. If you are interested in looking at a complete list of messages, refer to the Messages section of the Windows Development Toolkit *Programmer's Reference Manual*.

6 System Messages

A PROGRAM: SIX

The following program, SIX, incorporates system messages into the program FIVE2. Whenever a WM_PAINT message is received, such as when the size of the window changes, the text cursors are reset to the upper left corner of the screen. If the left mouse button is pressed, the text cursors are set to the mouse position (see Figure 6.1).

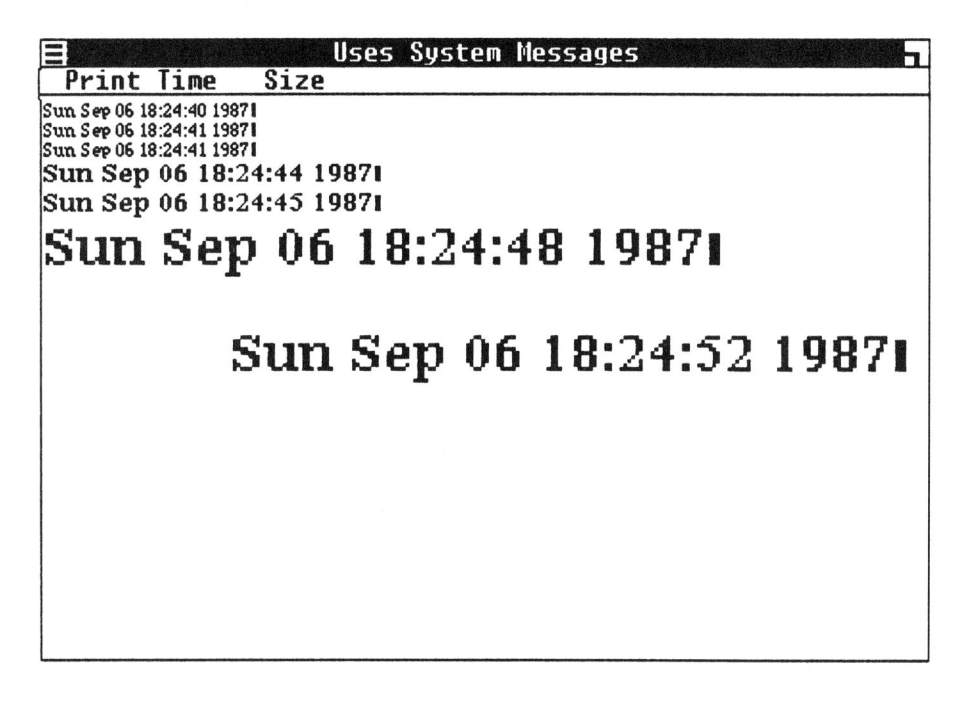

Figure 6.1   The program SIX.

Look over the code. The differences between FIVE2 and SIX occur in the **MsgServer** routine. Notice the use of the switch statement and the processing of the WM_PAINT and WM_LBUTTONUP messages. Also note that **DefWindowProc** is called after both of these messages, which lets WM_PAINT paint the screen as it normally does. WM_LBUTTONUP doesn't need to call **DefWindowProc**, but there is no harm in it doing so.

6 System Messages

When you run this program, make sure to load several copies of it at the same time. Note how the text cursors are reset after the windows are resized or moved. Move the text cursors around by clicking the left mouse button and then pressing the Print Time command.

```
/----------------------------------------------\
|                                              |
| The files for this program are in the SIX    |
| directory.  The make file is SIX.  SIX.RC is |
| the resource file.  SIX.H is the include file.|
| SIX.C is the code and SIX.DEF is the module  |
| definition file.  SIX.ICO is the icon.  The  |
| cursor, MIKE.CUR, is located in the root     |
| directory.  The executable file is SIX.EXE.  |
|                                              |
\----------------------------------------------/
```

The Make File: SIX

```
#
#  Make file for program from Chapter 6
#

cc=cl -d -c -AS -Gsw -Os -Zpe

.c.obj:
    $(cc) $*.c


six.obj: six.c  six.h

six.res: six.rc six.h six.ico mike.cur
    rc -r six.rc

six.exe: six.obj six.res six.def
    link4 six, /align:16, NUL, slibw, six.def
    rc six.res
```

The Resource File: SIX.RC

```
/***********************************************************
    Resource file for SIX
***********************************************************/

#include "windows.h"
#include "six.h"


face       CURSOR     mike.cur
six        ICON       six.ico

six MENU
BEGIN
    MENUITEM  "Print Time",  IDM_PRINT
    POPUP     "Size"
    BEGIN
        MENUITEM "10",   IDM_SIZE_10,   CHECKED
        MENUITEM "15",   IDM_SIZE_15,
        MENUITEM "30",   IDM_SIZE_30
    END
END
```

The Include File: SIX.H

```
/***********************************************************
    Include file for the program from Chapter 6.  Contains
    typedefs, constants, and external declarations.
***********************************************************/


extern int PASCAL WinMain();
extern int register_window();
extern long FAR PASCAL MsgServer();
extern long process_menu_cmds();
extern init_font();
extern create_font();
```

continued...

6 System Messages

...from previous page

```
extern int       text_size_glbl;
extern int       cur_text_y_glbl;
extern int       cur_text_x_glbl;
extern LOGFONT   LogFont_glbl;
extern HANDLE    hFont_glbl;
extern int       font_changed_glbl;


/* constants declarations for menus */

#define  IDM_PRINT      100
#define  IDM_SIZE       200
#define  IDM_SIZE_10    210
#define  IDM_SIZE_15    215
#define  IDM_SIZE_30    230
```

The Code: SIX.C

```
/*************************************************************
        File:     six.c
        Program:  six

        This is the Windows program from Chapter 6.  It
        demonstrates using system messages and reading the
        mouse position.  For example, if the window is resized
        or moved, the text location resets to the upper left
        corner of the screen.  If the left button is pushed on
        the screen, the text position is set to the mouse
        position.
*************************************************************/


#include "windows.h"
#include "string.h"
#include "time.h"
#include "stdio.h"
#include "six.h"
```

continued...

...from previous page

```
/*------------------------------------------------
    Global variables
--------------------------------------------------*/

int       cur_text_x_glbl;
int       cur_text_y_glbl;
int       text_size_glbl;
LOGFONT   LogFont_glbl;
HANDLE    hFont_glbl;
int       font_changed_glbl;



/*------------------------------------------------
    This is the Start Up procedure and message relayer
--------------------------------------------------*/

int PASCAL
WinMain(hInstance, hPrevInstance, lpszCmdLine, cmdShow)
HANDLE    hInstance, hPrevInstance;
LPSTR     lpszCmdLine;
int       cmdShow;
{
    HWND      hWnd;
    MSG       msg;

    /* If this is the first instance, register the
       window class
    */
    if (!hPrevInstance)
        register_window(hInstance);

    /* initialize the font characteristics */
    init_font();
```

continued...

6 System Messages

...from previous page

```
    /* Create a tiled window */
    hWnd = CreateWindow( (LPSTR) "Chap6WIN",     /* class */
                (LPSTR) "Uses System Messages", /* title */
                WS_TILEDWINDOW,            /* style */
                0, 0, 0, 0,
                (HWND) NULL,               /* parent */
                (HMENU) NULL,              /* use class menu */
                (HANDLE) hInstance,        /* instance */
                (LPSTR) NULL );

    /* now display the window */
    ShowWindow(hWnd,cmdShow);
    UpdateWindow(hWnd);


    /* initialize global variables */
    cur_text_x_glbl = 0;
    cur_text_y_glbl = 0;
    text_size_glbl = 10;
    hFont_glbl = NULL;
    font_changed_glbl = TRUE;


    /* relay all messages to the message server */
    while (GetMessage( (LPMSG) &msg, NULL, 0, 0) ) {
        TranslateMessage( (LPMSG) &msg);
        DispatchMessage( (LPMSG) &msg);
    }

    exit(msg.wParam);
}


/*----------------------------------------------------------
   This procedure registers the window.
  ----------------------------------------------------------*/

int
register_window( hInstance )
HANDLE   hInstance;
{
```

continued...

...from previous page

```
    PWNDCLASS       pClass;

    pClass = (PWNDCLASS) LocalAlloc(LPTR, sizeof(WNDCLASS));
    pClass->hCursor = LoadCursor(hInstance, (LPSTR) "face");
    pClass->hIcon = LoadIcon(hInstance, (LPSTR) "six");
    pClass->lpszMenuName = (LPSTR) "six";
    pClass->lpszClassName = (LPSTR) "Chap6WIN";
    pClass->hbrBackground = GetStockObject(WHITE_BRUSH);
    pClass->hInstance = hInstance;
    pClass->style = CS_HREDRAW | CS_VREDRAW;
    pClass->lpfnWndProc = MsgServer;

    RegisterClass( (LPWNDCLASS) pClass);
    LocalFree( (HANDLE) pClass);
}




/*-----------------------------------------------------------
  This routine processes commands from the menu
-------------------------------------------------------- */

long
process_menu_cmds( hWnd, command )
HWND    hWnd;
WORD    command;
{
    HMENU       hMenu;
    HDC         hDC;
    char        *time_string;
    long        ltime;


    /* get the handle for the menu */
    hMenu = GetMenu(hWnd);
```

continued...

6 System Messages

...from previous page

```
    /* now process the commands */
    switch (command) {
    case IDM_PRINT:
        /* print the time.  It is the same as in Chapter
           5, only now we also set the x location of the
           font also
         */
        time(&ltime);
        time_string = asctime( localtime( &ltime ) );
        hDC = GetDC(hWnd);
        create_font(hDC);
        TextOut(hDC, cur_text_x_glbl, cur_text_y_glbl,
            (LPSTR) time_string, strlen(time_string));
        ReleaseDC(hWnd, hDC);
        cur_text_y_glbl += text_size_glbl;
        break;
    case IDM_SIZE_10:
    case IDM_SIZE_15:
    case IDM_SIZE_30:
        /* get rid of old check */
        CheckMenuItem(hMenu, text_size_glbl + IDM_SIZE,
            MF_UNCHECKED | MF_BYCOMMAND);

        /* add new check */
        CheckMenuItem(hMenu, command, MF_CHECKED |
            MF_BYCOMMAND);

        /* update the font size */
        text_size_glbl = command - IDM_SIZE;
        LogFont_glbl.lfHeight = text_size_glbl;
        font_changed_glbl = TRUE;
        break;
    }
    return(0L);

}
```

continued...

System Messages 6

...from previous page

```
/*-----------------------------------------------------------
    This procedure receives the messages and decides what to
    do with them.  Note that in addition to processing menu
    commands, it also takes action if the mouse button is
    pressed in the window, or if the screen needs to be
    repainted (such as after the window is moved or sized)
    ----------------------------------------------------------- */

long FAR PASCAL
MsgServer(hWnd,message,wParam,lParam)
HWND     hWnd;
unsigned message;
WORD     wParam;
LONG     lParam;
{
    switch (message) {
    case WM_COMMAND:
        return( process_menu_cmds(hWnd, wParam) );
    case WM_PAINT:
        /* reset text position to upper left corner */
        cur_text_x_glbl = 0;
        cur_text_y_glbl = 0;
        break;
    case WM_LBUTTONUP:
        /* set the text position to the mouse position.
           The mouse position is passed in lParam.
        */
        cur_text_x_glbl = LOWORD(lParam);
        cur_text_y_glbl = HIWORD(lParam);
        break;
    }
    /* do the default processing */
    return(DefWindowProc(hWnd,message,wParam,lParam));

}
```

continued...

6 System Messages

...from previous page

```
/*-----------------------------------------------------------
    This procedure sets up the characteristics for the font.
    It is the same as in FIVE2.
------------------------------------------------------------ */
init_font()
{

    LogFont_glbl.lfHeight = 10;
    LogFont_glbl.lfWidth = 0;
    LogFont_glbl.lfEscapement = 0;
    LogFont_glbl.lfOrientation = 0;
    LogFont_glbl.lfWeight = 400;
    LogFont_glbl.lfItalic = 0;
    LogFont_glbl.lfUnderline = 0;
    LogFont_glbl.lfStrikeOut = 0;
    LogFont_glbl.lfCharSet = ANSI_CHARSET;
    LogFont_glbl.lfOutPrecision = OUT_DEFAULT_PRECIS;
    LogFont_glbl.lfClipPrecision = CLIP_DEFAULT_PRECIS;
    LogFont_glbl.lfQuality = DEFAULT_QUALITY;
    LogFont_glbl.lfPitchAndFamily = DEFAULT_PITCH
        | FF_ROMAN;
    LogFont_glbl.lfFaceName[0] = (BYTE) NULL;
}




/*-----------------------------------------------------------
    This procedure creates the font.  It sets the text color
    to red.
------------------------------------------------------------ */
create_font( hDC )
HDC     hDC;
{
```

continued...

...from previous page

```
    /* create a new font if the characteristics have
       changed
    */
    if (font_changed_glbl == TRUE) {
        /* delete old font */
        DeleteObject( hFont_glbl );

        /* create the font from its description */
        hFont_glbl = CreateFontIndirect( (LPLOGFONT)
            &LogFont_glbl);

        font_changed_glbl = FALSE;
    }

    /* select it */
    SelectObject(hDC, hFont_glbl);

    /* set text color to red */
    SetTextColor(hDC, (LONG) 255);

}
```

The Module Definition File: SIX.DEF

```
NAME      Six
DESCRIPTION   'Sixth Window Program'
STUB      'winstub.exe'
CODE      MOVEABLE
DATA      MOVEABLE MULTIPLE
HEAPSIZE 4096
STACKSIZE 4096
EXPORTS
          MsgServer @1
```

6 System Messages

SUMMARY

- Windows sends messages to the program when keys are pressed, the mouse is moved, or the window is modified. Processing these messages can enhance your programs.

- Window-related messages occur when a window is opened, closed, moved, resized, or made iconic.

- Dialog messages allow a program to initialize dialog boxes.

- Mouse messages occur when the mouse is moved or mouse buttons are used.

- Keyboard messages occur when keys are pressed.

- Timer messages relate to the system timer and timed events.

- Scroll messages are used by windows with scroll bars.

CHAPTER 7

GRAPHICS

7 Graphics

Graphics are an important part of any Windows program. This chapter discusses GDI, Windows' graphics language. You will learn about the different mapping modes, zooming and panning, pens and brushes, the built-in graphics functions, and metafiles.

AN INTRODUCTION TO GDI

GDI—the *graphics device interface*—is Windows' set of graphics routines. The GDI includes a wide variety of commands, performing such diverse functions as setting a coordinate system and filling polygons and regions.

GDI is important because it provides a standard set of device-independent graphics routines. What will work in one size window on one computer will work on any other setup or on a printer, which saves the programmer a great deal of hassle.

A program's window is broken into two areas: the *system area* and the *application area*. The system area includes the menus, title bar, and scroll bars. The application area is the rest of the window (Figure 7.1). All graphics appear in the application area.

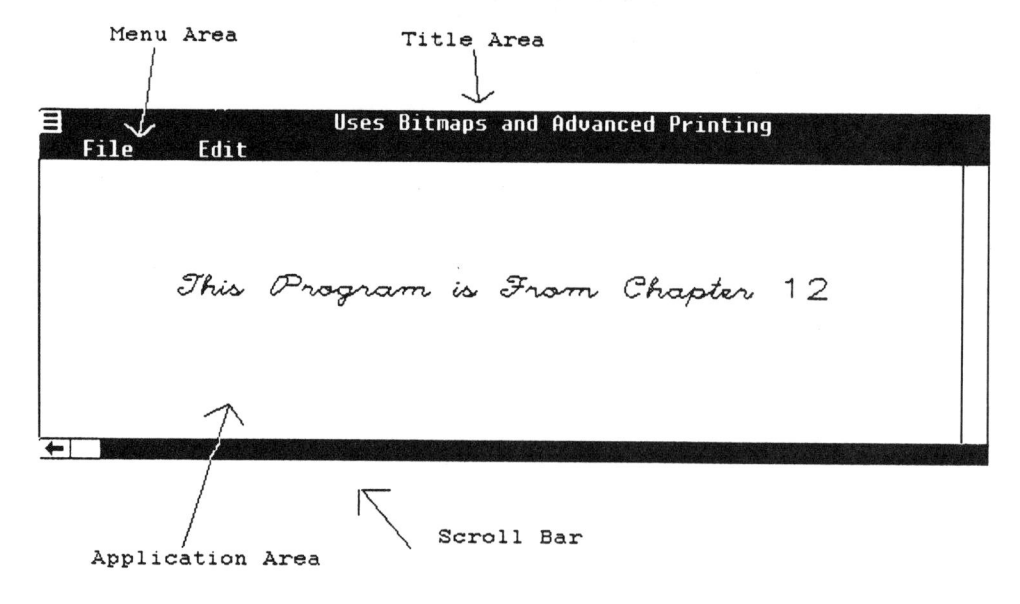

Figure 7.1 The system and application areas of a window. The title area, menu area, and scroll bar are all part of the system area.

To display graphics, you must perform the following steps:

- Get the display context
- Set the coordinate system
- Set the window and viewport
- Perform the graphics calls
- Release the display context

You have already learned about the display context. The next few sections will cover the coordinate systems, windows and viewports, and graphics calls.

THE MAPPING MODES

Every graphics display must have a *coordinate system* to provide a way to describe the position of objects. All Windows coordinate systems are *Cartesian*. An object's position is defined in terms of a horizontal (x) and vertical (y) position, with respect to a particular origin (Figure 7.2). You are probably familiar with such a system. Another common system is the polar coordinate system.

Windows provides several choices for defining the coordinate system's axes. There are three basic groups. The first is a *device-related coordinate system*. Each graphics unit corresponds to a dot on the screen. Horizontal and vertical units can have different sizes. Windows has one such mode (the default mode) called MM_TEXT, which is the coordinate system used in Chapter 5. In the second type of coordinate system, a unit in the x direction has the same size as a unit in the y direction. Windows has six such modes:

MM_LOMETRIC
MM_HIMETRIC
MM_LOENGLISH
MM_HIENGLISH
MM_TWIPS
MM_ISOTROPIC

7 Graphics

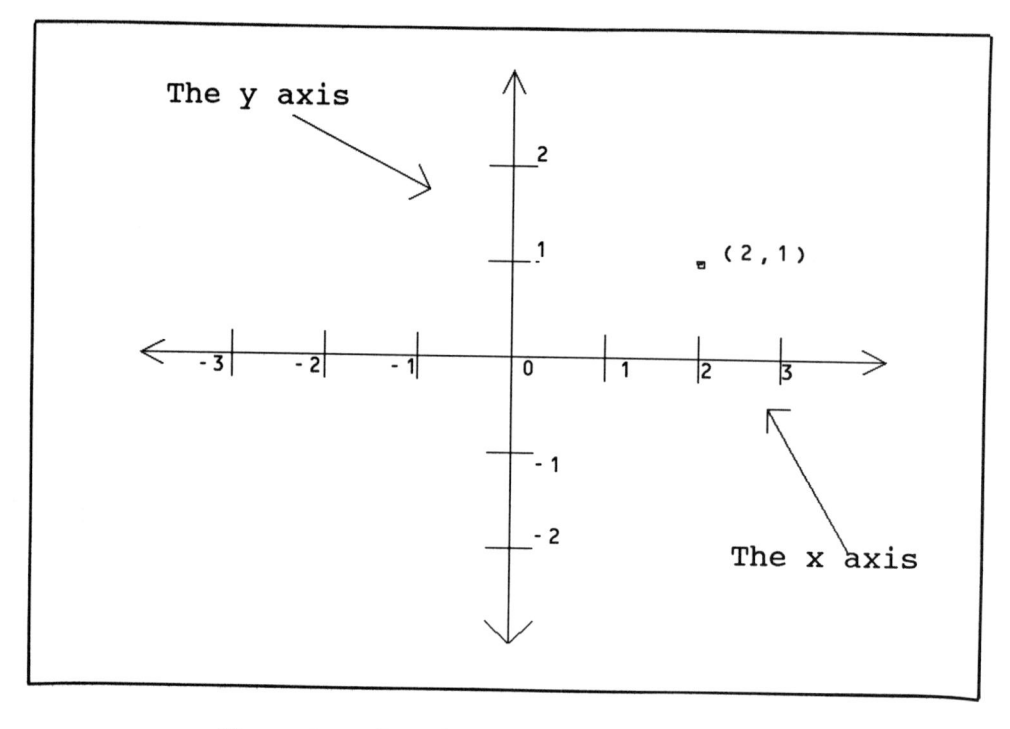

Figure 7.2 The Cartesian coordinate system.

Five of the modes provide units defined in terms of fixed units: inches, meters, or points. The sixth mode lets you define the units. The third type of coordinate system — MM_ANISOTROPIC — has no relation to the screen or a measurement unit and has no fixed relationship between the two axes. This system provides complete freedom for defining the axes.

MM_TEXT is the default mode, and, as its name suggests, it is convenient for text-based applications. MM_LOMETRIC, MM_HIMETRIC, MM_LOENGLISH, MM_HIENGLISH, and MM_TWIPS are useful for applications that must relate to actual physical measurements, such as in desktop publishing or drafting programs. MM_ISOTROPIC is useful for programs that need to maintain equal units for the x and y axes but do not relate to a particular physical system. Scientific and statistical graphics packages are a good example. MM_ANISOTROPIC is useful for programs that want more flexibility of scale; it can be used to ensure that a complete picture is always displayed in the application area.

Now, examine these mapping modes in more detail:

MM_TEXT

Each coordinate unit corresponds to one dot (pixel) on the screen. X and y units can have different sizes. X units increase going to the right and y units increase going down.

MM_LOMETRIC

Each coordinate unit corresponds to .1 millimeters. X units increase going right; y units increase going up.

MM_HIMETRIC

Each coordinate unit corresponds to .01 millimeters. X units increase going right; y units increase going up.

MM_LOENGLISH

Each coordinate unit corresponds to .01 inches. X units increase going right; y units increase going up.

MM_HIENGLISH

Each coordinate unit corresponds to .001 inches. X units increase going right; y units increase going up.

MM_TWIPS

Each coordinate unit corresponds to 1/20th of a printer's point (1/1440 inches). X units increase going right; y units increase going up.

MM_ISOTROPIC

A coordinate unit in the x direction is the same size as a coordinate unit in the y direction. **SetViewportExt** and **SetWindowExt** determine the coordinate system units and in which direction the coordinates increase.

MM_ANISOTROPIC

SetViewportExt and **SetWindowExt** define the coordinate axes and determine in which direction the units increase. X and y units are not necessarily of the same size.

Use the **SetMapMode** to choose the mapping system. Its format is as follows:

```
short
SetMapMode( hDC, Mode )
```

hDC is a handle to the display context, and **Mode** is one of the eight mapping modes just discussed. The function returns the previous mapping mode.

WINDOW AND VIEWPORT

The mapping mode determines the units for the coordinates. The window and viewport determine how the coordinate system maps to the screen.

Coordinates in the user-chosen coordinate system are called *logical coordinates*. At the same time, there is a *device coordinate system*. The device coordinate system refers to actual pixels on the screen. The system's units are the same as MM_TEXT: each coordinate represents one dot, and (0,0) is the upper left corner.

The *viewport* and *window* define how to map the logical coordinates onto the device coordinates, i.e., they tell Windows how to take a point in the user's system (the logical coordinate system) and decide where to plot it on the screen (the device coordinate system).

The viewport defines a region of the screen. It has a point called the *origin*, and it has *extents*. The extents define how far the viewport extends beyond the origin. The viewport is always defined in device coordinates. The window also has an origin and extents, and it is always described in logical coordinates.

The window origin defines the logical coordinate point to map the viewport origin. For example, suppose the viewport origin is the upper left corner of the application area, and the window origin is (10,10). If you plot the point (10,10), it will appear in the upper left corner of the application area.

The window and viewport extents are only used for MM_ISOTROPIC and MM_ANISOTROPIC modes. For these modes, the window extents define the logical coordinate points to map to the viewport extents, which tells the size of logical coordinates with respect to device coordinates. For example, suppose the viewport origin is (0, 0), and its extents are (2, 3). (Here, the x coordinate of the extent indicates the x extent and the y value indicates the y extent.) Suppose the window origin is (10, 10) and its extents are (6, 9). Then, the logical point (10 + 6, 10 + 9) corresponds to the device point (0 + 2, 0 + 3). Similarly, the logical point (10 - 6, 10) corresponds to the device point (0 - 2, 0). For MM_ISOTROPIC mode, the scales will be adjusted to ensure that x and y units have the same size.

An image can be drawn at any point in the coordinate system, but because of screen size, only part of the image can be seen at once. The window defines the visible portion of the image. Changing the window changes the visible portion of the image. For example, the coordinates between x = 0 and 50 and y = 60 and 110 could be mapped to the screen, or any part of an image between -1 inch and 1 inch in the x axis and -2 inches and 2 inches in the y direction could be displayed (Figure 7.3).

There are several effects you can create by using window and viewport:

Displaying a whole object: Suppose that all points of an object fall within the bounds (a0, b0) and (a1, b1). To ensure that the entire object is always displayed on the screen, set the viewport origin to the center of the screen and the viewport extents to half the screen size. (Get the screen size with **GetClientRect**.) Set the window origin to the center of the object: ((a0 + a1)/2, (b0 + b1)/2). Set the window extents to half the object's size: ((a1 - a0)/2, (b1 - b0)/2). Use MM_ANISOTROPIC mode.

7 Graphics

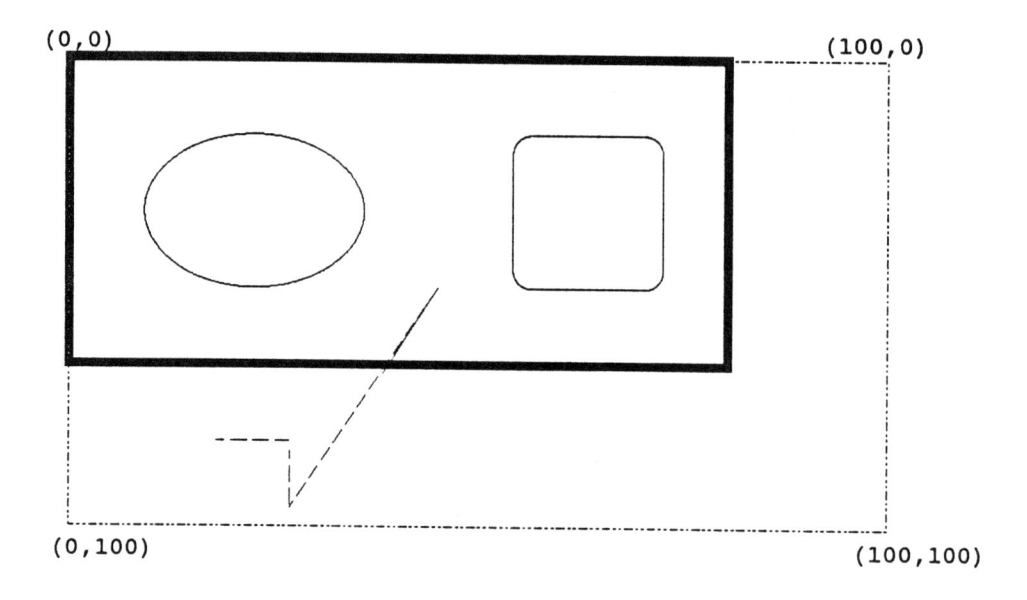

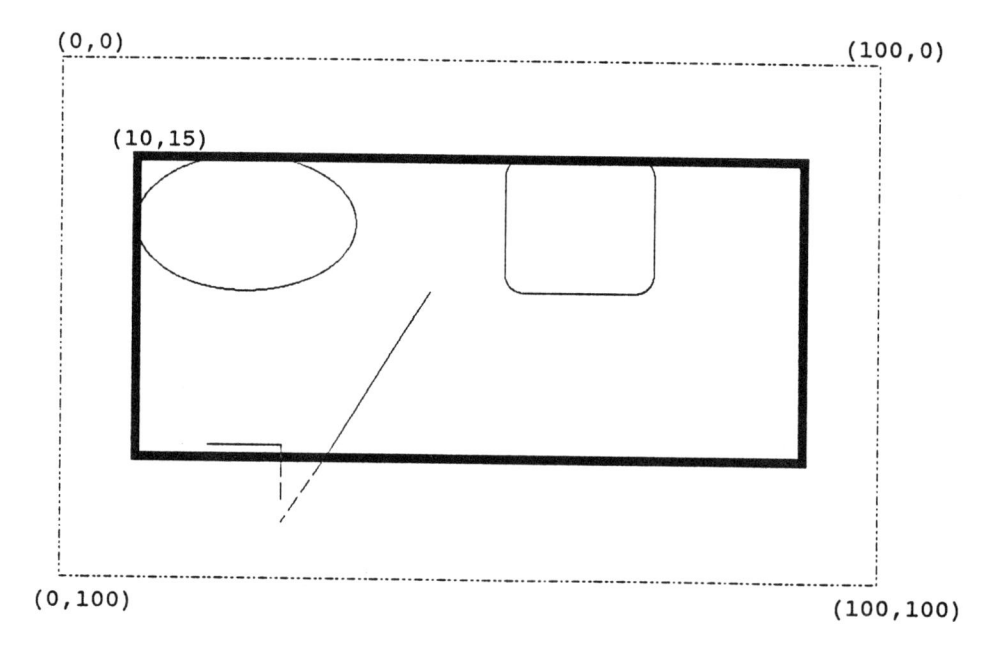

Figure 7.3 Windowing. The bold box is the display screen. The dotted box is the logical screen. In the upper figure, the window origin is (0,0). In the lower figure, the window origin is (10,15). Note what objects appear in the different screens. Changing the window scrolls the screen.

Keeping an object's position and size constant: Keep the viewport and window origin constant. For MM_ISOTROPIC and MM_ANISOTROPIC modes, keep the window and viewport extents constant, which is useful with text windows; it makes the application area act as a sheet of paper pinned to the application area.

Panning (Scrolling): To pan across an object, keep the window extents constant and move the window origin. Move the origin opposite to the panning direction. For example, to pan left, move the origin right; to pan down, move the origin up.

Zooming: Keep the window origin constant, and increase or decrease the window extents. To zoom in, decrease the window extents. To zoom out, increase the window extents. This procedure will only work in the MM_ISOTROPIC and MM_ANISOTROPIC modes. You can also switch between MM_HIMETRIC and MM_LOMETRIC modes or MM_HIENGLISH and MM_LOENGLISH modes.

Displaying several graphs: To display several graphs, define several viewports. If you want each graph to have the same coordinate axes, use the same window origins and extents. To use different axes, change the window origin and extents. Define the *clipping region* (discussed later in this chapter) to each of the viewports before you draw the graph.

Creating a (0,0) centered screen: To keep (0,0) in the center of the screen, set the viewport origin to the center of the screen. Set the window origin to (0,0). Set viewport and window extents as desired.

Setting axis direction: With MM_ISOTROPIC and MM_ANISOTROPIC modes, you can control the direction of the axes. Set window origin, viewport origin, and viewport extents as desired. To make the x axis increase going right, make the window and viewport x extents have the same sign. To make the x axis increase going left, set the window and viewport x extents to the opposite sign. To make the y axis increase going up, make the viewport and window y extents have opposite signs. Give the window and viewport y extents the same sign if you want the y axis to increase going down.

Note that you cannot change the axis direction in the MM_HIENGLISH, MM_LOENGLISH, MM_HIMETRIC, MM_LOMETRIC, and MM_TWIPS mapping modes. Unless you change the window origin, the y coordinates on the screen will always be negative.

7 Graphics

Use **SetViewportOrg** and **SetViewportExt** to define the viewport. Remember, viewport parameters are always in device coordinates, i.e., each unit represents one dot. (0,0) is the upper left corner of the application area. Points will not be clipped to the viewport bounds. Use **SelectClipRgn** to clip points to the viewport.

Following are the viewport and window commands:

```
LONG
SetViewportOrg( hDC, x, y)
```

hDC is a handle to the display context, and (x, y) is the viewport origin. The return value is the previous viewport origin.

```
LONG
SetViewportExt( hDC, xext, yext )
```

hDC   is a handle to the display context.

xext   tells how many units to extend left and right from the viewport origin.

yext   tells how many units to extend up and down from the viewport origin.

The return value is the previous extents.

To define the window, use **SetWindowOrg** and **SetWindowExt**. Window coordinates are logical coordinates, i.e., they are defined in terms of the selected mapping mode.

```
LONG
SetWindowOrg( hDC, x, y )
```

hDC is a handle to the display context, and **(x, y)** is the point that will be mapped to the viewport origin. The return value is the previous window origin.

```
LONG
SetWindowExt( hDC, xext, yext )
```

hDC is a handle to the display context. Call the viewport origin (xvo, yvo), the viewport extents (xve, yve), and the window origin (xwo, ywo). **xext** + xwo is the value to map to xvo + xve; **yext** + ywo is the value to map to yvo + yve.

You can determine the current window and viewport settings using the following functions:

```
LONG
GetWindowOrg( hDC )
```

hDC is a display context handle, and the return value is the window origin.

```
LONG
GetWindowExt( hDC )
```

hDC is a display context handle, and the return value is the window extents.

```
LONG
GetViewportOrg( hDC )
```

hDC is a display context handle, and the return value is the viewport origin.

```
LONG
GetViewportExt( hDC )
```

7 Graphics

hDC is a display context handle, and the return value is the viewport extents.

You must select the mapping mode and define the window and viewport each time you get the display context. Windows will not remember your previous selections.

DRAWING OBJECTS: BRUSHES, PENS, AND COLORS

Graphics commands draw and fill objects. Lines and object borders are drawn with a *pen*. Objects are filled with a *brush*. Several of the commands allow you to specify the brush or color to use. Normally, the pen draws a solid black line, and the brush paints a white region. Colors are defined by the RGB color scheme, as discussed in Chapter 5.

You can create a pen with the **CreatePen** command. Its format is as follows:

```
HPEN
CreatePen( PenStyle, Width, Color )
```

PenStyle specifies the pattern of the line the pen will draw. Set it to one of the following:

    0 Solid
    1 Dash
    2 Dot
    3 Dash and dot
    4 Dash and two dots
    5 Null

    The default is solid.

Width specifies the number of coordinates wide to make the pen. This measurement is in terms of logical y coordinates. In other words, if you set **Width** to 2, and two y points in the logical coordinate system correspond to five device points, the pen width will be five device points. If the pen is more than one device coordinate wide, the PenStyle will be ignored, and the pen will be solid.

Color RGB color of the pen.

The return value is a handle to the pen.

To create a colored brush, use the following command:

```
HBRUSH
CreateSolidBrush( Color )
```

Color is the RGB color for the brush. The function returns a handle to the brush.

To create a brush that doesn't paint a solid pattern, use the following command:

```
HBRUSH
CreateHatchBrush( Style, Color )
```

Style is one of the following:

HS__HORIZONTAL	horizontal hatch
HS__VERTICAL	vertical hatch
HS__FDIAGONAL	45-degree negative slope hatch
HS__BDIAGONAL	45-degree positive slope hatch
HS__CROSS	horizontal and vertical hatch
HS__DIAGCROSS	45-degree cross hatch

7 Graphics

Color   is the RGB color for the brush.

The function returns a handle to the brush.

As with fonts, select the pen or brush with **SelectObject**. When you are finished using a pen or brush, delete it with **DeleteObject** to free memory.

You may want to create the pens and brushes you will use in **register_window** and store their handles in global variables. Later instances can access these resources with **GetInstanceData**. Free the resources before terminating.

THE GRAPHICS COMMANDS

The following section details the various graphics commands. They are broken into commands for points and lines, polygons and curves, and regions.

Coordinates are always integer values.[1]

Point and Line Commands

SetPixel fills a point with a particular color. Its format is as follows:

```
RGB
SetPixel( hDC, x, y, Color )
```

hDC   is a display context handle.

x   is the x coordinate of the point.

y   is the y coordinate of the point.

---

[1] Coordinates can be specified by two means: *absolute* and *relative* position. The default is *absolute* position; in this method, position parameters refer to an actual coordinate. In *relative* mode, position parameters are a vector indicating how to get to a coordinate from the last drawn point.
 As of Windows 1.03, relative mode has not been implemented.

Graphics 7

Color   is the RGB color for the point. This color will be matched as closely as possible, given Windows' color palette. (For a discussion of color matching, see **SetTextColor** in Chapter 5.)

The return value is the actual color value used.

GetPixel is the opposite of **SetPixel**. It returns the color of a particular point. Its format is as follows:

```
RGB
GetPixel( hDC, x, y )
```

hDC   is a display context handle.

x   is the x coordinate of the point.

y   is the y coordinate of the point.

To draw a line, use the **MoveTo** and **LineTo** commands. Use **MoveTo** to define the location of one of the endpoints. Call **LineTo** with the other coordinate. A line will be drawn (using the current pen) between the two coordinates. **LineTo** always draws a line starting from the last point drawn or the point set by **MoveTo**. To draw a group of connected lines, set the first endpoint with **MoveTo**. Then, repeatedly call **LineTo** with the other coordinates. You can also use **Polyline**. **MoveTo**'s format is as follows:

```
POINT
MoveTo( hDC, x, y )
```

hDC   is the display context handle.

x   is the x coordinate of the line's endpoint.

y   is the y coordinate of the line's endpoint.

The return value is the last drawn point.

171

7 Graphics

Once **MoveTo** or **LineTo** has defined a point, the **LineTo** command will draw a line to the new point:

```
LineTo( hDC, x, y )
```

hDC   is a display context handle.

x   is the x coordinate to which the line will be drawn.

y   is the y coordinate to which the line will be drawn.

To draw line segments between a set of coordinates, use the **Polyline** command. Pass the command an array of endpoints. This array should be in the form as follows:

```
POINT    var_name[ num_points ];
```

Polyline will connect all of the endpoints; it will do a **MoveTo** to the first coordinate (var_name[0]) and then **LineTos** for the rest of the coordinates.

```
Polyline( hDC, lpPoints, Count )
```

hDC   is the display context handle.

lpPoints   is a long pointer to the array of endpoints.

Count   is the number of points to draw. **Polyline** will connect the first **Count** endpoints, starting with **lpPoints[0]**.

Polygon, Curve, and Fill Commands

There are several polygon and curve commands. In general, these commands create objects whose borders are drawn with the pens and whose interiors are filled with a brush.

There are several commands for drawing rectangles. **Rectangle** draws a normal, filled rectangle. **RoundRect** rounds the edges of the rectangle. **FrameRect** uses a brush to paint the border of a rectangle. **FillRect** uses a brush to fill the interior of a rectangle.

Rectangles are defined by their left, right, top, and bottom coordinates. For the FillRect and FrameRect commands, the rectangle will not be drawn if the left value is greater than the right value or the top value is greater than the bottom value. If your coordinate system's y axis increases while going up, switch the bottom and top values. In other words, in coordinate systems where the y value increases while going up, the top of a rectangle will have a higher coordinate value than the bottom. Passing the parameters this way, however, will prevent the rectangle from being drawn. Passing the bottom value—which is lower—as the top and the top as the bottom will result in the bottom value being higher than the top value; thus, the rectangle will be drawn.

```
Rectangle( hDC, left, top, right, bottom )
```

hDC is the display context handle.

left is the coordinate of the left side of the rectangle.

top is the coordinate of the top side of the rectangle.

right is the coordinate of the right side of the rectangle.

bottom is the coordinate of the bottom side of the rectangle.

7 Graphics

RoundRect(hDC, left, top, right, bottom, width, height)

hDC	is the display context handle.
left	is the coordinate of the left side of the rectangle.
top	is the coordinate of the top side of the rectangle.
right	is the coordinate of the right side of the rectangle.
bottom	is the coordinate of the bottom side of the rectangle.
width	is the width of the ellipse used for rounding the edges. In other words, it is the distance from the vertical sides where rounding should start.
height	is the height of the ellipse used for rounding the edges, i.e., it is the distance from the vertical sides where rounding should start.

FrameRect(hDC, lpRect, hBrush)

hDC	is the display context handle.
lpRect	is a long pointer to a RECT structure defining the rectangle.
hBrush	is a handle to the brush used for drawing the rectangle's border.

FillRect(hDC, lpRect, hBrush)

hDC	is the display context handle.
lpRect	is a long pointer to a RECT structure defining the rectangle.
hBrush	is a handle to the brush used for filling in the rectangle.

The **Polygon** command creates a polygon from a list of endpoints. The last and first endpoints are automatically connected. The polygon is filled with the current brush.

```
Polygon( hDC, lpPoints, Count )
```

hDC   is the display context handle.

lpPoints   is a long pointer to an array of endpoints. Its structure is the same as for **Polyline**.

Count   is the number of endpoints to use. The first **Count** endpoints in the point array are used.

The **Ellipse** command draws and fills an ellipse. The ellipse is described by a bounding rectangle.

```
Ellipse( hDC, left, top, right, bottom )
```

hDC   is the display context handle.

left   is the coordinate of the left side of the ellipse.

top   is the coordinate of the top of the ellipse.

right   is the coordinate of the right side of the ellipse.

bottom   is the coordinate of the bottom of the ellipse.

Arc draws a portion of an ellipse. Like **Ellipse**, the arc is defined by a bounding rectangle. In addition, the arc is passed a starting and ending coordinate. The section of the ellipse between these two points, traveling counterclockwise, is drawn.

```
Arc( hDC, left, top, right, bottom, xstart, ystart, xend,
yend )
```

7 Graphics

hDC   is the display context handle.

left   is the coordinate of the left side of the ellipse from which the arc will be drawn.

top   is the coordinate of the top of the ellipse from which the arc will be drawn.

right   is the coordinate of the right side of the ellipse from which the arc will be drawn.

bottom   is the coordinate of the bottom of the ellipse from which the arc will be drawn.

xstart, ystart define the starting point of the arc. These values should be close to, but not necessarily on, the ellipse.

xend, yend   define the ending point of the arc. These values should be close to, but not necessarily on, the ellipse.

Pie is similar to **Arc**, except that lines are drawn from the arc edges to the center of the ellipse. The center is then filled with the current brush. **Pie** is useful for creating pie charts.

```
Pie( hDC, left, top, right, bottom, xstart, ystart, xend,
yend )
```

hDC   is the display context handle.

left   is the coordinate of the left side of the ellipse from which the pie will be drawn.

top   is the coordinate of the top of the ellipse from which the pie will be drawn.

right   is the coordinate of the right side of the ellipse from which the pie will be drawn.

bottom   is the coordinate of the bottom of the ellipse from which the pie will be drawn.

xstart, ystart   define the starting point of the pie. These values should be close to, but not necessarily on, the pie.

xend, yend   define the ending point of the pie. These values should be close to, but not necessarily on, the pie.

Use the **FloodFill** function to fill in an irregular area of the screen that is bounded by a given color. You can use this feature to fill in regions in a drawing program. **FloodFill** starts at a point and recursively spreads out until it hits the boundary color.

```
FloodFill( hDC, startx, starty, BoundColor )
```

hDC   is the display context handle.

startx   is the x coordinate of the point at which to start painting.

starty   is the y coordinate of the point at which to start painting.

BoundColor   is the color of the boundary. The screen will be filled up to a border of this color. If there is no such continuous boundary, the entire screen will be filled.

Region Commands

A *region* is an area of the screen. The area need not be polygonal; rather, it can be a combination of polygons and arcs. Regions can be combined, outlined, and filled. In addition, regions are used to define the screen-clipping area.

Regions are defined using **CreateRectRgn**, **CreatePolygonRgn**, **CreateEllipticRgn**, and **CombineRgn**. **PtInRegion** tells if a particular point is within a particular region.

```
HRGN
CreateRectRgn( left, top, right, bottom )
```

7 Graphics

hDC is the display context handle.

left is the coordinate of the left side of the rectangular region.

top is the coordinate of the top side of the rectangular region.

right is the coordinate of the right side of the rectangular region.

bottom is the coordinate of the bottom side of the rectangular region.

The function returns a handle to the region.

You can also use the following:

```
HRGN
CreateRectRgnIndirect( lpRect )
```

lpRect is a long pointer to a RECT structure describing the rectangular region. The function returns a handle to the region.

```
HRGN
CreatePolygonRgn( lpPoints, Count, FillMode )
```

lpPoints is a long pointer to an array of endpoints. Its structure is the same as for **Polygon**.

Count is the number of endpoints to use. The first **Count** endpoints in the point array are used.

FillMode defines what parts of a self-crossing polygon to use. It can be one of the following:

- ALTERNATE
- WINDING

Graphics 7

If it is set to ALTERNATE, alternating regions of a self-crossing polygon will be used. If it is WINDING, the entire interior of a self-crossing polygon will be used. WINDING is the more useful selection.

The return value is a handle to the polygonal region.

```
HRGN
CreateEllipticRgn( left, top, right, bottom )
```

left   is the coordinate of the left side of the elliptic region.

top   is the coordinate of the top of the elliptic region.

right   is the coordinate of the right side of the elliptic region.

bottom is the coordinate of the bottom of the elliptic region.

The return value is a handle to the elliptic region.

You can also use the following:

```
HRGN
CreateEllipticRgnIndirect( lpRect )
```

lpRect is a long pointer to a RECT structure defining the boundary of the elliptic region. The function returns a handle to the region.

Use **CombineRgn** to form a new region from two other regions:

```
CombineRgn( Dest, Source1, Source2, Mode )
```

Dest   is a handle for the new region.

Source1 is a handle for the first source region.

Source2 is a handle for the second source region.

7 Graphics

Mode defines how to combine the two source regions. It can be as follows:

RGN_AND The new region is the intersection of the two source regions.

RGN_OR The new region is the union of the two source regions.

RGN_XOR The new region is the union of the two source regions, minus the intersecting portion of the source regions.

RGN_DIFF The new region is formed by the parts of the first source region that are not part of the second source region.

RGN_COPY The new region is a copy of the first source region.

Eliminate any regions you no longer need with **DeleteObject**.

To determine if a given point falls within a region, use the **PtInRegion** command:

```
BOOL
PtInRegion( hRgn, x, y )
```

hRgn is a handle for a region.

x is the x coordinate of the point in question.

y is the y coordinate of the point in question.

The function returns FALSE if the point is not in the region, and a non-zero value if the point is in the region.

Graphics 7

FrameRgn paints the border of a region. **PaintRgn** and **FillRgn** paint the interior of a region.

```
FrameRgn( hDC, hRgn, hBrush, width, height )
```

hDC	is the display context handle.
hRgn	is a handle to the region to frame.
hBrush	is a handle for the brush to use.
width	tells how wide to make vertical brush strokes.
height	tells how wide to make horizontal brush strokes.

```
PaintRgn( hDC, hRgn )
```

hDC	is a handle to the display context.
hRgn	is a handle to the region to fill.

```
FillRgn( hDC, hRgn, hBrush )
```

hDC	is a handle to the display context.
hRgn	is a handle to the region to fill.
hBrush	is a handle to the brush used to paint the region.

7 Graphics

SOME EXAMPLES OF USING GDI: CLEARING THE SCREEN, USING THE MOUSE, AND CHANGING THE CLIPPING AREA

To clear the screen, create a brush with the background color, get a rectangle for the screen, and fill it. If you have set your own coordinate system, define the rectangle as the bounds of the screen area, in logical coordinates. If you are in the default coordinate system (as if you are clearing because of a WM_PAINT message), fill the client rectangle:

```
hDC = GetDC(hWnd);
GetClientRect(hWnd, (LPRECT) &rect);
hBr = CreateSolidBrush( GetBkColor( hDC ) );
hBrOld = SelectObject(hDC, hBr);
FillRect(hDC, (LPRECT) &rect, hBr);
SelectObject(hDC, hBrOld);
DeleteObject(hBr);
ReleaseDC(hWnd, hDC);
```

If you are using the mouse as a graphics input device, remember that it always reports its position in device coordinates. To convert device coordinates, use the **DPtoLP** function:

DPtoLP(hDC, lpPoints, Count)

hDC is the display context handle.

lpPoints is an array of points to convert. It must be an array of POINTs. The points will be converted in place; that is, the new values are returned in the array.

Count is the number of points to convert. The first **Count** points are converted, starting with **lpPoints[0]**.

For example, you could do the following:

```
case WM_LBUTTONUP:
    /* add a point at the mouse position, making sure that
    the coordinates are in logical units */
    hDC = GetDC( hWnd );
    set_coordinate_system( hWnd, hDC );
    pt = MAKEPOINT( lParam );
    DPtoLP( hDC, (LPPOINT) &pt, 1 );
    pt_list_glbl[ cur_pt_glbl++ ] = pt;
    ReTeaseDC( hWnd, hDC );
    break;
```

You can convert from logical coordinates to device coordinates using **LPtoDP**:

LPtoDP(hDC, lpPoints, Count)

hDC is the display context handle.

lpPoints is an array of points to convert. It must be an array of POINTs. The points will be converted in place; that is, the new values are returned in the array.

Count is the number of points to convert. The first **Count** points are converted, starting with **lpPoints[0]**.

Normally, all graphics commands are clipped to the program's application area. You can easily change this convention. Change the clipping area whenever you break the screen into more than one area. For example, if you want to simultaneously display several graphs on the screen, change the clipping area to the viewport for each of the graphs. Change the clipping area with the **SelectClipRgn** command:

SelectClipRgn(hDC, hRgn)

hDC is the display context handle, and **hRgn** is a handle to the region to use for the clipping region. Any points drawn outside of the area defined by **hRgn** will not be drawn.

7 Graphics

Remember, every time you release the display context, the coordinate system, window, viewport, brushes, pens, and clipping region will not be saved. You must reset these each time you get the display context.

If you plan to use the display context for a very limited number of commands, such as when you are only clearing the screen, you might not want to reset the coordinate system, viewport, and so forth. Instead, you can execute your limited set of commands in the device coordinate system.

A PROGRAM: SEVEN

The following program uses GDI (see Figure 7.4). It keeps an array of endpoints. Every time the left mouse button is pressed, the point at the mouse location is added to the point array, and a line is drawn from the last point to the new point. As an option, the coordinates of the point are printed. This process illustrates combining graphics and text and converting numbers into text.

Whenever the screen is moved or sized, the whole picture is redrawn. A menu command clears the screen and clears out the points.

The program's operation is fairly simple. The endpoints are kept in a POINT array. A global variable keeps track of the number of points. This variable also indicates where in the array to add new points, and it is used to draw the lines. **MsgServer** checks for WM_COMMAND, WM_PAINT, and WM_LBUTTONUP. The procedure **set_up_coords** sets up an ANISOTROPIC coordinate system so that the whole image is always displayed. The procedure defines a screen with (0, 0) in the lower left corner and (100, 100) in the upper right corner. Note how this is done using **GetClientRect** and how the signs of the window and viewport extents make the y axis increase in the upward direction.

As each point is added, it is drawn with a **MoveTo** and **LineTo** pair. The whole object is drawn with the **Polyline** command.

Graphics 7

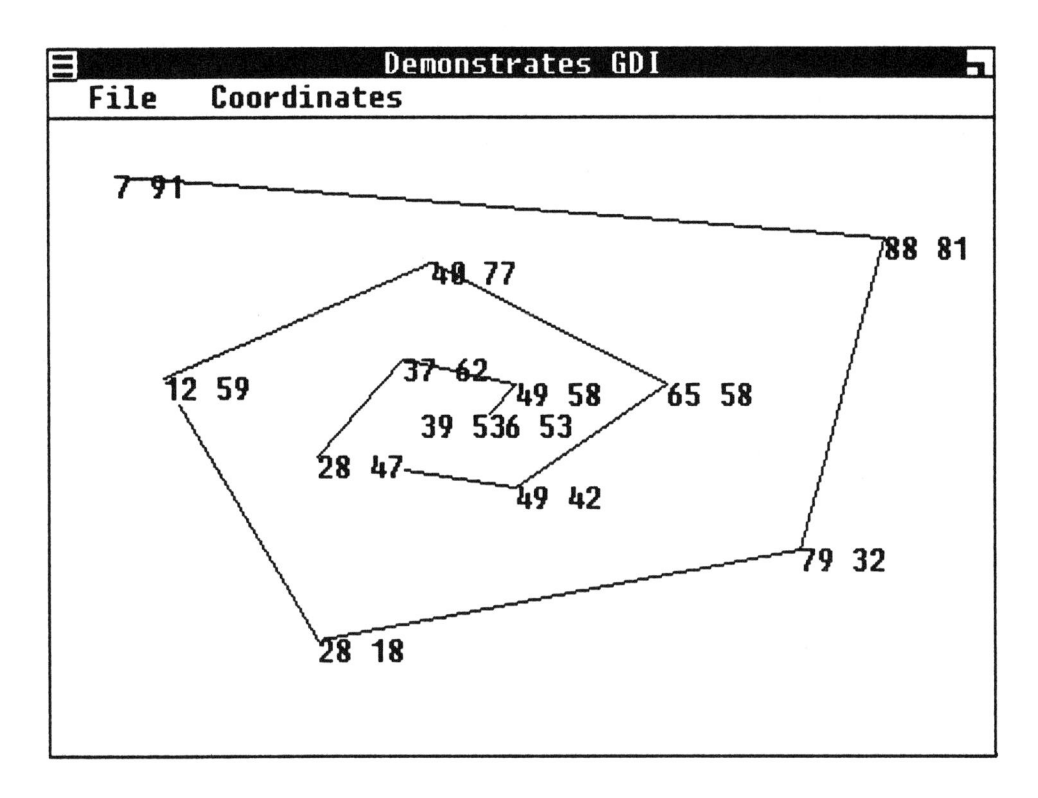

Figure 7.4 The program SEVEN.

When you run this program, be sure to try all the menu options. Draw with and without coordinates being displayed. Clear the screen and add more points. Bring up another application, and resize the screen. Note how the whole object is always displayed. Also note that regardless of the screen size, pressing the mouse button adds a point at the mouse's location.

Final note: lines will only appear after you add the second point. The first time you click the mouse, nothing will change. When you click the mouse again, a line will appear.

7 Graphics

```
/----------------------------------------------\
|                                              |
| The files for this program are in the SEVEN  |
| directory.  SEVEN is the make file.  SEVEN.RC|
| is the resource file, and SEVEN.H is the     |
| include file.  SEVEN.C is the code.  The icon|
| is SEVEN.ICO.  SEVEN.DEF is the module       |
| definition file.  The cursor, MIKE.CUR, is in|
| the root directory.  SEVEN.EXE is the        |
| executable.                                  |
|                                              |
\----------------------------------------------/
```

The Make File: SEVEN

```
#
#  Make file for the program from Chapter 7
#

cc=cl -d -c -AS -Gsw -Os -Zpe

.c.obj:
    $(cc) $*.c


seven.obj: seven.c  seven.h

seven.res: seven.rc seven.h seven.ico mike.cur
    rc -r seven.rc

seven.exe: seven.obj seven.res seven.def
    link4 seven, /align:16, NUL, slibw, seven.def
    rc seven.res
```

The Resource File: SEVEN.RC

```
/*
    Resource file for the program from Chapter 7
*/

#include "windows.h"
#include "seven.h"


face    CURSOR   mike.cur
seven   ICON     seven.ico

seven MENU
BEGIN
    POPUP    "File"
    BEGIN
        MENUITEM "New",     IDM_CLEAR
    END
    POPUP    "Coordinates"
    BEGIN
        MENUITEM "Print Values",        IDM_COORDS_SHOW,
                                            CHECKED
        MENUITEM "Don't Print Values", IDM_COORDS_NOSHOW
    END
END
```

The Include File: SEVEN.H

```
/***********************************************************
    Include file for the program from Chapter 7.  Contains
    typedefs, constants, and external declarations.
***********************************************************/
```

continued...

7 Graphics

...from previous page

```
extern int PASCAL WinMain();
extern int register_window();
extern long FAR PASCAL MsgServer();
extern long process_menu_cmds();
extern set_up_coords();
extern draw_all_lines();
extern add_point();



extern    POINT     *pt_list_glbl;
extern    int       cur_pt_glbl;
extern    int       show_coords_glbl;


#define  MAX_POINTS       100

/* constants for menus   */

#define  IDM_CLEAR            100
#define  IDM_COORDS_SHOW      210
#define  IDM_COORDS_NOSHOW    220
```

Graphics 7

The Code: SEVEN.C

```
/************************************************************
    File:     seven.c
    Program:  seven

    This is the program from Chapter 7.  It demonstrates
    GDI.  In particular, it sets the window and viewport
    and uses the line drawing command.  In addition, it
    shows how to convert from device points to logical
    points, which is needed when interfacing mouse input
    to a program that sets its own window and viewport. It
    adjusts the window so that the whole object is displayed
    no matter the size of the window.  It also redraws the
    scene whenever the screen is cleared because the window
    was moved or sized (that is, from WM_PAINT).  It clears
    the screen on command by making a brush having the
    background color.

    As an option, the program prints the coordinates of
    the points it draws.  This further illustrates the
    functioning of the window and viewport commands.

    The program keeps an array of points.  Adjacent points
    are connected together.  The variable cur_pt_glbl tells
    the number of points, and is an index to the location
    where the next point will be added.
************************************************************/


#include "windows.h"
#include "string.h"
#include "time.h"
#include "stdio.h"
#include "stdlib.h"
#include "seven.h"
```

continued...

7 Graphics

...from previous page

```
/*----------------------------------------------------
    global variables
----------------------------------------------------*/

POINT       pt_list_glbl[MAX_POINTS];
int         cur_pt_glbl;
int         show_coords_glbl;




/*----------------------------------------------------
    This is the Start Up procedure and message relayer
----------------------------------------------------*/
int PASCAL
WinMain(hInstance, hPrevInstance, lpszCmdLine, cmdShow)
HANDLE      hInstance, hPrevInstance;
LPSTR       lpszCmdLine;
int         cmdShow;
{
    HWND        hWnd;
    MSG         msg;

    /* If this is the first instance, register the
       window class
    */
    if (!hPrevInstance)
        register_window(hInstance);

    /* Create a tiled window */
    hWnd = CreateWindow( (LPSTR) "Chap7WIN",     /* class */
                (LPSTR) "Demonstrates GDI",     /* title */
                WS_TILEDWINDOW,           /* style */
                0, 0, 0, 0,
                (HWND) NULL,              /* parent */
                (HMENU) NULL,      /* use class menu */
                (HANDLE) hInstance,       /* instance */
                (LPSTR) NULL );
```

continued...

...from previous page

```
    /* now display it */
    ShowWindow(hWnd,cmdShow);
    UpdateWindow(hWnd);


    /* initialize global variables */
    cur_pt_glbl = 0;
    show_coords_glbl = IDM_COORDS_SHOW;

    /* relay all messages to the message server */
    while (GetMessage( (LPMSG) &msg, NULL, 0, 0) ) {
         TranslateMessage( (LPMSG) &msg);
         DispatchMessage( (LPMSG) &msg);
    }
     exit(msg.wParam);
}



/*-----------------------------------------------------------
   This procedure registers the window.
------------------------------------------------------------*/

int
register_window( hInstance )
HANDLE   hInstance;
{
    PWNDCLASS      pClass;

    pClass = (PWNDCLASS) LocalAlloc(LPTR, sizeof(WNDCLASS));
    pClass->hCursor = LoadCursor(hInstance, (LPSTR) "face");
    pClass->hIcon = LoadIcon(hInstance, (LPSTR) "seven");
    pClass->lpszMenuName = (LPSTR) "seven";
    pClass->lpszClassName = (LPSTR) "Chap7WIN";
    pClass->hbrBackground = GetStockObject(WHITE_BRUSH);
    pClass->hInstance = hInstance;
    pClass->style = CS_HREDRAW | CS_VREDRAW;
    pClass->lpfnWndProc = MsgServer;

    RegisterClass( (LPWNDCLASS) pClass);
    LocalFree( (HANDLE) pClass);
}
```

continued...

7 Graphics

...from previous page

```
/*-------------------------------------------------------------
    This procedure receives the messages and decides what to
    do with them.  Note that for WM_PAINT, it first does the
    default processing, then redraws the screen.  If the left
    button is pushed, it adds a point at that position on
    the screen.
-------------------------------------------------------------*/
long FAR PASCAL
MsgServer( hWnd, message, wParam, lParam )
HWND      hWnd;
unsigned  message;
WORD      wParam;
LONG      lParam;
{
    switch (message) {
    case WM_COMMAND:
        return( process_menu_cmds(hWnd, wParam) );
    case WM_PAINT:
        DefWindowProc(hWnd,message,wParam,lParam);
        draw_all_lines(hWnd);
        break;
    case WM_LBUTTONUP:
        /* add a point at the mouse position.  Note the
           use of MAKEPOINT
         */
        if (cur_pt_glbl < MAX_POINTS)
            add_point(hWnd,MAKEPOINT(lParam));
        break;
    default:
        return(DefWindowProc(hWnd,message,wParam,lParam));

    }
    return(0L);
}
```

continued...

...from previous page

```
/*-----------------------------------------------------
  This routine processes commands from the menu
------------------------------------------------------*/
long
process_menu_cmds( hWnd, command )
HWND     hWnd;
WORD     command;
{
    HDC      hDC;
    HBRUSH   hBr,hBrOld;
    RECT     rect;
    HMENU    hMenu;

    switch (command) {
    case IDM_CLEAR:
        /* clear out all points */
        cur_pt_glbl = 0;

        /* now clear the screen.  Because set_up_coords
           sets the screen coordinates to (0,0) - (100,100),
           we automatically know where the screen bounds
           are.

           Note:  the top and bottom are the reverse of
           the true top and bottom, but in order for a
           rectangle to be filled, its bottom must be a
           bigger coordinate than its top.  (This
           is a problem of the command, not a feature.)
        */
        hDC = GetDC(hWnd);
        set_up_coords( hWnd, hDC );
        rect.left = 0;
        rect.right = 100;
        rect.top = 0;
        rect.bottom = 100;

        /* create a brush having the background color */
        hBr = CreateSolidBrush( GetBkColor(hDC) );
        hBrOld = SelectObject(hDC, hBr);
        FillRect(hDC, (LPRECT) &rect, hBr);
```

continued...

7 Graphics

...from previous page

```
            /* now clear out this brush and release the
                display context
            */
            SelectObject(hDC, hBrOld);
            DeleteObject(hBr);
            ReleaseDC(hWnd, hDC);
            break;

        case IDM_COORDS_NOSHOW:
        case IDM_COORDS_SHOW:
            hMenu = GetMenu(hWnd);
            CheckMenuItem(hMenu,show_coords_glbl,MF_UNCHECKED |
                MF_BYCOMMAND);
            CheckMenuItem(hMenu,command,MF_CHECKED |
                MF_BYCOMMAND);
            show_coords_glbl = command;
            break;
    }
    return(0L);

}




/*-----------------------------------------------------------
    Sets up the coordinate system.  Places the origin (0,0)
    at the lower left corner of the window and the point
    (100,100) at the upper right corner of the window.  In
    this manner, no matter the size of the window, the
    whole picture will always be seen.

    Note that the mapping mode is set to ANISOTROPIC.  This
    is the only mode that allows for different scales along
    the x and y axes.
-----------------------------------------------------------*/
```

continued...

...from previous page

```
set_up_coords( hWnd, hDC )
HWND    hWnd;
HDC     hDC;
{
    RECT    client_rect;

    /* determine bounds of window */
    GetClientRect(hWnd, (LPRECT)&client_rect);

    /* set mapping mode */
    SetMapMode(hDC,MM_ANISOTROPIC);

    /* set the window and viewport origins and extents */
    SetWindowOrg(hDC,0,0);
    SetWindowExt(hDC,100,100);
    SetViewportOrg(hDC,client_rect.left,client_rect.bottom);
    SetViewportExt(hDC, client_rect.right - client_rect.left,
        client_rect.top - client_rect.bottom);
}




/*----------------------------------------------------------
    This procedure draws all the lines
------------------------------------------------------------*/

draw_all_lines( hWnd )
HWND    hWnd;
{
    HDC     hDC;

    /* get the display context and set the screen mapping
       system
    */
    hDC = GetDC(hWnd);
    set_up_coords( hWnd, hDC );
```

continued...

7 Graphics

...from previous page

```
    /* if there are at least two points, draw all the
       lines
    */
    if (cur_pt_glbl >= 2)
        Polyline(hDC, (LPPOINT) pt_list_glbl, cur_pt_glbl);

    ReleaseDC(hWnd,hDC);
}




/*-----------------------------------------------------------
    This procedure adds a point to the list structure at the
    particular point
-------------------------------------------------------*/
add_point( hWnd, pt )
HWND    hWnd;
POINT   pt;
{
    HDC     hDC;
    char    coords[35],temp[10];

    /* get the display context and set the screen mapping
       system
    */
    hDC = GetDC(hWnd);
    set_up_coords( hWnd, hDC );

    /* convert the point from device coordinates to screen
       coordinates
    */
    DPtoLP(hDC, (LPPOINT) &pt, 1);
```

continued...

...from previous page

```
    /* add the point and draw the new line */
    pt_list_glbl[cur_pt_glbl] = pt;
    if (cur_pt_glbl >= 1) {
        MoveTo(hDC, pt_list_glbl[cur_pt_glbl - 1].x,
            pt_list_glbl[cur_pt_glbl - 1].y);
        LineTo(hDC, pt_list_glbl[cur_pt_glbl].x,
            pt_list_glbl[cur_pt_glbl].y);
    }
    cur_pt_glbl++;

    /* if desired, print the point's coordinates */
    if (show_coords_glbl == IDM_COORDS_SHOW) {
        itoa(pt.x,coords,10);
        itoa(pt.y,temp,10);
        strcat(coords," ");
        strcat(coords,temp);
        TextOut(hDC, pt.x,pt.y, (LPSTR) coords,
            strlen(coords));
    }

    ReleaseDC(hWnd,hDC);
}
```

The Module Definition File: SEVEN.DEF

```
NAME        Seven
DESCRIPTION 'Seventh Window Program'
STUB        'winstub.exe'
CODE        MOVEABLE
DATA        MOVEABLE MULTIPLE
HEAPSIZE 4096
STACKSIZE 4096
EXPORTS
        MsgServer @1
```

7 Graphics

ADVANCED CONCEPTS: METAFILES

Metafiles are a convenient way of storing graphics images in a device-independent form. Metafiles record the series of actions undertaken to create an image. Metafiles are useful for transferring images between graphics programs and for inserting graphics objects into a text program.

Metafiles are useful because they provide a convenient and easy way to recreate a complex object without requiring a lot of code to decode information about the object. For example, it only takes one command to display a very complex object created by a metafile.

The usefulness of metafiles is limited by the inability to examine the actual data implied by an object. For example, if you used a metafile to display a polygon, you would be unable to determine the coordinates of the points in the polygon.

Use metafiles when you must transfer an image and are not concerned about the coordinate values of items in the image. In other words, use metafiles when you are only interested in the image itself. If you are interested in the coordinate values of objects, you will need to store a mathematical description of the objects, such as an endpoint list.

To use a metafile, you create a display context for the metafile and then execute all your graphics calls as normal. When you are finished, you close the metafile and perhaps save it to disk. To draw the image stored in a metafile, you open the metafile and *play* it.

Use the **CreateMetaFile** command to start a metafile. It returns a display context for the metafile as follows:

```
HDC
CreateMetaFile( lpFilename )
```

lpFilename   is a long pointer to an ASCIIZ string naming the file in which to save the metafile. If you do not want to save the commands to a file (for example, if you wanted to transfer the image using the clipboard), set this value to NULL. The metafile will be stored in memory.

Once you have the display context for the metafile, go through your normal graphics routines, but use the metafile display context instead of the display context you would get with **GetDC**.

When you are finished with your graphics commands, close the metafile:

```
HANDLE
CloseMetaFile( hDC )
```

hDC is the display context used for the metafile. This function returns a handle to the metafile.

If you created the metafile in memory but want to save it, you can do so with the **CopyMetaFile** command. You can also use this command to copy a disk metafile to another disk file or to memory.

```
HANDLE
CopyMetaFile( hMF, lpFilename)
```

hMF   is a handle to the source metafile.

lpFilename   is a long pointer to an ASCIIZ string naming the file to copy the source metafile to. If **lpFilename** is NULL, the metafile will be copied into memory.

The return value is a handle to the new metafile.

To open an existing metafile, use the following:

```
HANDLE
GetMetaFile( lpFilename )
```

lpFilename is a long pointer to the ASCIIZ name of the metafile to open. The return value is a handle to this metafile.

Use the **PlayMetaFile** command to display the graphics figure defined in a metafile:

7 Graphics

```
PlayMetaFile( hDC, hMF )
```

hDC is the handle of the display context. If you want to display the object on the screen, use the display context handle returned by **GetDC**.

hMF is the handle of the metafile you want to display.

To free up the memory used to store a metafile, use the **DeleteMetaFile** command. This command will not erase a metafile from disk. It simply frees the RAM used for the metafile:

```
DeleteMetaFile( hMF )
```

hMF is a handle to the metafile to free.

SUMMARY

- Windows provides a useful, versatile set of device-independent graphics commands.

- There are eight different modes for defining the coordinate axes:

    MM_TEXT
    MM_HIMETRIC
    MM_LOMETRIC
    MM_HIENGLISH
    MM_LOENGLISH
    MM_TWIPS
    MM_ISOTROPIC
    MM_ANISOTROPIC

Graphics 7

- The coordinate system that refers to actual dots in the application area is called the *device coordinate* system. Coordinates in the system defined by the programmer are called *logical coordinates*.

- The *viewport* and *window* define what coordinates are mapped to the screen and where they are mapped. In MM_ISOTROPIC and MM_ANISOTROPIC modes, they control the scale of the axes.

- You can create many special effects, such as panning and zooming, by modifying the viewport and window.

- Lines and outlines of objects are drawn with a *pen*. Interiors are filled with a *brush*. There are several commands for creating pens and brushes.

- Colors are RGB colors.

- There are many commands for drawing points, lines, polygons, and curves.

- There are also commands for defining, combining, and filling complex regions.

- You can control the clipping area with the **SetClipRgn** command.

- To use the mouse position in a graphics program, you may have to convert it to logical coordinates with the **DPtoLP** command. You can convert from logical points to device points using **LPtoDP**.

- Metafiles provide a convenient way of transferring and saving graphics images.

CHAPTER 8

DIALOG BOXES

8 Dialog Boxes

This chapter discusses the use of dialog boxes—a very versatile tool for inputting data. You will learn to set up the dialog boxes and use buttons, text and number boxes, and list boxes. You will also see how to select files using dialog boxes.

WHY USE DIALOG BOXES?

Dialog boxes are pop-up windows into which you can enter data; they contain buttons, lists, and boxes for entering text and numbers. If you need more flexibility in entering data than a menu can provide, you must use a dialog box.

For example, to get the name of a file, read in birth data, or get aquifer parameters, you must use a dialog box.

Dialog boxes contain great editing features. You move the mouse to buttons you want to push. To enter a number or text, you move the mouse to the associated box. You can insert and delete characters or, by moving the mouse, edit the middle of a string. You can also specify default values for all items.

As with menus, dialog boxes are described by an outlining language in the resource file.

DIALOG BOXES ARE WINDOWS

Dialog boxes are windows that run within another window. Dialog boxes communicate by sending messages; thus, to use a dialog box, you add a procedure akin to **MsgServer** that processes dialog box messages. When a dialog box item is processed, this message routine receives a WM_COMMAND message. When the dialog box is closed, the message routine receives a WM_CLOSE message. Because the message receiver is called by Windows, it must be declared as a FAR PASCAL procedure. In addition, it must be declared in the EXPORT list in the module definition file.

Following is a sample dialog box message receiver. Don't worry about the specific commands; pay attention to the overall structure. Like **MsgServer**, **SelectFile** passes WM_COMMAND messages to a special procedure.

Dialog Boxes 8

```c
/*-----------------------------------------------------------
    This procedure processes commands for the dialog box.
    Note that it is set up just like the MsgServer.  The
    dialog box is just a window with buttons and other
    input features.  Selecting the various buttons sends
    messages just like any other window.

    Because this routine is called by Windows, it must be
    declared as a FAR PASCAL.
------------------------------------------------------------*/

short FAR PASCAL
SelectFile( hDlg, message, wParam, lParam )
HWND        hDlg;
unsigned    message;
WORD        wParam;
LONG        lParam;
{
    switch (message) {
    case WM_COMMAND:
        process_dlg_commands(hDlg, wParam);
        break;
    case WM_INITDIALOG:
        /* fill the directory list box with the file
            names from the default drive.  ID_DIR_SELECTED
            indicates what list box to fill.  It is the
            menu value for the list box as defined in
            eight.rc.
        */
        DlgDirList(hDlg, (LPSTR) "*.*", ID_DIR_SELECTED,
            0, (unsigned) 0);
        break;
    default:
        return (FALSE);
    }
    return(TRUE);
}
```

8 Dialog Boxes

Instead of using **DefWindowProc** for messages it doesn't process, a dialog box routine returns FALSE if it didn't process the message, which instructs Windows to use a default response.

There are two types of dialog box windows: modal and modeless. *Modal* boxes are the more common. When a modal dialog box appears, the window that called it gives up control until the user is finished with the dialog box; thus, the program won't continue until all the information the dialog box requested is entered. Use modal dialog boxes to get data that is immediately used in the program.

Modeless dialog boxes allow the main program to continue while the dialog box is still active. Use these boxes when the program doesn't immediately rely on the information entered through the dialog box.

THE DIALOG BOX INPUT FEATURES

There are several items for entering data in dialog boxes: check boxes, push buttons, radio buttons, text entry boxes, and list boxes. All of these items have a text title or label associated with them.

Check boxes and *radio buttons* are useful for selecting features such as italics. Check boxes and radio buttons are small boxes that appear next to a text label. When the user clicks on them, the devices send messages to the Windows program. The program can then toggle the devices' states. Check boxes are boxes, and radio buttons are circles. Use radio buttons for mutually exclusive choices and check boxes for non-exclusive choices.

Push buttons are useful for selecting items. When they are pressed, a message is sent to the program. Push buttons are most often used to accept or cancel items entered in a dialog box. The text label is enclosed within the button.

Text entry boxes are useful for entering text and numbers; they are boxes into which text can be typed and edited. The mouse and edit keys can be used to edit the text, and Windows automatically displays a text cursor while the text is being modified. Though text boxes do not have labels, a label can be added with a *text control*. Text controls are rectangles that contain text. The text cannot be edited; it simply serves as a label.

To use text entry boxes to input numbers, when you examine text, convert it to a number. There is also a special command for reading integer values from text entry boxes.

List boxes are a great feature; they present a list of items from which the user can select. The items appear in a box with a scroll bar. Moving the scroll position automatically scrolls the list of items. List boxes are useful for selecting files or devices or for editing arrays of numbers. You can request that Windows automatically sort the items in a list box. List boxes send messages when their items are selected.

PUTTING TOGETHER A DIALOG BOX

Dialog boxes are a combination of the various dialog box items. The easiest way to create a dialog box is to use the dialog box editor, DIALOG.EXE, which comes with the Microsoft Windows Development Toolkit.

With the dialog editor, you use a mouse to create a dialog box and fill it with the various dialog box items. You see the dialog box as it will look when your program calls it. As you add items, you specify the message they will send to the program, which is the same as specifying the number in a MENUITEM command. Use a constant. Place these constants in an .H file before you begin creating the dialog box. The editor has a command to load in include files.

Save the file in RC format. The dialog box description will be saved in a file with a .DLG extension. Load this file into your resource file with the **rcinclude** command. For example, if the dialog file is named eight.dlg, you would add the following:

```
rcinclude eight.dlg
```

Note that you do not surround the file name with quotation marks.

8 Dialog Boxes

Always include "OK" and "CANCEL" buttons in your dialog boxes so the user can verify or cancel any changes. These buttons should return the value IDOK and IDCANCEL respectively. IDOK and IDCANCEL are defined in **windows.h**. They are defined as follows:

```
#define  IDOK       1
#define  IDCANCEL   2
```

THE FORMAT OF THE .DLG FILE

You can create dialog boxes without the DIALOG editor, but it is much more difficult. You should, however, be familiar with the dialog box description language in case you want to manually make a few minor changes to a dialog box description.

The basic format of a dialog description is as follows:

```
name     DIALOG[load option,] [memory option,] left, top, width,
         height
STYLE    param1 | param2 | ....
CAPTION  title
BEGIN
     commands
END
```

name is a single-word text string naming the dialog box. This string is the name your programs will use to refer to the dialog box. **left, top, width,** and **height** define the size of the pop-up and its suggested screen location. **left** and **top** are meaured in device coordinates. **width** is measured in 1/4-character widths and **height** is measured in 1/8-character heights. You can use the load and memory option defaults. The load option is either PRELOAD or LOADONCALL. PRELOAD forces the dialog box to be loaded when the program is loaded. LOADONCALL, the default, causes the dialog box to be loaded as needed, which conserves memory. The memory option is either FIXED, MOVEABLE, or DISCARDABLE and refers to how the dialog box will be stored in memory. These options are discussed in more detail in Chapter 9. The default, MOVEABLE, allows the box definition to be moved in memory to free space. MOVEABLE DISCARDABLE is a good choice.

STYLE determines what type of a window to use for the dialog box; it can use any of the parameters for the **CreateWindow** call. Use WS_POPUP | WS_CAPTION | WS_BORDER for modal dialog boxes. Use WS_POPUP | WS_SYSMENU | WS_BORDER | WS_CAPTION for modeless dialog boxes. If you want the user to be able to change the dialog box size, add the WS_SIZEBOX parameter. You can also add the WS_SYSMENU option to modal boxes, which allows the user to reposition the dialog box.

CAPTION sets the text for the dialog box's title. Use this command with the WS_CAPTION | WS_BORDER option. Enclose the text within double quotes.

A variety of commands can appear within the BEGIN and END statements. They all have the following format:

```
type     text,    id_value,    x, y, width, height
```

type describes the item; **text** is the label for the item; and **id_value** is the message number sent to the program when the item is used. The positioning parameters use the same units as the DIALOG command, but the **x** and **y** values are calculated with respect to the application area of the dialog box.

type can be one of the following:

LTEXT	a left-justified text control box
RTEXT	a right-justified text control box
CTEXT	a centered text control box
CHECKBOX	a check box
RADIOBUTTON	a radio button
PUSHBUTTON	a push button
DEFPUSHBUTTON	a push button with a thicker border
EDITTEXT	a box for editing text
LISTBOX	a list box
GROUPBOX	a rectangle used to visually group items
ICON	an area in which to display an icon. Height and width are ignored.

8 Dialog Boxes

In addition, dialog boxes can contain **CONTROL** statements with the following format:

```
CONTROL   text, id, class, style, x, y, width, height
```

CONTROL statements can describe any of the dialog box items, such as buttons, list boxes, and so forth. The **class** determines whether the item is an edit control, a text control, a button, or a list box. **style** specifies the item. The remaining items specify the position.

For this command, there are too many options to list. The format is similar enough to other dialog box commands that you will be able to figure out what the CONTROL statement is doing. Again, use the DIALOG.EXE tool to create dialog boxes; it is much easier and lets you view and test the dialog boxes as you create them.

ADDING DIALOG BOXES TO A PROGRAM

As mentioned, dialog boxes act as separate windows; they need a routine like **MsgServer** to receive messages from Windows. This function must be declared in the EXPORTS section of the module definition file. For example, suppose the message server for the dialog box is called **DlgMsgServer**. The module definition file would contain the following:

```
EXPORTS
        MsgServer         @1
        DlgMsgServer      @2
```

You will pass a pointer to **DlgMsgServer** to Windows when you create the dialog box. Before you do so, you must register the procedure with Windows so that Windows will know the proper data segment to use with the procedure. Perform this task in **WinMain**, using the **MakeProcInstance** command. Its format is as follows:

```
FARPROC
MakeProcInstance( lpProc, hInstance )
```

lpProc is a long pointer to the function. You can create this pointer by casting the procedure name as a FARPROC.

hInstance is the instance handle passed to **WinMain**.

The return value is a handle to a function that loads the proper data segment and then calls the procedure.

For example, you could use the following:

```
lpprocDlgMsgServer_glbl = MakeProcInstance( (FARPROC)
    DlgMsgServer, hInstance );
```

Note: exported functions are called by Windows. If your program must call an exported function, call it by indirectly calling the pointer returned by **MakeProcInstance**. For example, you could do the following:

```
(*lpprocDlgMsgServer_glbl) ( [params] );
```

When you want to pop up a dialog box, use the **CreateDialog** or **DialogBox** commands. **CreateDialog** creates a modeless dialog box; its format is as follows:

```
HWND
CreateDialog( hInstance, lpBoxName, hWndParent,
    lpDlgMsgServer )
```

hInstance is the instance handle of the program creating the dialog box.

lpBoxName is the name of the dialog box as defined in the resource file.

hWndParent is a handle for the window of the program creating the dialog box.

8 Dialog Boxes

lpDlgMsgServer is a FARPROC pointer to the routine to handle the dialog box messages, which should be the value returned by **MakeProcInstance**.

The function returns a handle to the dialog box. Because the dialog box is just a window, this is a HWND handle.

To create a modal dialog box, use the following:

```
DialogBox( hInstance, lpBoxName, hWndParent, lpDlgMsgServer )
```

hInstance   is the instance handle of the program creating the dialog box.

lpBoxName   is the name of the dialog box as defined in the resource file.

hWndParent   is a handle for the window of the program creating the dialog box.

lpDlgMsgServer is a FARPROC pointer to the routine to handle the dialog box messages, which should be the value returned by **MakeProcInstance**.

The dialog box should contain an OK and Cancel pair that allows the user to leave the dialog box. The pair will send the IDOK and IDCANCEL messages. When these messages are received, close the dialog box with the following:

```
EndDialog( hDlg, TRUE )
```

hDlg is a handle to the dialog box; it is the parameter passed to the dialog message server. (It serves the same function as the hWnd parameter passed to **MsgServer**.) **TRUE** is the constant TRUE.

Dialog Boxes 8

When the dialog box is opened, the dialog message server will receive the WM_INITDIALOG message. Trap this message to initialize any of the items in the dialog box. For example, you can use the message to check or uncheck check boxes or supply default string values. After receiving an IDOK message, read in the new values from the dialog box. Following are the commands for initializing and reading dialog box items.

To set the status of a radio button or check box, use the **CHeckRadioButton** and **CheckDlgButton** commands:

```
CheckRadioButton( hDlg, FirstUncheck, LastUncheck, ToCheck )
```

hDlg   is a handle to the dialog box.

FirstUncheck   is the value (as set by id_value) of the first of a list of sequential radio buttons to uncheck before the radio button is checked.

LastUncheck   is the value of the last radio button to uncheck before the radio button is checked.

ToCheck   is the number of the radio button to check.

Remember that radio buttons are used to choose from a mutually exclusive list. Set FirstUncheck and LastUncheck to the first and last buttons in the list. These buttons will be cleared; then, ToCheck will be set. For example, suppose the commands numbered 100 to 160 selected text size, and the user selected 150. You could use the following:

```
CheckRadioButton( hDlg, 100, 160, 150 );
```

```
CheckDlgButton( hDlg, ToCheck, Param )
```

hDlg   is a handle to the dialog box.

ToCheck   is the value of the button (check box) to check.

213

8 Dialog Boxes

Param   is FALSE to remove a check and TRUE to add a check. If you are checking a three-state button, set Param to 2 to gray the button.

To determine if a button or check box is checked, use the following:

```
BOOL
IsDlgButtonChecked( hDlg, Button )
```

hDlg is a handle to the dialog box, and **Button** is the value of the button to examine. The return value is TRUE if the button is checked and FALSE if it is not. For three state buttons, the return value is 2 if it is grayed.

Use text entry boxes to get string and numeric values. For integers, use **SetDlgItemInt** to initialize the text entry box and **GetDlgItemInt** to read the box:

```
SetDlgItemInt( hDlg, BoxId, Value, Signed )
```

hDlg   is a handle to the dialog box.

BoxId   is the value identifying the text entry box.

Value   is the integer value to put in the box.

Signed   is TRUE if Value is a signed integer, and FALSE if it is an unsigned integer.

```
int
GetDlgItemInt( hDlg, BoxId, lpTrans, Signed )
```

hDlg   is a handle to the dialog box.

BoxId   is the value identifying the text entry box.

Dialog Boxes 8

lpTrans   is a long pointer to a Boolean variable. This variable will be set to a non-zero value if the number was translated without error and zero if an error occurred. Set this parameter to NULL if you do not want to be informed about errors.

Signed   is FALSE if you want the returned value to be unsigned, and TRUE if you want it translated as a signed integer.

The return value is the integer typed in the text entry box.

If you want to read a string or a float value, use the **SetDlgItemText** and **GetDlgItemText** commands:

```
SetDlgItemText( hDlg, BoxId, lpString )
```

hDlg   is a handle for the dialog box.

BoxId   is the number identifying the text entry box.

lpString   is a long pointer to an ASCIIZ string to place in the text entry box.

```
int
GetDlgItemText( hDlg, BoxId, lpString, Count )
```

hDlg   is a handle for the dialog box.

BoxId   is the number identifying the text entry box.

lpString   is a long pointer to a string buffer where the string will be stored.

Count   is the maximum number of characters to read into the string buffer, which must not be greater than the size of the string buffer pointed to by lpString.

The function returns the number of characters actually read.

8 Dialog Boxes

To read float values, convert the text string to a float with **strtod**, which is part of the standard C library. You can also use any of the other strings to number conversion routines.

To use a list box to select a file name, fill it with a directory listing when the dialog box is initialized. Do so using the following:

```
DlgDirList( hDlg, lpPathSpec, BoxId, PathDisplayId, FileType )
```

hDlg is a handle to the dialog box.

lpPathSpec is a long pointer to an ASCIIZ string defining the drive and path from which to list the files. For example, (LPSTR) "*.*" will list all the files in the current directory.

BoxId is the value identifying the list box.

PathDisplayId is the value identifying a text control box into which the current drive and directory will be displayed. Use 0 if you have no such box.

FilePath is a word that determines what type of files to use for the list. The values can be combined. The values are as follows:

0	normal files
1	read only files
2	hidden files
4	system files
16	subdirectories
32	archived files
0x4000	available drives
0x8000	do not show normal files

To display a list of all normal files, directories, and drives, use 0x4010.

Dialog Boxes 8

To determine what file, drive, or subdirectory was chosen, use the following:

```
DlgDirSelect( hDlg, lpString, ListBoxId )
```

hDlg is a handle to the dialog box.

lpString is a long pointer to a buffer in which to place the file name, directory name, or drive name. Make sure that this name is at least 13 characters long.

ListBoxId is the number identifying the list box containing the directory list.

You can use list boxes for lists of any items (not just files). To do this, you must fill and read the list box by sending messages to the list box with **SendDlgItemMessage**. Its format is as follows:

```
long
SendDlgItemMessage( hDlg, ListBoxId, wMsg, wParam, lParam )
```

hDlg is a handle for the dialog box.

ListBoxId is the value identifying the list box.

wMsg is the message to send to the list box, which will be discussed shortly.

wParam and **lParam**

are parameters associated with the message.

List boxes are actually windows; thus, they have a procedure to analyze messages sent to them. The wMsg, wParam, and lParam values are the parameters passed to the list box window. **SendDlgItemMessage** returns the value returned by the list box message processor.

8 Dialog Boxes

You can send many messages to control list boxes; the important ones are as follows:

LB_ADDSTRING

adds a string to the list box. If the list box is sorted, the string will be added in sorted order; if not, it will be added to the end. wParam is not used. Set lParam to a long pointer to the ASCIIZ string to add to the list box.

LB_ERR is returned if there was an error; LB_ERRSPACE is returned if there wasn't enough room for the new string.

If the addition was successful, the position of the added string is returned.

LB_INSERTSTRING

adds a string without sorting. wParam is the position to place the new string before. Use -1 to add the string to the end. Set lParam to a long pointer to an ASCIIZ string to add.

The return value is the same as for LB_ADDSTRING.

LB_DELETESTRING

removes a string from the list box. wParam is the position of the item to remove.

The return value is the number of items remaining in the list or LB_ERR if there was an error.

LB_GETCURSEL

returns the position of the currently selected item. Use this message to determine what is selected. wParam and lParam aren't used.

The return value is the position of the selected item; LB_ERR is returned if there was an error.

Dialog Boxes 8

LB_GETTEXTLEN tells the length of a particular string in the list box. wParam is the position of the string, and lParam is not used.

The return value is the length of the string or LB_ERR.

LB_GETTEXT retrieves a string from the list box. Set wParam to the position of the string. Set lParam to a char buffer to copy the string to. This buffer must have enough room for the string; at a minimum, this buffer should be the length of the string, as reported by LB_GETTEXTLEN, plus 1 for the ending null character.

The return value is the length of the string or LB_ERR.

LB_RESETCONTENT

Removes all strings from the list box.

LB_DIR Adds a directory list from the current directory to the list box. wParam is the same as the FileType parameter of **DlgDirList**. lParam is a long pointer to an ASCIIZ string with the file specification.

The return value is the number of items in the list; LB_ERRSPACE is returned if there wasn't enough room, or LB_ERR is returned if there was some other error.

As an option, list boxes can allow more than one item to be selected. This option is specified when describing the list box in the resource file. For such list boxes, you must use the LB_GETSEL command instead of the LB_GETCURSEL command:

LB_GETSEL tells whether a particular item is selected. wParam is the position of the item, and lParam is not used.

The return value is positive if the item is selected; the return value is 0 if it is not. LB_ERR is returned if there is an error.

8 Dialog Boxes

LB_GETCOUNT

returns the number of items in the list. Use this to loop through the items to determine which of a group are selected. wParam and lParam are not used.

The return value is the number of items in the list or LB_ERR.

A PROGRAM: EIGHT

The following program, EIGHT, uses a dialog box to get the name of a disk file. When the File command is selected, a dialog box appears. This box contains a list box of the file names in the current directory, an OK button, and a Cancel button (see Figure 8.1). After the dialog box is closed, the selected file name is printed.

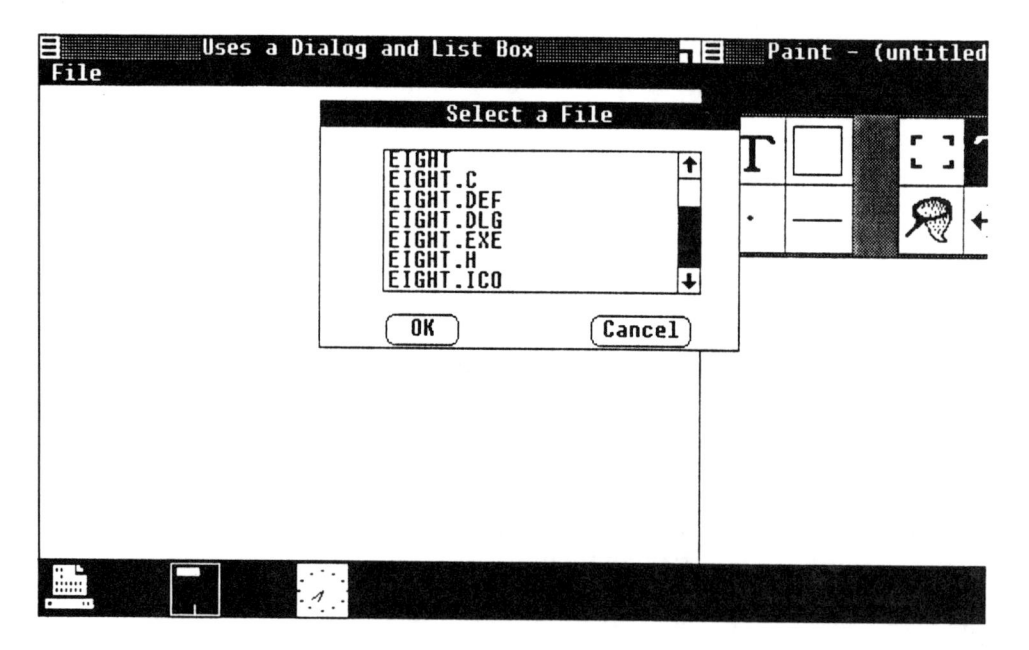

Figure 8.1 The program EIGHT.

Dialog Boxes 8

Be sure to examine the resource file, EIGHT.RC, and the dialog file, EIGHT.DLG. Note the description of the dialog box and the use of the **rcinclude** command.

The dialog box message server is called **SelectFile**. Note how it is declared in EIGHT.DEF and how it is registered in **WinMain**. See how the dialog box is opened when the File command is entered.

Examine the structure of **SelectFile** and **process_dlg_commands**. Note how they are similar to **MsgServer** and **process_menu_cmds**. SelectFile traps WM_INITDIALOG to fill the directory list box. The selected item is read when the IDOK command is received. If the IDCANCEL command is received, the selected item is ignored; thus, the old value isn't changed. Note how the box is ended with **EndDialog**.

After you test the program, simultaneously run a few copies of it. Note what happens when you open the dialog box from several of the windows at the same time. Then, change the **DlgDirList** parameters so that drives and subdirectories are listed. Add routines to let the user change the drive and directory.

```
/------------------------------------------------\
|                                                |
| The files for this program are in the EIGHT    |
| directory.  The make file is EIGHT. EIGHT.RC   |
| is the resource file. EIGHT.DLG describes the  |
| dialog box. EIGHT.H is the include file.       |
| EIGHT.C is the code. EIGHT.DEF is the module   |
| definition file. EIGHT.ICO is the icon.  The   |
| cursor, MIKE.CUR, is in the root directory.    |
| EIGHT.EXE is the executable version.           |
|                                                |
\------------------------------------------------/
```

8 Dialog Boxes

The Make File: EIGHT

```
#
#  Make file for the program from Chapter 8
#

cc=cl -d -c -AS -Gsw -Os -Zpe

.c.obj:
    $(cc) $*.c

eight.obj: eight.c  eight.h

eight.res: eight.rc eight.h eight.dlg eight.ico mike.cur
    rc -r eight.rc

eight.exe: eight.obj eight.res eight.def
    link4 eight, /align:16, NUL, slibw, eight.def
    rc eight.res
```

The Resource File: EIGHT.RC

```
/*************************************************************
    Resource file for the program from Chapter 8.
    Note the use of rcinclude to bring in the definition
    for the dialog box
*************************************************************/


#include "windows.h"
#include "eight.h"


rcinclude eight.dlg
```

continued...

...from previous page

```
face     CURSOR    mike.cur
eight    ICON      eight.ico

eight MENU
BEGIN
    MENUITEM "File",    IDM_FILE
END
```

The Dialog Description File: EIGHT.DLG

```
directory      DIALOG  LOADONCALL     MOVEABLE DISCARDABLE
               89, 16, 130, 88

CAPTION        "Select a File"
STYLE          WS_BORDER | WS_CAPTION | WS_DLGFRAME |
                WS_POPUP
BEGIN
    CONTROL    "OK"     IDOK,      "button",   BS_PUSHBUTTON |
        WS_TABSTOP | WS_CHILD,     20, 74, 24, 14
    CONTROL    "Cancel" IDCANCEL,  "button",   BS_PUSHBUTTON |
        WS_TABSTOP | WS_CHILD,     84, 74, 32, 14
    LISTBOX    ID_DIR_SELECTED,    20, 9, 98, 57,
        LBS_NOTIFY | LBS_SORT | WS_BORDER | WS_VSCROLL
END
```

The Include File: EIGHT.H

```
/************************************************************
    Include file for the program from Chapter 8.  Contains
    typedefs, constants, and external declarations.
************************************************************/
```

continued...

8 Dialog Boxes

...from previous page

```
extern int PASCAL WinMain();
extern int register_window();
extern long FAR PASCAL MsgServer();
extern long process_menu_cmds();
extern short FAR PASCAL SelectFile();
extern process_dlg_commands();



extern HANDLE    instance_glbl;
extern FARPROC   lpprocSelectFile_glbl;
extern char      *filename_glbl;


/* constant definitions for menu and dialog box. */

#define IDM_FILE          200
#define ID_DIR_SELECTED   100
```

The Code: EIGHT.C

```
/***************************************************************
    File:     eight.c
    Program:  eight

    This is the program from Chapter 8. It demonstrates
    using dialog boxes. In particular, it creates a dialog
    box with two push buttons and a list box. This list
    box contains a directory of disk files on the current
    drive. The program lets the user select a file from
    this list.
***************************************************************/
```

continued...

...from previous page

```c
#include "windows.h"
#include "string.h"
#include "time.h"
#include "stdio.h"
#include "eight.h"




/*----------------------------------------------------------
    global variables
  ----------------------------------------------------------*/

FARPROC   lpprocSelectFile_glbl;
HANDLE    hInstance_glbl;
char      filename_glbl[30];




/*----------------------------------------------------------
   This is the Start Up procedure and message relayer
  ----------------------------------------------------------*/

int PASCAL
WinMain(hInstance, hPrevInstance, lpszCmdLine, cmdShow)
HANDLE    hInstance, hPrevInstance;
LPSTR     lpszCmdLine;
int       cmdShow;
{
    HWND      hWnd;
    MSG       msg;

    /* If this is the first instance, register the
       window class
    */
    if (!hPrevInstance)
        register_window(hInstance);
```

continued...

...from previous page

```
    /* Create a tiled window */
    hWnd = CreateWindow( (LPSTR) "Chap8WIN",
             (LPSTR) "Uses a Dialog and List Box",
             WS_TILEDWINDOW,
             0, 0, 0, 0,
             (HWND) NULL,
             (HMENU) NULL,
             (HANDLE) hInstance,
             (LPSTR) NULL );

    /* now display it */
    ShowWindow(hWnd,cmdShow);
    UpdateWindow(hWnd);


    /* initialize global variables.  Note the use of
       MakeProcInstance to create a pointer to the
       procedure for processing the dialog box messages
    */
    lpprocSelectFile_glbl = MakeProcInstance((FARPROC)
        SelectFile, hInstance);
    hInstance_glbl = hInstance;

    /* relay all messages to the message server */
    while (GetMessage( (LPMSG) &msg, NULL, 0, 0) ) {
        TranslateMessage( (LPMSG) &msg);
        DispatchMessage( (LPMSG) &msg);
    }

    exit(msg.wParam);
}



/*----------------------------------------------------------
    This procedure registers the window.
------------------------------------------------------------*/

int
register_window( hInstance )
```

continued...

Dialog Boxes 8

...from previous page

```
HANDLE    hInstance;
{
    PWNDCLASS      pClass;

    pClass = (PWNDCLASS) LocalAlloc(LPTR, sizeof(WNDCLASS));
    pClass->hCursor = LoadCursor(hInstance, (LPSTR) "face");
    pClass->hIcon = LoadIcon(hInstance, (LPSTR) "eight");
    pClass->lpszMenuName = (LPSTR) "eight";
    pClass->lpszClassName = (LPSTR) "Chap8WIN";
    pClass->hbrBackground = GetStockObject(WHITE_BRUSH);
    pClass->hInstance = hInstance;
    pClass->style = CS_HREDRAW | CS_VREDRAW;
    pClass->lpfnWndProc = MsgServer;

    RegisterClass( (LPWNDCLASS) pClass);
    LocalFree( (HANDLE) pClass);
}


/*----------------------------------------------------------
   This procedure receives the messages and decides what to
   do with them.
------------------------------------------------------------*/

long FAR PASCAL
MsgServer( hWnd, message, wParam, lParam )
HWND      hWnd;
unsigned  message;
WORD      wParam;
LONG      lParam;
{
    switch (message) {
    case WM_COMMAND:
        return( process_menu_cmds(hWnd, wParam) );
    default:
        return(DefWindowProc(hWnd,message,wParam,lParam));

    }
    return(0L);
}
```

continued...

8 Dialog Boxes

...from previous page

```
/*-----------------------------------------------------
    This routine processes commands from the menu.  Note the
    use of the command DialogBox.  This creates a dialog box
    -- a child window.  The dialog box becomes the active
    window until its OK or Cancel buttons are pressed.  Then
    control returns to the line after the DialogBox command.
-------------------------------------------------------*/
long
process_menu_cmds( hWnd, command )
HWND      hWnd;
WORD      command;
{
    HDC       hDC;

    switch (command) {
    case IDM_FILE:
        /* create a dialog box called directory.  Have it
            send its messages to the SelectFile procedure.
        */
        DialogBox(hInstance_glbl, (LPSTR) "directory",
            hWnd, lpprocSelectFile_glbl);

        /* once a file has been selected, print out its
            name
        */
        hDC = GetDC(hWnd);
        TextOut(hDC, 0, 0, (LPSTR) filename_glbl,
            strlen((LPSTR) filename_glbl));
        ReleaseDC(hWnd,hDC);
        break;
    }
    return(0L);

}
```

continued...

...from previous page

```
/*----------------------------------------------------------
    This procedure processes commands for the dialog box.
    Note that it is set up just like the MsgServer.  The
    dialog box is just a window with buttons and other
    input features.  Selecting the various buttons sends
    messages just like any other window.

    Because this routine is called by Windows, it must be
    declared as a FAR PASCAL.
------------------------------------------------------------*/

short FAR PASCAL
SelectFile( hDlg, message, wParam, lParam )
HWND     hDlg;
unsigned message;
WORD     wParam;
LONG     lParam;
{
    switch (message) {
    case WM_COMMAND:
        process_dlg_commands(hDlg, wParam);
        break;
    case WM_INITDIALOG:
        /* fill the directory list box with the file
            names from the default drive.  ID_DIR_SELECTED
            indicates what list box to fill.  It is the
            menu value for the list box as defined in
            eight.rc.
        */
        DlgDirList(hDlg, (LPSTR) "*.*", ID_DIR_SELECTED,
            0, (unsigned) 0);
        break;
    default:
        return (FALSE);
    }
    return(TRUE);
}
```

continued...

8 Dialog Boxes

...from previous page

```
/*-----------------------------------------------------------
    This procedure processes commands sent to the "File"
    dialog box.  Note its similarity to
    process_menu_commands().
-------------------------------------------------------------*/
process_dlg_commands( hDlg, command )
HWND    hDlg;
WORD    command;
{
    switch (command) {
    case IDOK:
        /* enter or OK has been pressed.  This means
           accept the current selection.  Because it was
           a directory listing, DlgDirSelect is used.
        */
        DlgDirSelect(hDlg, (LPSTR) filename_glbl,
            ID_DIR_SELECTED);
        /* once the selection is made, end the dialog
           box
        */
        EndDialog(hDlg, TRUE);
        break;

    case IDCANCEL:
        /* escape or Cancel has been pressed.  This means
           don't accept the current selection, so return
           immediately.
        */
        EndDialog(hDlg, TRUE);
        break;
    default:
        break;
    }
}
```

Dialog Boxes 8

The Module Definition File: EIGHT.DEF

```
NAME         Eight
DESCRIPTION  'Eighth Window Program'
STUB         'winstub.exe'
CODE         MOVEABLE
DATA         MOVEABLE MULTIPLE
HEAPSIZE  4096
STACKSIZE 4096
EXPORTS
        MsgServer        @1
        SelectFile       @2
```

SUMMARY

- Dialog boxes are a great way to make selections and enter text and numbers. Windows provides built-in editing features.

- Dialog boxes are windows that run within the program; they receive and process messages just like any other window.

- Modal dialog boxes require the user to enter data before the program continues. Modeless dialog boxes let the program continue before the data is entered.

- Dialog boxes should have OK and Cancel buttons.

- Dialog boxes can contain buttons, text entry boxes, and list boxes.

- Dialog boxes are described with an outline language in the resource file.

- Use the DIALOG.EXE program to create dialog boxes.

- Use the **CreateDialog** or **DialogBox** commands to open a dialog box. Use the **EndDialog** command to close a dialog box.

8 Dialog Boxes

- There are many commands for examining and setting buttons, text entry boxes, and list boxes.

- There are special commands for making a list box of file names.

CHAPTER 9

SYSTEM RESOURCES

9 System Resources

In this chapter, how to use memory and disk files will be covered. In addition, you will learn how to interface Assembly Language programs with Windows programs and how to use memory models.

MEMORY

In conventional C programs, you use **malloc** and **free** to access memory. Windows has analogous functions, though there are a few important differences. First, there are two types of memory: *local* and *global*. Second, memory can be relocated during program operation; thus, memory is initially maintained by handles, not addresses.

Local memory is near memory. It is created from the program's local heap. You can allocate up to the amount of memory in the local heap for local memory. This amount is at least the amount specified by the LOCALHEAP command in the module definition file and, depending on what other programs are running, can be up to 64K. When a program terminates, its local memory is automatically freed.

Global memory is far memory. It is allocated from the system heap and can be any size. When a program terminates, its global memory is not automatically freed.

To use memory, you first allocate it, which returns a handle—not an address—to a memory block. When you want to use the block, you lock it, which returns an address for the memory block. As long as the block is locked, it stays in one place, and the address is valid. Once you are finished reading from or writing to the memory block, you unlock it, which allows Windows to move the memory block to create bigger contiguous memory spaces. When you are finished with the memory block, you free it.

Use the **LocalAlloc** command to allocate local memory and the **GlobalAlloc** command to allocate global memory. If more than one procedure will use the memory, save the resulting handle in a global variable. Both alloc commands have parameters defining whether the memory should always stay in a fixed position, whether it can be moved or discarded, and whether the memory should be initialized to zero. In general, it is best to allow memory blocks to move.

```
LOCALHANDLE
LocalAlloc( MemStyle, Size )
```

MemStyle is a combination of the following:

LMEM_FIXED	the memory block location will not move.
LMEM_MOVEABLE	the memory block can move.
LMEM_DISCARDABLE	the memory block can be discarded.
LMEM_ZEROINT	initialize the memory to zeros.
LPTR	do not use this with the other options. The memory block will be fixed, and **LocalAlloc** will return an address to the block instead of a handle. Only use with the small and medium models.

Size   is an unsigned short specifying the number of bytes for the block.

If the memory was allocated, the function returns a handle to the memory block; otherwise, it returns NULL.

```
GLOBALHANDLE
GlobalAlloc( MemStyle, Size )
```

MemStyle is a combination of the following:

GMEM_FIXED	the memory block location will not move.
GMEM_MOVEABLE	the memory block can move.

9 System Resources

       GMEM__DISCARDABLE the memory block can be discarded.

       GMEM__ZEROINT   initialize the memory to zeros.

Size   is an unsigned long specifying the number of bytes for the block.

The function returns a handle to the memory block if it is successful and returns NULL if it isn't.

Before you read from or write to the memory, lock it with **LocalLock** or **GlobalLock**. These functions return pointers to the block of memory. Typecast them as necessary, as you would with a **malloc** call:

```
PSTR
LocalLock( LocMemHandle )
```

LocMemHandle is a handle for a block of local memory. The function returns a pointer to the block of memory.

```
LPSTR
GlobalLock( GlobMemHandle )
```

GlobMemHandle is a handle for a block of local memory. The function returns a pointer to the block of memory.

You can access locked memory as you would any memory. For example, if you stored an array in local memory, and the address resulting from the lock was stored in Array__ptr, then the first element in the array would be Array__ptr[0].

When you are finished accessing the memory block, unlock it using **LocalUnlock** or **GlobalUnlock**:

```
LocalUnlock( LocMemHandle )
```

LocMemHandle is a handle for a block of local memory.

```
GlobalUnlock( GlobMemHandle )
```

GlobMemHandle is a handle for a block of global memory.

When you no longer need the memory, free it. Memory must be unlocked before it can be freed.

```
LocalFree( LocMemHandle )
```

LocMemHandle is a handle for a block of local memory.

```
GlobalFree( GlobMemHandle )
```

GlobMemHandle is a handle for a block of global memory.

You must free all global memory before a program terminates. To ensure that this process occurs, store all handles to global memory in global variables. Trap the WM_DESTROY message in **MsgServer**. When it is received, unlock and free all global memory used by the program.

Use the **LocalReAlloc** and **GlobalReAlloc** commands to change the size of a memory block. You can also use these commands to make fixed blocks moveable and so forth.

```
LOCALHANDLE
LocalReAlloc( LocMemHandle, NewSize, MemStyle )
```

LocMemHandle is a handle to the block of local memory that you want to resize.

NewSize is an unsigned short specifying the new size of the block.

9 System Resources

MemStyle is a combination of the following:

LMEM__FIXED	the memory block location will not move.
LMEM__MOVEABLE	the memory block can move.
LMEM__DISCARDABLE	the memory block can be discarded.
LMEM__ZEROINT	initialize the memory to zeros.

The return value is a handle to the new block of memory.

```
GLOBALHANDLE
GlobalReAlloc( GlobMemHandle, NewSize, MemStyle )
```

GlobMemHandle
is a handle to the block of global memory that you want to resize.

NewSize is an unsigned long specifying the new size of the block.

MemStyle is a combination of the following:

GMEM__FIXED	the memory block location will not move.
GMEM__MOVEABLE	the memory block can move.
GMEM__DISCARDABLE	the memory block can be discarded.
GMEM__ZEROINT	initialize the memory to zeros.

The return value is a handle to the new block of memory.

As an example of using memory, you could do the following:

```
LOCALHANDLE         buf_handle;
PSTR                buf;

buf_handle = LocalAlloc( LMEM_MOVEABLE, 1000 );
buf = LocalLock( buf_handle );
strcpy( buf, "Put this string in local memory");
LocalUnlock( buf_handle );
```

You must be very careful if you use global memory. Global memory pointers are far pointers. While most Windows functions work with far pointers, the standard C functions will not, unless the memory model is *compact, large,* or *huge.* If you plan to use standard C functions, such as **strcpy** or **itoa**, with global memory blocks, be sure that you use a model that supports far pointers. For more information on changing the memory model, refer to the "Advanced Concepts" section in this chapter.

MEMORY, LINKED LISTS, AND POINTERS

Because memory is accessed via handles, linked lists should contain a handle to the next element instead of a pointer to the next element. Lock and unlock these handles to traverse the list.

Do not create long pointers; set them to the address of a local memory variable, and use them later. The address of the data segment could move, and the long pointer would become invalid. Always use short pointers for local memory variables. If you want to pass the address of a local memory structure to a function that requires a long pointer, typecast it to long when you pass it.

9 System Resources

For example, suppose you use a LOGFONT structure to define a font, as was done in Chapter 5. The following would be incorrect:

```
LPLOGFONT   lpFont_glbl;
LOGFONT     Font_glbl;

init_font()
{
    lpFont_glbl = (LPLOGFONT) &Font_glbl;
    .
    .
}

create_font()
{
    CreateFontIndirect( lpFont_glbl );
}
```

If the data segment for the instance moved, then **lpFont_glbl** would be invalid, and the **CreateFontIndirect** call would have unpredictable results.

Instead, use the following:

```
CreateFontIndirect( (LPLOGFONT) &Font_glbl );
```

USING DISK FILES

Using disk files is somewhat tricky. Remember that many programs could be operating at the same time. These different programs could use files from different disks. Because the user could swap these disks in and out at any time, never assume that the proper disk is in the drive when you open a file.

Also, because several programs could need disks, but the number of programs that can use disks at one time is limited, don't keep files open for a long time; instead, open a file, access it immediately, then close it. If you will infrequently write to a sequential file, open and close it after each write. Move the file pointer to the end of the file each time that you open it. Don't keep a disk file open after you have processed one menu command and are waiting for another.

In addition, if you store information in a temporary disk file, make sure that each instance of your program uses a unique name. There is a Windows command that guarantees this protection.

The final complication with using files is that, despite the manuals' claims, you can't use the normal C file routines, such as **fopen**, **fread**, and **fscanf**, to access disk files; instead, you must use the low-level disk access routines: **read**, **lseek**, **write**, **close**, and so forth.

The low-level disk access routines read and write data in binary format. They transfer data directly from or to a buffer in memory, which saves disk space and reduces decoding time but can be somewhat more difficult to code. If you want to write data in text format, you can **sprintf** it into a buffer, then write the buffer to disk.

Because the low-level routines directly write to and read from memory, they are limited by the memory model. For example, if a small model program wants to transfer data from disk to a variable in global memory, it must read the data into a local variable, then copy it to the global variable. You can get around this limitation by making your own Assembly Language disk access routines.

The *Windows Guide Diskette* contains a set of small model disk access routines that allow you to directly read from or write to local and global memory. You may want to use these routines. They are discussed in full in the Advanced Concepts section of this chapter, which explains interfacing Assembly Language with Windows programs.

9 System Resources

```
/------------------------------------------------\
|                                                |
| To use the Windows Guide Diskette disk access  |
| routines, you must #include the file FILEIO.H  |
| into your source code.  This file contains     |
| external declarations for the three Assembly   |
| Language commands, fileread, filewrite, and    |
| fileclose.  You also need to link the file     |
| FILEIO.OBJ along with your other object        |
| modules.  You can look at the make file and    |
| source code from this chapter's program for an |
| example.                                       |
|                                                |
| The disk access routines are in the FILEIO     |
| directory.  FILEIO.H is the file to include    |
| in your programs.  FILEIO.OBJ is the file      |
| to link with your program's object files.      |
| FILEIO.ASM, the source listing, is discussed   |
| at the end of this chapter.                    |
|                                                |
\------------------------------------------------/
```

To use a file, you open it, access it, then close it. You can open the file with **OpenFile** or **open**.

WORD
OpenFile(lpFileName, lpOfStruct, Style)

lpFileName   is a long pointer to the ASCIIZ name of the file to open.

lpOfStruct   is a long pointer to a variable of OFSTRUCT type. This structure stores information about the file.

Style   is a combination of the following:

> OF_READ   opens the file as a read-only file.
>
> OF_WRITE   opens the file as a write-only file.
>
> OF_READWRITE   opens the file for reading and writing.

OF_CREATE	creates the file. If one already exists, truncates its length to 0.
OF_REOPEN	reopens the file using information in the OFSTRUCT variable pointed to by lpOfStruct. This option causes the file to be reopened using the previous parameters.
OF_EXIST	checks if the file exists. Returns an error if it doesn't.
OF_PARSE	fills the lpOfStruct variable, but does nothing else.
OF_PROMPT	prompts the user for permission to create a file if the file does not exist.
OF_CANCEL	adds a cancel button to the OF_PROMPT message. If the cancel button is selected, **OpenFile** returns -1.
OF_VERIFY	checks that the date and time of the file are the same as when previously opened. Use with the OF_REOPEN option.
OF_DELETE	erases the file.

The return value is a file handle that can be used by the low-level disk access routines or by DOS interrupts. If the open was unsuccessful, the command returns -1.

If you want to prompt the user to insert the disk for a file, use the OF_CANCEL | OF_PROMPT options. Also OR in OF_READ, OF_WRITE, or one of the other similar parameters. If the file is not found, a message will pop up instructing the user to enter the disk containing the file. The user puts in the proper disk and presses the OK button. The message will continue to appear until the proper disk is inserted. The user can also press the Cancel button to cancel the file request. Once the proper disk is inserted, the file will be opened. For example, you could use the fowing:

9 System Resources

```
filehandle = OpenFile( (LPSTR) filename, (LPOFSTRUCT) &fileinfo,
    OF_PROMPT | OF_CANCEL | OF_READ );
```

Once you have opened a file, you can reopen it (after having closed it) by repeating the original **OpenFile**, or by passing a pointer to the OFSTRUCT variable and using the OF_REOPEN option:

```
filehandle = OpenFile( (LPSTR) filename, (LPOFSTRUCT) &fileinfo,
    OF_REOPEN );
```

You can use the OF_EXIST option to determine if a file is already present. It will return an error if the file is not present. If the file does exist, call **OpenFile** again to get a valid handle for it. You can use this function to check if a scratch file is already present. If it is, you could append to the end of it. If it isn't, you could create one.

If you want to create a file with a unique name, such as for a scratch file, use the **GetTempFileName** command:

```
GetTempFileName( Drive, lpPrefixString, 0, lpFileName )
```

Drive is the drive letter where the file will be stored. If you use 0, Windows will use the TEMP drive or a hard disk for the file.

lpPrefixString is a long pointer to an ASCIIZ string that will form the prefix for the file name. Windows will fill the end of the name with a number and the .TMP extension.

lpFileName is a long pointer to a character buffer where the resulting unique file name will be stored. Make sure that the buffer is long enough.

System Resources 9

Once you have opened a file, you can read to and write from it with the **read** and **write** commands or with the *Windows Guide Diskette* commands **fileread** and **filewrite**:

```
WORD
fileread( filehandle, lpBuffer, Count )
```

filehandle is a handle for the file, as returned by **OpenFile** or **open**.

lpBuffer is a long pointer to the buffer where the read data will be stored. This value can be the address of a variable. Make sure that you do not overflow this buffer.

Count is the number of bytes to read into the buffer.

The function will return the number of bytes actually read or 0 if there was an error. This number will be less than **Count** if an end of file was encountered.

```
WORD
filewrite( filehandle, lpBuffer, Count )
```

filehandle is a handle for the file

lpBuffer is a long pointer to the buffer from which the data will be read. This value can be the address of a variable.

Count is the number of bytes to write.

The function returns the number of bytes actually written. If there was an error, it will return 0.

When you are finished accessing a file, close it using **close** or the *Windows Guide Diskette* **fileclose** command.

```
WORD
fileclose( filehandle )
```

filehandle is the handle for the file to close. This function returns 0 if it was successful, and -1 if it was not successful.

STYLISTIC CONSIDERATIONS

Most Windows programs group file access commands in a pop-up menu entitled "File," which is usually the first item in a menu and has at least the following items:

```
MENUITEM  "New",          ....
MENUITEM  "Open...",      ....
MENUITEM  "Save",         ....
MENUITEM  "Save As...",   ....
MENUITEM  "Print",        ....
```

You can see such a menu in the program from this chapter.

A PROGRAM: NINE

The following program illustrates how to use global memory and how to access files (see Figure 9.1). It builds on the program from Chapter 8.

When the Open command in the File menu is selected, the program pops up a dialog box that prompts the user to select a file name from a list box. When the name is selected, the program attempts to read the first 1000 bytes from the file. It displays the number of bytes it could read. The Show File command displays what was read from the file.

There are several interesting aspects to this program. First, it has two object files in the **link4** statement in the make file because it uses commands for accessing disk files; these commands are located in the FILEIO.OBJ file.

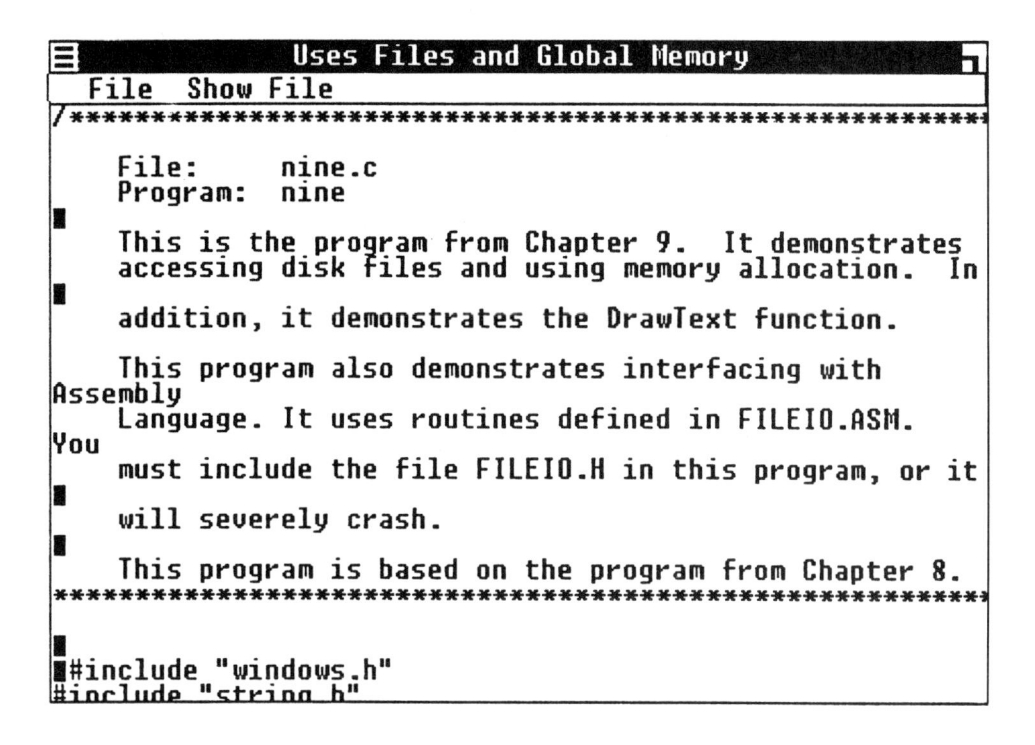

```
┌─────────────────────────────────────────────────────────┐
│ ≡         Uses Files and Global Memory              ┐   │
│   File  Show File                                       │
│/**********************************************************
│                                                         │
│      File:     nine.c                                   │
│      Program:  nine                                     │
│■                                                        │
│      This is the program from Chapter 9.  It demonstrates│
│      accessing disk files and using memory allocation.  In│
│■                                                        │
│      addition, it demonstrates the DrawText function.   │
│                                                         │
│      This program also demonstrates interfacing with    │
│Assembly                                                 │
│      Language. It uses routines defined in FILEIO.ASM.  │
│You                                                      │
│      must include the file FILEIO.H in this program, or it│
│■                                                        │
│      will severely crash.                               │
│■                                                        │
│      This program is based on the program from Chapter 8.│
│ **********************************************************
│                                                         │
│                                                         │
│■                                                        │
│■#include "windows.h"                                    │
│#include "string.h"                                      │
└─────────────────────────────────────────────────────────┘
```

Figure 9.1   The program NINE.

Second, the program uses global memory. The global memory block serves as the buffer for disk information. It is allocated in **WinMain** and freed in **MsgServer** when the WM_DESTROY message is received. Before the buffer is written to or read from, it is locked. This locking is done in **read_file** and **show_file**. Also note how **read_file** uses the disk access commands.

Finally, note how the **DrawText** command is used in **show_file**. This command is quite useful for displaying the text read in from files.

9 System Resources

Also note the use of the standard File menu.

When you compile this program, make sure that the FILEIO.OBJ and FILEIO.H files are in the current directory.

Run this program and read and display several files. Try reading files that are less than 1000 bytes long. Then, load up another application. Change the size of NINE's window several times, redisplaying the text each time. Observe how the **DrawText** command reacts to the different window sizes. In particular, note how the word-wrapping feature operates.

If you feel adventurous, change the program so that it uses a dialog box to input the number of bytes to read and a starting offset.

```
/--------------------------------------------------\
|                                                  |
| The files for this program are located in the    |
| NINE directory.  NINE is the make file.          |
| NINE.RC is the resource file and NINE.DLG is     |
| the dialog description file.  NINE.H is the      |
| include file.  NINE.C contains the code.         |
| NINE.ICO is the icon.  NINE.DEF is the module    |
| definition file.  NINE.EXE is the executable     |
| file.  The cursor, MIKE.CUR, is found in the     |
| root directory.                                  |
|                                                  |
| The files FILEIO.H and FILEIO.OBJ must also be   |
| copied to the working directory.  They are       |
| located in the FILEIO directory.                 |
|                                                  |
\--------------------------------------------------/
```

The Make File: NINE

```
#
#   Make file for the program from Chapter 9
#   Note that it uses fileio.obj
#

cc=cl -d -c -AS -Gsw -Os -Zpe

.c.obj:
    $(cc) $*.c


nine.obj: nine.c  nine.h

nine.res: nine.rc nine.h nine.dlg nine.ico mike.cur
    rc -r nine.rc

nine.exe: nine.obj fileio.obj nine.res nine.def
    link4 nine fileio, /align:16, NUL, slibw, nine.def
    rc nine.res
```

The Resource File: NINE.RC

```
/************************************************************
     Resource file for NINE
*************************************************************/

#include "windows.h"
#include "nine.h"


rcinclude nine.dlg



face        CURSOR      mike.cur
nine        ICON        nine.ico
```

continued...

...from previous page

```
nine    MENU
BEGIN
    POPUP       "File"
    BEGIN
        MENUITEM    "New",          IDM_NULL, GRAYED
        MENUITEM    "Open...",      IDM_FILE
        MENUITEM    "Save",         IDM_NULL, GRAYED
        MENUITEM    "Save As...",   IDM_NULL, GRAYED
        MENUITEM    "Print",        IDM_NULL, GRAYED
    END
    MENUITEM    "Show File",    IDM_SHOW
END
```

The Dialog Description File: NINE.DLG

```
directory   DIALOG   LOADONCALL   MOVEABLE DISCARDABLE
            89, 16, 130, 88

CAPTION     "Select a File"
STYLE       WS_BORDER | WS_CAPTION | WS_DLGFRAME |
            WS_POPUP
BEGIN
    CONTROL     "OK"        IDOK,       "button",
        BS_PUSHBUTTON | WS_TABSTOP | WS_CHILD,
        20, 74, 24, 14
    CONTROL     "Cancel"    IDCANCEL,   "button",
        BS_PUSHBUTTON | WS_TABSTOP | WS_CHILD,
        84, 74, 32, 14
    LISTBOX     ID_DIR_SELECTED,    20, 9, 98, 57 ,
        LBS_NOTIFY | LBS_SORT | WS_BORDER | WS_VSCROLL
END
```

The Include File: NINE.H

```
/***********************************************************
    Include file for the program from Chapter 9.  Contains
    typedefs, constants, and external declarations.
***********************************************************/


extern int PASCAL WinMain();
extern int register_window();
extern long FAR PASCAL MsgServer();
extern long process_menu_cmds();
extern short FAR PASCAL SelectFile();
extern process_dlg_commands();
extern read_file();
extern show_file();


extern HANDLE      instance_glbl;
extern FARPROC     lpprocSelectFile_glbl;
extern char        *filename_glbl;
extern GLOBALHANDLE  file_buffer_glbl;
extern int         amt_read_glbl;



#define  BUFFER_SIZE       1000

/* constant definitions for menus */

#define  IDM_NULL          0
#define  IDM_FILE          100
#define  IDM_SHOW          200
#define  ID_DIR_SELECTED   1000
```

9 System Resources

The Disk File Access Include File: FILEIO.H

```
/***********************************************************
        This file declares the assembly language disk
        routines from fileio.asm
***********************************************************/


extern WORD far fileread();
extern WORD far filewrite();
extern WORD far fileclose();
```

The Code: NINE.C

```
/***********************************************************
        File:       nine.c
        Program:    nine

        This is the program from Chapter 9.  It demonstrates
        accessing disk files and using memory allocation.  In
        addition, it demonstrates the DrawText function.

        This program also demonstrates interfacing with Assembly
        Language. It uses routines defined in FILEIO.ASM.  You
        must include the file FILEIO.H in this program, or it
        will severely crash.

        This program is based on the program from Chapter 8.
***********************************************************/


#include "windows.h"
#include "string.h"
#include "time.h"
#include "stdio.h"

#include "fileio.h"
#include "nine.h"
```

continued...

...from previous page

```
/*-------------------------------------------------------
   global variables
----------------------------------------------------*/

FARPROC      lpprocSelectFile_glbl;
HANDLE       hInstance_glbl;
char         filename_glbl[30];
GLOBALHANDLE file_buffer_glbl;
int          amt_read_glbl;




/*-------------------------------------------------------
   This is the Start Up procedure and message relayer
----------------------------------------------------*/

int PASCAL
WinMain(hInstance, hPrevInstance, lpszCmdLine, cmdShow)
HANDLE    hInstance, hPrevInstance;
LPSTR     lpszCmdLine;
int       cmdShow;
{
    HWND      hWnd;
    MSG       msg;

    /* If this is the first instance, register the
       window class
    */
    if (!hPrevInstance)
        register_window(hInstance);

    /* Create a tiled window */
    hWnd = CreateWindow( (LPSTR) "Chap9WIN",
             (LPSTR) "Uses Files and Global Memory",
             WS_TILEDWINDOW,
             0, 0, 0, 0,
             (HWND) NULL,
             (HMENU) NULL,
             (HANDLE) hInstance,
             (LPSTR) NULL );
```

continued...

9 System Resources

...from previous page

```
    /* display the window */
    ShowWindow(hWnd,cmdShow);
    UpdateWindow(hWnd);


    /* initialize variables */
    lpprocSelectFile_glbl = MakeProcInstance((FARPROC)
        SelectFile, hInstance);
    hInstance_glbl = hInstance;
    amt_read_glbl = 0;

    /* Allocate a chunk of global memory for the file buffer.
       Declare it as moveable so that Windows has the
       flexibility of moving it around
    */
    file_buffer_glbl = GlobalAlloc(GMEM_MOVEABLE,
        (unsigned LONG) BUFFER_SIZE + 5);

    /* relay all messages to the message server */
    while (GetMessage( (LPMSG) &msg, NULL, 0, 0) ) {
        TranslateMessage( (LPMSG) &msg);
        DispatchMessage( (LPMSG) &msg);
    }

    exit(msg.wParam);
}




/*-----------------------------------------------------
This procedure registers the window.
-----------------------------------------------------*/

int
register_window( hInstance )
HANDLE    hInstance;
{
    PWNDCLASS        pClass;
```

continued...

...from previous page

```
    pClass = (PWNDCLASS) LocalAlloc(LPTR, sizeof(WNDCLASS));
    pClass->hCursor = LoadCursor(hInstance, (LPSTR) "face");
    pClass->hIcon = LoadIcon(hInstance, (LPSTR) "nine");
    pClass->lpszMenuName = (LPSTR) "nine";
    pClass->lpszClassName = (LPSTR) "Chap9WIN";
    pClass->hbrBackground = GetStockObject(WHITE_BRUSH);
    pClass->hInstance = hInstance;
    pClass->style = CS_HREDRAW | CS_VREDRAW;
    pClass->lpfnWndProc = MsgServer;

    RegisterClass( (LPWNDCLASS) pClass);
    LocalFree( (HANDLE) pClass);
}


/*-----------------------------------------------------------
    This procedure receives the messages and decides what to
    do with them.  Note that when the window is destroyed,
    all global memory must be freed.
------------------------------------------------------------*/

long FAR PASCAL
MsgServer( hWnd, message, wParam, lParam )
HWND     hWnd;
unsigned message;
WORD     wParam;
LONG     lParam;
{
    switch (message) {
    case WM_COMMAND:
        return( process_menu_cmds(hWnd, wParam) );
    case WM_DESTROY:
        /* free all global memory */
        GlobalUnlock( file_buffer_glbl);
        GlobalFree( file_buffer_glbl );
        return(DefWindowProc(hWnd,message,wParam,lParam));
    default:
        return(DefWindowProc(hWnd,message,wParam,lParam));
    }
    return(0L);
}
```

continued...

9 System Resources

...from previous page

```
/*-----------------------------------------------------------
    This routine processes commands from the menu.  Note the
    addition of read_file and show_file.
-------------------------------------------------------------*/
long
process_menu_cmds( hWnd, command )
HWND     hWnd;
WORD     command;
{
    switch (command) {
    case IDM_FILE:
        DialogBox(hInstance_glbl, (LPSTR) "directory",
            hWnd, lpprocSelectFile_glbl);
        read_file(hWnd);
        break;
    case IDM_SHOW:
        show_file(hWnd);
    }
    return(0L);
}




/*-----------------------------------------------------------
    This procedure processes commands for the dialog box.
    It is the same as in Chapter 8.
-------------------------------------------------------------*/
short FAR PASCAL
SelectFile( hDlg, message, wParam, lParam )
HWND       hDlg;
unsigned   message;
WORD       wParam;
LONG       lParam;
```

continued...

...from previous page

```c
{
    switch (message) {
    case WM_COMMAND:
        process_dlg_commands(hDlg, wParam);
        break;
    case WM_INITDIALOG:
        DlgDirList(hDlg, (LPSTR) "*.*", ID_DIR_SELECTED,
            0, (unsigned) 0);
        break;
    default:
        return (FALSE);
    }
    return(TRUE);
}




/*-----------------------------------------------------------
    This routine processes commands sent to the select file
    dialog box.  It is the same as in Chapter 8.
-------------------------------------------------------------*/

process_dlg_commands( hDlg, command )
HWND    hDlg;
WORD    command;
{
    switch (command) {
    case IDOK:
        DlgDirSelect(hDlg, (LPSTR) filename_glbl,
            ID_DIR_SELECTED);
        EndDialog(hDlg, TRUE);
        break;
    case IDCANCEL:
        EndDialog(hDlg, TRUE);
        break;
    default:
        break;
    }
}
```

continued...

9 System Resources

...from previous page

```
/*-------------------------------------------------------------
    This procedure reads a portion of a file from disk.  It
    locks the global buffer and uses one of the Assembly
    Language disk routines to read in a block from disk to
    the buffer.  It then unlocks the buffer.  Note the use
    of OpenFile.  Also, note that file handles are declared
    as integers rather than FILE *.  This is because file
    handles for low level DOS calls are integers.  Also
    note that all pointers passed to the disk file routines
    are passed as long pointers.

    Note that message must be long enough to hold the full
    filename and bytes read message.
-------------------------------------------------------------*/
read_file( hWnd )
HWND     hWnd;
{
    LPSTR      buffer;
    int        file_handle;
    OFSTRUCT   file_info;
    HDC        hDC;
    char       message[40], temp[10];


    /* first lock the global buffer.  This returns a
       memory address
    */
    buffer = (LPSTR) GlobalLock( file_buffer_glbl );

    /* only proceed if could allocate the memory */
    if (buffer != NULL) {
        /* open the file for reading only */
        amt_read_glbl = 0;
        file_handle = OpenFile( (LPSTR) filename_glbl,
            (OFSTRUCT FAR *) &file_info, OF_READ);
```

continued...

...from previous page

```
            /* try to fill the buffer by reading a chunk from
                disk.  amt_read_glbl contains the number of
                bytes actually read.
            */
            amt_read_glbl = fileread(file_handle, buffer,
                (WORD) BUFFER_SIZE);

            /* close the file */
            (VOID) fileclose(file_handle);

            /* now unlock the buffer */
            GlobalUnlock( file_buffer_glbl);

            /* print out the number of bytes read */
            hDC = GetDC(hWnd);
            if (file_handle == NULL)
                strcpy(message,"Could not open!");
            else {
                strcpy(message,"Read ");
                strcat(message,itoa(amt_read_glbl,temp,10));
                strcat(message," bytes from ");
                strcat(message,filename_glbl);
            }
            TextOut(hDC, 0, 0, (LPSTR) message,
                strlen(message));
            ReleaseDC(hWnd,hDC);
        }
}


/*-----------------------------------------------------------
    This procedure displays the data read from the disk
    file.  Note how it locks the buffer before it reads it
    and unlocks the buffer when it is finished.  Also note
    the use of DrawText.  This is a very powerful command
    for displaying text.  Change the size of the window
    several times and observe what DrawText does.
-----------------------------------------------------------*/
```

continued...

9 System Resources

...from previous page

```
show_file( hWnd )
HWND    hWnd;
{
    char      FAR *buffer;
    HDC       hDC;
    RECT      screen;
    HBRUSH    hBr,hBrOld;

    /* first lock the global buffer */
    buffer = (char FAR *) GlobalLock( file_buffer_glbl );

    /* get the display context and clear the screen */
    hDC = GetDC(hWnd);
    GetClientRect(hWnd, (LPRECT) &screen);
    hBr = CreateSolidBrush(GetBkColor(hDC));
    hBrOld = SelectObject(hDC, hBr);
    FillRect(hDC, (LPRECT) &screen, hBr);
    SelectObject(hDC, hBrOld);
    DeleteObject(hBr);

    /* now use DrawText to fill the whole screen with text.
       Left justify the text.  If a word would go across
       the right edge, wrap it around to the next column.
       Expand tabs.  Text that goes off the bottom of the
       screen will be clipped.
    */
    DrawText(hDC, (LPSTR) buffer, amt_read_glbl,
        (LPRECT) &screen, DT_LEFT | DT_WORDBREAK |
        DT_EXPANDTABS);
    ReleaseDC(hWnd, hDC);

    /* now unlock the buffer */
    GlobalUnlock( file_buffer_glbl);
}
```

The Module Definition File: NINE.DEF

```
NAME        Nine
DESCRIPTION 'Ninth Window Program'
STUB        'winstub.exe'
CODE        MOVEABLE
DATA        MOVEABLE MULTIPLE
HEAPSIZE    4096
STACKSIZE   4096
EXPORTS
        MsgServer       @1
        SelectFile      @2
```

ADVANCED CONCEPTS: USING ASSEMBLY LANGUAGE AND MEMORY MODELS

To create Assembly Language programs, you must be familiar with Assembly Language programming, and you must have the Microsoft Macro Assembler. In addition, you should be familiar with the DOS and BIOS interrupts and should have your compiler reference manual nearby.[1]

Fortunately, it is not difficult to add Assembly Language commands to a Windows program. There is a file, CMACROS.INC, that comes with the Windows Development Toolkit and provides a number of macros to make Assembly Language interfacing relatively painless.

CMACROS.INC automatically formats your Assembly Language routines so that they can be called by a high-level language, such as C or Pascal. It will format the routines for the different memory models and for the Windows protocol.

---

[1] If you are not familiar with the DOS and BIOS interrupts, it is suggested that you read *Memory Resident Utilities, Interrupts, and Disk Management with MS and PC DOS* (also by the author, MIS:Press, 1987).

9 System Resources

You must define the memory model, language, and Windows protocol options at the beginning of the Assembly Language file. Start by selecting the memory model. Set one of the following constants to 1:

```
memS          small model
memM          medium model
memL          large model
memC          compact model
memH          huge model
```

For example, to create a file of Assembly Language routines for a medium model program, you would use the following:

```
memM     EQU     1
```

If you are unfamiliar with the various memory models, refer to the end of this section.

Next, select the language. If you are interfacing with a Pascal program, use the Pascal interface; if you are interfacing with a C program, use the C interface. If your routines will be called by the Windows system, not just from a Windows program, you must use the Pascal calling convention.

Declare all the procedures you create as externals, as is done in the file FILEIO.H. If the routines use the Pascal calling convention, you must include the PASCAL keyword in the external declarations.

To choose the language, set the ?PLM flag. Set it to 0 for C convention and to 1 for Pascal convention. For example, if you want to use the C calling convention, you would use the following:

```
?PLM     =     0
```

Finally, indicate whether the procedures will be used by a Windows application. Since you are reading this book, you clearly want this convention. Set the ?WIN flag to 1 for the Windows interface and to 0 for a conventional program interface. For example, to create procedures with the Windows calling conventions, use the following:

```
?WIN      =    1
```

Now, include the CMACROS.INC file. It will use the flags you just set to determine how the macros will function:

```
include      cmacros.inc
```

You are now ready to create Assembly Language routines. Assembly Language programming gives much flexibility over segments and groups. This discussion assumes that you are making a few utility commands to add to Windows programs rather than creating a huge library or a complete Windows program. If you plan to create complete Assembly Language Windows programs, read over the "Assembly Language Macros" section of the Windows Development Toolkit.

Start your code with the following macros:

```
sBegin       CODE
assumes      CS, CODE
assumes      DS, NOTHING
```

These macros set up the segments for the code and data so that they will easily interface to Windows programs.

Next, write your Assembly Language routines. Declare procedures with the **cProc** macro. Follow this macro with the procedure name, a comma, and the following options: **<PUBLIC, FAR>**, **<si, di, ds>**. These options define the procedure as a FAR procedure and ensure that the si, di, and ds registers are restored at the end of the procedure. These registers must be restored when calling a procedure from C.

9 System Resources

For example, you could have the following:

```
cProc fileread, <PUBLIC, FAR>, <si, di, ds>
```

Then, list the parameters that will be passed to the routine. Declare them using the **parm**X keyword. Its format is as follows:

parmX   parameter name

You can use the following declarations:

parmB	byte parameter
parmW	word parameter (short integers)
parmD	double-word parameter (long integers)
parmQ	quad-word parameter
parmT	ten-byte word
parmCP	code pointer (pointer to a procedure; will be one or two words, depending on the memory model)
parmDP	data pointer (pointer to a variable; will be one or two words, depending on the memory model)

For example, the **fileread** command gets passed three parameters: a file handle, a long pointer to a buffer, and the number of bytes to read. It is declared as follows:

```
cProc   fileread, <PUBLIC, FAR>, <si, di, ds>
        parmW           filehandle
        parmD           buffer
        parmW           bytes_to_read
```

To access the file handle, you refer to the variable **filehandle**. For example, you could use the following:

```
mov     ax, filehandle
```

This command will load the ax register with the value passed in the file handle parameter.

You can use the **OFF_** and **SEG_** prefixes to access the offset and segment of double words. These prefixes are useful because long pointers are double words. For example, OFF_buffer refers to the offset of the buffer, and SEG_buffer refers to the segment of the buffer.

After you declare parameters, use the **cBegin** keyword. At the end of the procedure, use the **cEnd** keyword. Do not end your procedures with a **ret**. The **cEnd** macro will take care of returning from the procedure.

For example, following is a complete listing of the code for the **fileread** procedure:

```
;
; fileread
;
;
; Reads bytes_to_read bytes from the file with file handle
; filehandle and stores them in the array pointed to by
; the LONG pointer buffer.  Returns the numbers of bytes
; actually read.  Returns 0 bytes if there was an error.
; Updates the file position pointer.
;
; This is the same as fread, except for the order of
; parameters, the fact that the buffer is passed by a far
; pointer, and that size and count are multiplied before
; being passed.
;
;
; WORD
; fileread(filehandle, buffer, bytes_to_read)
; WORD      filehandle;
; BYTE      FAR * buffer;
; WORD      bytes_to_read;
;
```

continued...

9 System Resources

...from previous page

```
cProc   fileread, <PUBLIC, FAR>, <si,di,ds>
                parmW       filehandle
                parmD       buffer
                parmW       bytes_to_read
cBegin
                mov         ah,63
                mov         bx,filehandle
                mov         cx,bytes_to_read
                lds         dx,buffer
                int         21h
                jnc         fread_finished
                xor         ax,ax
fread_finished:
cEnd
```

End your Assembly Language file with the **sEnd** and **end** commands:

```
sEnd
end
```

If you need to use variables for your procedures, you can declare local variables with the **LocalX** command. Its format is the same as the **ParmX** command. You can use the following:

LocalB	byte variable
LocalW	word variable
LocalD	double-word variable
LocalQ	quad-word variable
LocalT	ten-byte word
LocalCP	code pointer (pointer to a procedure. will be one or two words, depending on the memory model)
LocalDP	data pointer (pointer to a variable; will be one or two words, depending on the memory model)

Place the local variable definitions after the parameter definitions and before the **cBegin**.

For example, to declare a word variable, you could use the following:

```
LocalW      string_length
```

If there are subroutines that your procedures will call, but that aren't called by a Windows application, you can create and call the subroutines without any special macros; that is, create them as you would in a conventional Assembly Language program.

If you want to call a procedure from an Assembly Language procedure, you can use the **cCall** macro, which lets you call high-level language procedures and Assembly Language procedures in your file that start with the **cProc** macro. Its format is as follows:

```
cCall   procedure [, <parameter list> ]
```

procedure is the name of the procedure to call, and **parameter list** is the list of values to pass as parameters.

For example, you could use the following:

```
cCall fileread, < ax, mybuf, cx >
```

Your procedure can return results. For example, **fileread** returns the number of bytes actually read. Put all return values in the ax register. If the return value is a double word or far pointer, put the high word or segment in dx, and put the low word or offset in ax.

Once you have written your procedures, assemble them. Create a .H file, declaring all of your procedures as external and far. If you used the Pascal convention, you must also declare them as PASCAL.

For example, this file could include the following:

```
extern WORD far fileread();
```

9 System Resources

For Pascal convention procedures, it would be as follows:

```
extern WORD far PASCAL fileread();
```

Include the object file from your Assembly Language procedures when you link4 a program that uses them. For example, the disk commands are assembled into the file FILEIO.OBJ. To use the disk commands, you would need to have the following:

```
link4 mainprog other_modules fileio, ......
```

You can look at the make file, NINE, discussed earlier in this chapter, for an example.

This section has outlined all you need to do to interface Assembly Language procedures with a Windows program. If you are at all confused, look over the following listing for FILEIO.ASM, and review how the procedures are used, declared, and linked in the program NINE.

As you examine FILEIO.ASM, note that the options at the beginning of the program make the procedures use the small model and Windows C calling convention. You can change the memS, ?PLM, and ?WIN parameters to change these options.

The procedures use DOS interrupts.

```
/--------------------------------------------------\
|                                                  |
| The files for this program are in the FILEIO     |
| directory.  FILEIO.H is the declarations for     |
| C programs.  FILEIO.ASM is the listing of the    |
| procedures.  FILEIO.OBJ is the object file.      |
|                                                  |
\--------------------------------------------------/
```

The Include File for C Programs: FILEIO.H

```
/************************************************************
        This file declares the assembly language disk
        routines from fileio.asm
*************************************************************/


extern WORD far fileread();
extern WORD far filewrite();
extern WORD far fileclose();
```

The Disk Access Assembly Language Routines: FILEIO.ASM

```
;
;       This file contains assembly language routines that allow
;       you to do disk IO.
;
;
;
;       For further information on the disk interrupts, see:
;               Memory Resident Utilities, Interrupts, and Disk
;               Management with MS and PC DOS
;       by Michael I. Hyman, published by MIS Press.
;

; Define the memory model.  Change this line if you do not
; want the small memory model.

memS    EQU     1

; Defines the calling convention.  Change this line if you
; want to use the Pascal calling convention instead of C.

?PLM    =       0


; Sets Windows option on.

?WIN    =       1
```

continued...

9 System Resources

...from previous page

```
include         cmacros.inc         ; comes with Windows
                                    ; toolkit


sBegin   CODE

assumes CS,CODE
assumes DS,NOTHING


;
;       fileread
;
;       Reads bytes_to_read bytes from the file with file handle
;       filehandle and stores them in the array pointed to by
;       the LONG pointer buffer.  Returns the numbers of bytes
;       actually read.  Returns 0 bytes if there was an error.
;       Updates the file position pointer.
;
;       This is the same as fread, except for the order of
;       parameters, the fact that the buffer is passed by a far
;       pointer, and that size and count are multiplied before
;       being passed.  Also, data is low level not stream.
;
;
;       WORD
;       fileread(filehandle, buffer, bytes_to_read)
;       WORD       filehandle;
;       BYTE       FAR * buffer;
;       WORD       bytes_to_read;
;

cProc   fileread, <PUBLIC, FAR>, <si,di,ds>
                parmW       filehandle
                parmD       buffer
                parmW       bytes_to_read
```

continued...

...from previous page

cBegin
```
        mov     ah,63
        mov     bx,filehandle
        mov     cx,bytes_to_read
        lds     dx,buffer
        int     21h
        jnc     fread_finished
        xor     ax,ax
fread_finished:
cEnd
```

```
;
;       filewrite
;
;       Writes bytes_to_write bytes to the file with file handle
;       filehandle from the array pointed to by
;       the LONG pointer buffer.  Returns the numbers of
;       bytes actually written.  Returns 0 bytes if there was an
;       error.  Updates the file position pointer.
;
;       This is the same as fwrite, except for the order of
;       parameters, the fact that the buffer is passed by a far
;       pointer, and that size and count are multiplied before
;       being passed.  Also, data is low level, not stream.
;
;
;       WORD
;       filewrite(filehandle, buffer, bytes_to_write)
;       WORD    filehandle;
;       BYTE    FAR * buffer;
;       WORD    bytes_to_write;
;
```

continued...

9 System Resources

...from previous page

```
cProc   filewrite, <PUBLIC, FAR>, <si,di,ds>
                parmW       filehandle
                parmD       buffer
                parmW       bytes_to_write
cBegin
                mov         ah,64
                mov         bx,filehandle
                mov         cx,bytes_to_write
                lds         dx,buffer
                int         21h
                jnc         fwrite_finished
                xor         ax,ax
fwrite_finished:
cEnd
```

```
;
;   fileclose
;
;   Closes a file handle.  Returns a zero if successful.
;
;
;   This routine is identical to fclose, except that it
;   returns -1 if the close wasn't successful.
;
;
;   WORD
;   fileclose(filehandle)
;   WORD        filehandle;
;

cProc   fileclose, <PUBLIC, FAR>, <si,di,ds>
                parmW       filehandle
```

continued...

...from previous page

cBegin

```
            mov     ah,62
            mov     bx,filehandle
            int     21h
            jnc     fclose_good
            mov     ax,-1
            jmp     fclose_end
fclose_good:
            xor     ax,ax
fclose_end:
cEnd
```

sEnd

end

CHANGING THE MEMORY MODELS

Programs are compiled using different memory models. The memory model indicates how much space can be used for the code and for data. For example, the small model, which you have been using so far, allows up to 64K of code and 64K of data, which is enough for most programs. Long programs might need more space for the code. Far more likely, a program could need more room for data.

With Windows programs, the needs are somewhat different. There is no restriction on the amount of data a program can use, as long as the data is in global memory. Unfortunately, though, in the small model only the Windows commands will work with global memory. The C commands use short pointers, and, as a result, can only work with local memory. If you want to use C commands such as **memcpy** and **strcat** with items in global memory, you will have to switch to a model that supports more than one data segment. The compact model is probably the best one to use.

9 System Resources

Fortunately, the -> and * commands will work with far pointers (global memory) in the small model. If you only need to use a few C library commands with global memory, write your own versions of the routines. This strategy will save space because the small memory model is the most space efficient. For example, the following routine is a **memcpy** that works with global memory:

```
/* copies memory from one location to another.  Unlike memcpy,
   it will work with global memory in the small model, but it
   will not check for memory overwriting.
*/

lmemcpy( dest, source, count )
LPSTR    *dest;
LPSTR    *source;
int      count;
{
     int    i;

     for (i = 0; i < count; i++)
          dest[i] = source[i];
}
```

Following is a list of the different memory models and their attributes:

Model	Size
small	64K code, 64K data
medium	unlimited code, 64K data
large	unlimited code, unlimited data
compact	64K code, unlimited data
huge	unlimited code, unlimited data, arrays can be bigger than 64K

You need to adjust the compiler /A option for the memory model you select. You also need to specify the appropriate Windows library to use with link4.

Model	/A flag	Library
small	/AS	slibw.lib
medium	/AM	mlibw.lib
large	/AL	llibw.lib
compact	/AC	clibw.lib
huge	/AH	llibw.lib

For large, compact, and huge memory models, you must also change the DATA statement in the module definition file. Use the FIXED option.

Windows 1.03 doesn't load unique data segments for repeat instances of large, compact, and huge memory programs. To get around this problem, change the NAME and .DEF file to something other than the file name. This forces a new data segment to be loaded (see ELEVEN.DEF for an example).

The program in Chapter 11 uses the compact memory model. You can look at it as an example of a different memory model.

SUMMARY

- There are two types of memory: local and global. You can use at most 64K for local memory. You can use any size for global memory.

- Memory blocks can stay in the same place or be moved by Windows.

- To use memory, first allocate it. Before you access it, lock it. Unlock it when you are finished accessing it. Free it when you are finished using it.

- You can change the size of a block of memory.

- Local memory is freed when a program ends. The program must free global memory itself. Trap the WM_DESTROY message to do so.

9 System Resources

- Don't keep a disk file open for long. In particular, never leave a disk file open between receiving menu messages. If you need to do sequential access, open the file, seek to the desired position, read or write, then close.

- If you store information in a temporary file, make sure that it has a unique name.

- You must use low-level commands to perform disk access. The *Windows Guide Diskette* provides disk file commands that work with global memory in the small model.

- The CMACROS.INC file provides a set of macros that makes it easy to interface Assembly Language programs with Windows programs.

- The memory model defines the maximum size of the code and data.

- If your program plans to use normal C commands for accessing global memory, you must change the memory model. There are several memory models that you can use.

CHAPTER 10

MISCELLANEOUS TOPICS

10 Miscellaneous Topics

This chapter covers a variety of Windows topics: how to use message boxes, string tables, continuously update icons, add scroll bars, create child windows, and use the timer. You will also review multiple instances, see how to change system menus, run background processes, and examine keyboard interfacing and debugging. In addition, you will look at using the WIN.INI file and learn how to print.

MESSAGE BOXES

Message boxes are pop-up windows used to display messages to the user. For example, you could pop up a message that a system resource was unavailable or that some error occurred. You will use message boxes in Chapter 11 to indicate clipboard errors.

Windows automatically places and sizes the message box. Message boxes contain buttons to select a response to the message and optionally can contain warning icons. Message boxes can be *application modal* or *system modal*. Application modal message boxes prevent the program from continuing before the user responds to the message. System modal boxes prevent all programs from operating before the user responds to the message. Only use system modal boxes for system emergencies, such as a hardware error.

Following is the command to create a message box:

```
int
MessageBox( hWnd, lpMessage, lpTitle, Style )
```

hWnd is a handle to the window creating the dialog box. For example, if you are creating the message box in **MsgServer**, use the hWnd parameter. If you are creating the message box from a dialog box, use the hDlg.

lpMessage is a long pointer to the ASCIIZ string that will be displayed in the message box.

lpTitle is a long pointer to an ASCIIZ string to use for the title of the message box. If this value is NULL, the title will be "Error!"

Miscellaneous Topics 10

Style   indicates what type of buttons will appear in the message box and whether it is system modal. It can be a combination of the following:

MB_OK   contains an OK button

MB_OKCANCEL   contains OK and Cancel buttons

MB_RETRYCANCEL
                  contains Retry and Cancel buttons

MB_ABORTRETRYIGNORE
                  contains Abort, Retry, and Ignore buttons

MB_YESNO   contains Yes and No buttons

MB_YESNOCANCEL
                  contains Yes, No, and Cancel buttons

MB_DEFBUTTON   use the first button as the default button

MB_DEFBUTTON2   use the second button as the default button

MB_DEFBUTTON3   use the third button as the default button

MB_ICONHAND   contains the hand icon. Use for severe warning messages.

MB_ICONQUESTION
                  contains the question mark icon.

10 Miscellaneous Topics

MB_ICONEXCLAMATION	contains the exclamation mark icon. Use for warning messages.
MB_ASTERISK	contains the asterisk icon. Use for information messages.
MB_APPLMODAL	the message box is application modal
MB_SYSTEMMODAL	the message box is system modal

The function returns the message from the button selected by the user. The message will be one of the following, all of which are defined in windows.h:

- IDOK
- IDCANCEL
- IDABORT
- IDRETRY
- IDIGNORE
- IDYES
- IDNO

System modal message boxes should use the hand icon. Do not use any of the other icons for system modal boxes.

Message boxes are a good place to use string resource tables, discussed in the next section. Do not use string resource table strings for system modal messages.

10 Miscellaneous Topics

STRING RESOURCE TABLES

There are two ways you can define a string in Windows. The first is what you have been doing so far: simply enclose a block of text within double quotes. For example, if you wanted to use "Hello World" as the title of a Window, you would pass (LPSTR) "Hello World" as a parameter to the **CreateWindow** call. This method is convenient and easy to use.

The second method is to load strings from a table in the resource file. This method has two advantages: first, the memory for the strings is used only if the string is used; second, having all strings in one place makes it easier to translate messages into foreign languages.

Window titles and message box messages are two good places to use string table entries. You can also use string tables to load the names of icons, cursors, and other resources, or for any text message.

Define the string table in the resource file with the **STRINGTABLE** command. Its format is as follows:

```
STRINGTABLE
BEGIN
    string_id,    "string"
        .
        .
END
```

Also define constants that tell the length of the strings. Include the ending null character when calculating this length. For example, you could have the following:

```
#define   IDS_CLIP_EMPTY_LGTH      23
#define   IDS_GREETING_LGTH        46

STRINGTABLE
BEGIN
    IDS_CLIP_EMPTY,       "The Clipboard is Empty"
    IDS_GREETING,         "Thank you for buying the Windows Guide
                           Diskette"
END
```

10 Miscellaneous Topics

To use the strings, allocate or define a buffer for them. Use the constant to determine the buffer length. Then, load the strings with **LoadString**:

```
int
LoadString( hInstance, StringId, lpString, Count )
```

hInstance is a handle to the program instance.

StringId is the constant that identifies the string, which could be IDS_GREETING from the previous example.

lpString is a long pointer to the buffer into which the string will be read.

Count is the number of characters to read into the buffer. Make sure that this number does not exceed the buffer length. Use the constants that define the string lengths.

The function returns the number of characters copied, which will be zero if the string doesn't exist.

CHANGEABLE ICONS

So far, you have created a program's icon using the built-in icons or with ICONEDIT. You can also use the GDI commands to create an icon, which is how CLOCK works. Even while it is iconic, its hands move.

It is easy to make an icon with GDI calls. First, set the class icon to NULL. Do so in the **register_window** procedure. Then, trap WM_PAINT. Every time an icon is made or moved, the program receives a WM_PAINT message. If you execute any GDI calls after receiving a WM_PAINT message, they will show up in the icon because **GetDC** will return a display context for the icon.

This process is surprisingly simple. In fact, to make the program SEVEN display the screen picture in the icon area, all you have to do is set the class icon to NULL.

Miscellaneous Topics 10

TEN, the program from this Chapter, puts the screen display on the icon.

SCROLL BARS

Scroll bars allow the user to change the portion of an image that is displayed on the screen. For example, list boxes contain scroll bars that let you scroll down a list of items. The PAINT and WRITE programs have scroll bars that let you change the part of a page you are editing.

Scroll bars are useful for programs that might not be able to display a whole image on the screen at once. For example, a desktop publishing program should have a scroll bar so that the user can look at any portion of a document, no matter the size of the window. Any program that uses the MM_HIMETRIC, MM_LOMETRIC, MM_HIENGLISH, MM_LOENGLISH, or MM_TWIPS modes should have scroll bars.

There are two types of scroll bars: horizontal and vertical. Horizontal scroll bars let you move a displayed image left and right. Vertical scroll bars let you move an image up and down.

Scroll bars have a small position box called the *thumb*. When the user moves this thumb, a message is sent to the program. The program reads the thumb position and updates the scroll bar and the display area.

There are two ways to scroll the screen image. The first is to use the **ScrollWindow** command. A much better way is to use **SetWindowOrg** to move the window origin, which causes a different portion of the coordinate system to be mapped to the screen. For example, suppose the thumb was in the middle of the scroll bar. You could set the window origin to the middle of the coordinate system. If the thumb was at the top of the scroll bar, you could set the window origin to the highest coordinate value.

Add scroll bars in the **CreateWindow** call in **WinMain**. To add a vertical scroll bar, add WS_VSCROLL to the style parameter. Add WS_HSCROLL to create a horizontal scroll bar. For example, you could have the following:

10 Miscellaneous Topics

```
/* Create a tiled window with a vertical scroll
   bar.  Note the use of WS_VSCROLL.
*/
hWnd = CreateWindow( (LPSTR) "Chap10WIN",
                     (LPSTR) "Scrolls and Changes Icon",
                     WS_TILEDWINDOW | WS_VSCROLL,
                     0, 0, 0, 0,
                     (HWND) NULL,
                     (HMENU) NULL,
                     (HANDLE) hInstance,
                     (LPSTR) NULL );
```

The scroll bar messages, WM__VSCROLL and WM__HSCROLL, are sent whenever the user positions the thumb. These two messages are detailed in Chapter 6. Process these messages to update a global variable indicating the thumb position. Update the scroll bar by setting the thumb to this position. (Windows will not do this step for you.) Then, update the screen, or pass a message indicating that the screen needs to be updated.

Normally, the thumb position ranges between 0 and 100. You can change this range if you like. **GetScrollRange** returns the current range, and **SetScrollRange** lets you set a new range:

GetScrollRange(hWnd, Bar, lpMinPos, lpMaxPos)

hWnd   is a handle to the window containing the scroll bars.

Bar   indicates for which bar to get the range. It can be one of the following:

      SB__VERT   looks at the vertical bar
      SB__HORZ   looks at the horizontal bar

lpMinPos   is a long pointer to a variable into which the minimum range will be stored.

lpMaxPos   is a long pointer to a variable into which the maximum range will be stored.

Miscellaneous Topics 10

```
SetScrollRange( hWnd, Bar, MinPos, MaxPos, Redraw )
```

hWnd　　　　is a handle for the window containing the scroll bar.

Bar　　　　indicates for which bar to set the range. It can be one of the following:

        SB_VERT　　　　vertical bar
        SB_HORZ　　　　horizontal bar

MinPos　　　　is the new minimum range for the bar.

MaxPos　　　　is the new maximum range for the bar.

Redraw　　　　indicates whether to redraw the screen after adjusting the scroll range. Set it to TRUE if you want to redraw, FALSE if you don't.

As mentioned, when you receive a message indicating scroll bar activity, you need to move the thumb to its new position. Do so with the **SetScrollPos** command:

```
int
SetScrollPos( hWnd, Bar, Position, Redraw )
```

hWnd　　　　is a handle to the window containing the scroll bar.

Bar　　　　indicates which bar to adjust. It can be one of the following:

        SB_VERT　　　　the vertical bar
        SB_HORZ　　　　the horizontal bar

Position　　　　is the new position. This value should be between the scroll bar minimum and maximum range. The default is 0 - 100. This value can be changed with **SetScrollRange**.

10 Miscellaneous Topics

The return value is the previous thumb position.

You can determine the current thumb position by using the following:

```
int
GetScrollPos( hWnd, Bar )
```

hWnd   is a handle for the window containing the scroll bar.

Bar   indicates which scroll bar to check. It can be one of the following:

         SB_VERT   the vertical bar
         SB_HORZ   the horizontal bar

The function returns the position of the thumb.

You can use the command **ScrollWindow** to scroll the window. This command moves one portion of the screen directly to another and specifies that a portion of the screen is invalid. First you move part of the screen using **ScrollWindow**; then, you draw in the empty parts of the screen, using **SetWindowOrg** to draw the proper sections. This process is a bit complicated. The advantage of this method is that you only have to redraw the sections of the scrolled screen that weren't present in the old screen. Unless you are dealing with images that have a great deal of detail, and thus take a long time to draw, you are much better off moving the window origin and redrawing the whole screen.

The **ScrollWindow** command has the following format:

```
ScrollWindow( hWnd, XAmount, YAmount, lpInvalidRect, lpClipRect )
```

Miscellaneous Topics 10

hWnd is a handle to the window.

XAmount is the amount to scroll horizontally. This amount is in device coordinates. Use a positive number to scroll the screen right; use a negative number to scroll the screen left.

YAmount is the amount to scroll vertically. This amount is in device coordinates. Use a positive number to scroll the screen down; use a negative number to scroll the screen up.

lpRect is a long pointer to a RECT structure that indicates what part of the window should be scrolled. If this value is NULL, the whole screen will be scrolled.

lpClipRect is a long pointer to a RECT structure that indicates what part of the screen can be updated by the scroll. If this value is NULL, the whole screen is affected.

Instead of using **ScrollWindow**, it is suggested that you clear the screen, change the coordinates that will appear with **SetWindowOrg**, and then redraw the image.

The program TEN has a vertical scroll bar. The program draws lines and is based on the program SEVEN. It can update the window using **ScrollWindow** or **SetWindowOrg**. Following are excerpts from the program that relate to scrolling:

```
/*-------------------------------------------------------
   This procedure receives the messages and decides how to
   process them.
---------------------------------------------------------*/
long FAR PASCAL
MsgServer( hWnd, message, wParam, lParam )
HWND      hWnd;
unsigned  message;
WORD      wParam;
LONG      lParam;
```

continued...

10 Miscellaneous Topics

...from previous page

```
{
    switch (message) {
    case WM_COMMAND:
        return( process_menu_cmds(hWnd, wParam) );
    case WM_PAINT:
        DefWindowProc(hWnd,message,wParam,lParam);

        /* A WM_PAINT message will be sent each time the
           screen is scrolled.  Only redraw the lines the
           scroll method is WINDOW or the scroll position
           didn't change.
        */
        if ((scroll_method_glbl == IDM_SCROLL_WINDOW) ||
            (scroll_chg_glbl == FALSE))
            draw_all_lines(hWnd);

        /* indicate that have updated for the scroll */
        scroll_chg_glbl = FALSE;
        break;

    case WM_LBUTTONUP:
        /* add a point at the mouse position */
        if (cur_pt_glbl < MAX_POINTS)
            add_point(hWnd,MAKEPOINT(lParam));
        break;

    case WM_VSCROLL:
        /* This is the message that there has been activity
           on the scroll bar.  The message can be that a
           new position has arrived, or that the thumb is
           in motion.  We are only interested in new
           positions.  process_scroll_cmds will return
           TRUE if a new position has been chosen.  If not,
           we just use the default scroll bar adjustment
           routines.
        */
        if (process_scroll_cmds(wParam,lParam) != TRUE)
            return( DefWindowProc( hWnd, message, wParam,
                lParam) );
```

continued...

...from previous page

```
            /* the new position is in scroll_pos_glbl.  Thus,
                we need to update the thumb position on the
                scroll bar.
            */
            SetScrollPos(hWnd, SB_VERT, scroll_pos_glbl, TRUE);
            scroll_chg_glbl = TRUE;

            /* if we use the screen scrolling method, scroll
                the screen.  If not, post a message that the
                current window display is invalid.
            */
            if (scroll_method_glbl == IDM_SCROLL_SCREEN)
                ScrollWindow(hWnd, 0, scroll_amt_glbl,
                    (LPRECT) NULL, (LPRECT) NULL);
            else
                InvalidateRect(hWnd, (LPRECT) NULL, TRUE);

            break;

        default:
            return( DefWindowProc( hWnd, message, wParam,
                lParam) );
    }
    return(0L);
}




/*-----------------------------------------------------------
    This procedure processes the scroll commands.  It only
    deals with commands that give a new scroll thumb
    position.  It returns TRUE if the command was processed,
    and FALSE if it wasn't.
------------------------------------------------------------*/
```

continued...

10 Miscellaneous Topics

...from previous page

```
int
process_scroll_cmds( command, pos)
WORD      command;
LONG      pos;
{
    int       retval;

    /* set defaults.  use scroll_amt_glbl = 0 in case try
       to move more than can.  That way, the screen won't
       change because of a thumb adjust position that was
       invalid.
    */
    retval = TRUE;
    scroll_amt_glbl = 0;


    /* scroll_pos_glbl stores the location of the scroll
       thumb.  This value will range between 0 and 100.
       scroll_amt_glbl stores the amount that the screen
       was scrolled.  scroll_amt_glbl is only needed for
       the SCREEN scrolling method.
    */

    switch (command) {
    case SB_LINEUP:
        /* move up one unit */
        if (scroll_pos_glbl > 0) {
            scroll_pos_glbl -= 1;
            scroll_amt_glbl = 1;
        }
        break;
    case SB_PAGEUP:
        /* move up one (arbitrarily sized) page */
        if (scroll_pos_glbl > 20) {
            scroll_pos_glbl -= 20;
            scroll_amt_glbl = 20;
```

continued...

...from previous page

```
            }
            break;
        case SB_LINEDOWN:
            /* move down one line */
            if (scroll_pos_glbl < 100) {
                scroll_pos_glbl += 1;
                scroll_amt_glbl = -1;
            }
            break;
        case SB_PAGEDOWN:
            /* move down one page */
            if (scroll_pos_glbl < 80) {
                scroll_pos_glbl += 20;
                scroll_amt_glbl = -20;
            }
            break;
        case SB_TOP:
            /* move to the top of the page */
            scroll_amt_glbl = scroll_pos_glbl;
            scroll_pos_glbl = 0;
            break;
        case SB_BOTTOM:
            /* move to the bottom of the page */
            scroll_amt_glbl = scroll_pos_glbl - 100;
            scroll_pos_glbl = 100;
            break;
        case SB_THUMBPOSITION:
            /* move to the position passed in pos */
            scroll_amt_glbl = scroll_pos_glbl - LOWORD(pos) ;
            scroll_pos_glbl = LOWORD(pos);
            break;
        default:
            retval = FALSE;
    }

    return (retval);
}
```

continued...

10 Miscellaneous Topics

...from previous page

```
/*-----------------------------------------------------
    Sets up the coordinate system.  If the scrolling method
    is IDM_SCROLL_SCREEN, it is just as in Chapter 7.  But
    if the method is IDM_SCROLL_WINDOW, something very
    different happens.  The point mapped to the viewport
    origin is no longer (0,0).  Instead, the y value is
    shifted down.  This means that the window coordinates
    that will be displayed on the screen are those with
    lower y values.  For example, if the screen is scrolled
    10 units, the coordinates that appear on the screen will
    be those between (0, -10) and (100, 90).

    The scrolling amount was taken directly from the scroll
    position.  The range of values this has is controlled
    by the user.  Thus, it is very easy to scroll over a
    much larger or smaller range.
-------------------------------------------------------*/
set_up_coords( hWnd, hDC )
HWND       hWnd;
HDC        hDC;
{
    RECT       client_rect;

    /* sets mapping mode */
    GetClientRect(hWnd,(LPRECT)&client_rect);
    SetMapMode(hDC,MM_ANISOTROPIC);

    /* if scrolling by adjusting the window, move the
       screen up if the THUMB moves down.  Moving to the
       bottom moves one whole screen full (100 units).
       The window is moved in the opposite direction of
       the thumb to give the effect of moving down (the
       direction of the thumb) the page.  That is, the
       "paper" moves in an equal but opposite direction
       of the thumb.
    */
    if (scroll_method_glbl == IDM_SCROLL_WINDOW)
        SetWindowOrg(hDC, 0, -scroll_pos_glbl);
    else
        SetWindowOrg(hDC,0,0);

    continued...
```

...from previous page

```
    /* the rest is unchanged */
    SetWindowExt( hDC, 100, 100);
    SetViewportOrg( hDC, client_rect.left,
       client_rect.bottom);
    SetViewportExt(hDC, client_rect.right -
       client_rect.left, client_rect.top -
       client_rect.bottom);
}
```

Note the use of **InvalidateRect** in **MsgServer**. This command indicates that a portion of the screen needs adjusting and sends a WM_PAINT message. Its format is as follows:

InvalidateRect(hWnd, lpRect, TRUE)

hWnd is a handle to the window.

lpRect is a long pointer to a RECT structure. This structure should mark (in device coordinates) the area that must be drawn. Set it to NULL to force update of the entire window.

CHILD WINDOWS

You can create a separate window within your program. This window is essentially another program. When the mouse cursor is within the child windows, all system messages are sent to it. When the mouse is in the parent window, all messages are sent to the parent.

There are many uses for child windows. You can use them to set up more powerful dialog-box-like windows for special graphics displays and for utility features. They are also very useful for breaking a window's screen into separate areas of functionality. Dialog boxes are really collections of child windows.

10 Miscellaneous Topics

Like normal windows, child windows can have scroll bars, be moved and sized, call up dialog boxes and message boxes, create their own child windows, and use all system resources. They are essentially a Windows program within a Windows program.

You create a child window with **CreateWindow**. As you may recall from Chapter 2, its format is as follows:

```
HWND
CreateWindow( lpClass, lpTitle, style, xpos, ypos, width, height,
     parent_window, menu, instance, params )
```

Set **lpClass** to the class for the child window. Most likely this class will be different than the parent window's class. The lpfnWndProc parameter of the class determines what procedure gets the messages for the child window. The child window class should be registered in **register__window**.

style can be a combination of the following:

WS__POPUP   creates a window that can appear anywhere on the screen. Don't combine with **WS__CHILD**.

WS__CHILD   creates a window that is clipped to the parent window's area. Don't combine with **WS__POPUP**.

WS__BORDER   gives the window a border.

WS__CAPTION

      gives a caption bar. The text in this bar is specified by lpTitle.

WS__DLGFRAME

      gives the window a double border. Cannot have a caption bar.

Miscellaneous Topics 10

WS__SYSMENU

> gives the window a system menu box with the close option. Combine this with WS__CAPTION.

WS__SIZEBOX

> lets the window be sized. Combine this with WS__CAPTION.

WS__VSCROLL

> adds a vertical scroll bar.

WS__HSCROLL

> adds a horizontal scroll bar.

WS__CLIPCHILDREN

> sets this parameter for all windows that have child windows. In particular, make sure that you include this option for the main window.

xpos and **ypos** specify in device coordinates the location of the upper left corner of the child window. For WS__CHILD windows, these coordinates are relative to the parent's application area. For WS__POPUP windows, these coordinates are relative to the upper left corner of the whole screen.

width and **height** specify the size of the child window in device coordinates.

parent__window should be set to the handle (hWnd) of the parent window.

For WS__CHILD windows, **menu** should be set to a number identifying the child window. Use a different number for each child window you create. Pass this number to the parent window if the child window sends messages to the parent.

Set **instance** to the hInstance value passed to **WinMain**.

10 Miscellaneous Topics

When messages arrive for the child window, they are sent to the procedure specified by its class. This procedure must be an exported FAR PASCAL procedure and should be similar in format to **MsgServer**.

To remove a child window, call **DestroyWindow**. Its format is as follows:

DestroyWindow(hWnd)

hWnd is a handle to the window to destroy.

The parent can send messages to the child window, and vice versa, using **SendMessage** or **PostMessage**. **SendMessage** waits until the message is processed before returning and receives a return value; **PostMessage** does not wait and does not receive a return value.

LONG
SendMessage(hWnd, wMsg, wParam, lParam)

hWnd   is the handle for the window to send the message to.

wMsg   is the message value.

wParam and **lParam** are additional message parameters.

The return value is that returned by the message processing routine of the window to which the message is sent.

PostMessage(hWnd, wMsg, wParam, lParam)

The parameters are the same as for **SendMessage.**

Miscellaneous Topics **10**

USING THE TIMER

Windows has a command, **SetTimer**, that will send a message to your program after a given number of milliseconds has elapsed. This command provides a very useful feature. For example, you could use it in a clock or alarm program to update a display every second or minute. You could also use it to pop up a message after a certain amount of time has elapsed.

Another use is to send messages periodically to an inactive or iconic program, which lets the program check system status or do calculations. Or, if a program wasn't used for an hour, you could reactivate it and ask the user if it was still needed.

The command **SetTimer** sets a timer. Up to sixteen timers can operate at one time. Be sure to check the return value to make sure you could start the timer. After the given amount of time elapses, a WM_TIMER message is sent to the application. This message continues to be sent until the timer is turned off. **SetTimer**'s format is as follows:

```
int
SetTimer( hWnd, TimerId, TimerLength, lpTimerFunc )
```

hWnd   is a handle to the window.

TimerId   is an integer identifying the timer. Use a unique number for each timer a program has running at the same time.

TimerLength   is a WORD indicating the number of milliseconds that should elapse before the timer stops.

297

10 Miscellaneous Topics

lpTimerFunc   should be NULL if you want the timer to send a WM_TIMER message when the timer elapses. Instead of sending this message, you can have the timer automatically call a function. In this case, set **lpTimerFunc** to a long pointer to the function that will be called when the timer elapses. This long pointer should be returned by **MakeProcInstance**. The routine should have the following format:

```
far PASCAL
procedure_name( hWnd, wMsg, nTimerId, dwCurTime )
HWND      hWnd;
WORD      wMsg;
short     nTimerId;
long      CurTime;
```

It is suggested that you set this parameter to NULL and process the WM_TIMER message.

The return value is 0 if the timer wasn't set.

Process the WM_TIMER message as you would any other message. If your program depends on the current time, such as with a clock, you should also want to trap the WM_TIMECHANGE message. This message is sent when the user changes the system time.

Use the **KillTimer** command to stop a timer before or after it elapses. Remember that the WM_TIMER message will continue to be sent until the timer is killed. As you must kill all timers a program uses before the program terminates, trap the WM_DESTROY message. When it is received, kill all timers.

KillTimer's format is as follows:

```
KillTimer( hWnd, TimerId )
```

hWnd   is a handle to the window.

TimerId   is the id number associated with the timer, as set in **SetTimer**.

Miscellaneous Topics 10

PROGRAMS WITH MULTIPLE INSTANCES

If several copies of a program are running, Windows saves memory by loading a new copy of the data but keeping the old copy of the code. In other words, the first time a program is loaded, its code and data are loaded. The next time, only the data is loaded. Since the code doesn't change, there is no need to have more than one copy of it.

You can examine the setting of variables in an earlier instance using the **GetInstanceData** command, as discussed in Chapter 4. **GetInstanceData** copies memory from the earlier instance's data area into the current instance's data area. Since both data areas have the same variables, the offset of the variable in the current instance's data area is the same as that in the earlier instance; thus, by passing Windows the address of the variable, it knows where to find the earlier instance data.

You can use **GetInstanceData** to determine settings of an earlier instance's variables, such as the font selection. You can also get handles to accelerator tables, brushes, and other resources.

CHANGING SYSTEM MENUS

The system menu is the menu that pops up when you click over the striped box in the upper left corner of a window. Normally, this menu allows you to move the window, close the window, and so forth.

You can change the items in the system menu just as you can change items in any other menu. In particular, you can add new options to the system menu. Though you can remove or disable system menu options, it is a dangerous and unrecommended practice.

10 Miscellaneous Topics

First, get a handle to the system menu. Do so with the following:

```
HMENU
GetSystemMenu( hWnd, Option )
```

hWnd   is a handle to the window

Option   is one of the following:

    0   to return a handle to the system menu

    non-zero   to return a copy to the original system menu and destroy a copy of the modified one

The return value is a handle to the system menu.

Add commands using the **ChangeMenu** command.

Trap the WM_SYSCOMMAND message in **MsgServer**. When the value for the commands you have added comes through, take appropriate action. For example, you could pop up a message box describing the program. Send the normal system commands to **DefWindowProc**.

PROGRAM COOPERATION

If your program performs a lot of calculations, the user may want to run another program while it is calculating. If a program enters a long calculation loop, it will have processing time until the loop is finished. The other programs won't get a chance to run.

Miscellaneous Topics 10

If you have a section of code that uses a lot of processing time, such as a lengthy calculation loop, you should add statements that let other programs run at the same time. First, stop all mouse and keyboard messages from being sent to the program; the program won't need to read them for a while, and they will just fill up the message queue. Then, call a procedure that passes messages to procedures for which they are waiting. When the loop finishes, reenable mouse and keyboard input for the window:

```
/* this section is a lengthy calculation loop */
EnableWindow( hWnd, FALSE);
for (i = 0; i  50000; i++) {
    do_long_math_formula( i );
    hog_some_more_time( i );
    pass_control( );
}
EnableWindow( hWnd, TRUE );
```

The procedure **pass_control** should use the **PeekMessage** command to see if there are any messages waiting for other programs. If there are messages, the command passes the messages to these other programs and allows the other programs to process them. When the other programs are finished processing these messages, Windows returns to **pass_control**, which, in turn, returns to the calculation loop:

```
/* this procedure gives other Windows programs a chance
   to run.
*/
pass_control()
{
    MSG      msg;

    if (PeekMessage( (LPMSG) &msg, NULL, NULL, NULL, TRUE )) {
        TranslateMessage( (LPMSG) &msg );
        DispatchMessage( (LPMSG) &msg );
    }
}
```

10 Miscellaneous Topics

To be fancier, you can set up a modeless dialog box with a cancel button. Have **pass_control** check for messages to this dialog box as well. The dialog box can set a global flag telling the calculation loop to terminate. The procedures **PrintAbort** and **DlgPrintAbort** in Chapter 12 perform this function.

The **EnableWindow** command's format is as follows:

```
EnableWindow( hWnd, command )
```

hWnd is a handle to the window to enable or disable.

command is either TRUE or FALSE. If **command** is TRUE, any mouse or keyboard messages that would be intended for the window are passed on to the window. If **command** is FALSE, all keyboard and mouse messages for the window are ignored.

If you disable a window that has a modeless dialog box, reenable the window before you destroy the dialog box.

The **PeekMessage** command checks the message queue for messages. Its format is as follows:

```
BOOL
PeekMessage( lpMsg, hWnd, MinMsg, MaxMsg, RemoveIt )
```

lpMsg is a long pointer to a variable of MSG type. On return from the function, **lpMsg->message** contains the window message, and **lpMsg->wParam** and **lpMsg->lParam** contain any message parameters.

hWnd is a handle to a window. If this value is NULL, **PeekMessage** looks at the message queue for all windows. If it is a particular handle, **PeekMessage** only looks at messages for the particular window.

MinMsg sets the minimum value of messages to examine. Set this value to 0.

MaxMsg	sets the maximum value of messages to examine. Set this value to 0.
RemoveIt	tells whether or not to remove the message from the message queue. If you are using this command to give other applications the chance to run while your program is in a heavy calculation loop, set this value to TRUE and translate and dispatch the corresponding message.

The return value is non-zero if a message was waiting.

If you use **PeekMessage** and another program gets processor time, the data segment of your program could change; thus, any long pointers to local memory variables could become invalid. Be especially careful of this problem for memory models with more than one data segment. You do not need to worry about pointers to global memory variables or short pointers to local memory variables (that is, the segment but not the offsets could change).

KEYBOARD STYLE

Normally, all interaction with Windows is done with a mouse or a similar pointing device. If you want to allow keyboard commands to move the mouse cursor, you must trap all keyboard messages and process them yourself. Refer to the *Application Style Guide* if you decide to do so.

Windows will automatically process certain Alt key combinations to select menu items and switch between Windows programs.

DEBUGGING HINTS

You need two monitors if you want to use SYMDEB to debug a Windows program. If you don't have such a setup, though, you can still debug your program by using standard techniques.

10 Miscellaneous Topics

Place **TextOut** messages or **MessageBox** messages at key points in your program. Use these to print variable values or indicate that a portion of a program was reached. Use a global variable to indicate whether or not these messages should be printed. Add a menu command to set this global variable value to true or false.

For example, you could add the following to a routine:

```
if (debug_glbl == TRUE)
    MessageBox( hWnd, (LPSTR) "Reached the calculation routine",
    (LPSTR) "Debug Message", MB_OK );
```

A PROGRAM: TEN

The following program has a scroll bar and updates the icon. It is based on the line drawing program from Chapter 7. When the thumb is moved on the scroll bar, the screen is updated appropriately. The result is a much larger drawing area (see Figure 10.1).

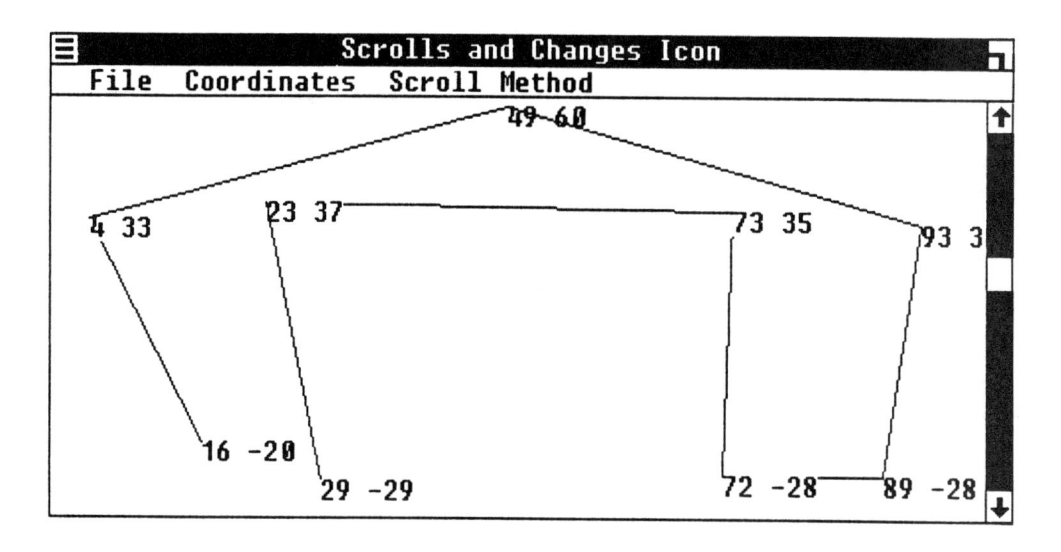

Figure 10.1 The program TEN.

Miscellaneous Topics 10

This program is very similar to SEVEN. Some key differences are the use of WS_VSCROLL in the **CreateWindow** style parameter and the setting of the hIcon parameter in the window class. The scrolling of the image is handled through the change to **set_up_coords**. **MsgServer** and **process_scroll_cmds** process the scrolling messages and decide where to position the thumb.

When you run the program, be sure to use the scroll bar. Note how it changes the values of the coordinates. Make the program iconic. Note how the position of the scroll thumb affects the icon. Also, try the two scrolling methods.

```
/------------------------------------------------\
|                                                |
| The files for this program are in the TEN      |
| directory.  TEN is the make file.  TEN.RC is   |
| the resource file.  TEN.H is the include file. |
| TEN.C is the code.  TEN.DEF is the module      |
| definition file.  The cursor, MIKE.CUR, is in  |
| the root directory.  TEN.EXE is the executable |
| file.                                          |
|                                                |
\------------------------------------------------/
```

The Make File: TEN

```
#
#   Make file for the program from Chapter 10
#

cc=cl -d -c -AS -Gsw -Os -Zpe

.c.obj:
    $(cc) $*.c


ten.obj: ten.c  ten.h

ten.res: ten.rc ten.h mike.cur
    rc -r ten.rc

ten.exe: ten.obj ten.res ten.def
    link4 ten, /align:16, NUL, slibw, ten.def
    rc ten.res
```

10 Miscellaneous Topics

The Resource File: TEN.RC

```
/***********************************************************
    Resource file for TEN
***********************************************************/

#include "windows.h"
#include "ten.h"



face        CURSOR      mike.cur

ten MENU
BEGIN
    POPUP       "File"
    BEGIN
        MENUITEM    "New",          IDM_CLEAR
        MENUITEM    "Open...",      IDM_NULL, GRAYED
        MENUITEM    "Save",         IDM_NULL, GRAYED
        MENUITEM    "Save As...",   IDM_NULL, GRAYED
        MENUITEM    "Print",        IDM_NULL, GRAYED
    END
    POPUP       "Coordinates"
    BEGIN
        MENUITEM    "Print Values",         IDM_COORDS_SHOW,
                                                CHECKED
        MENUITEM    "Don't Print Values",   IDM_COORDS_NOSHOW
    END
    POPUP       "Scroll Method"
    BEGIN
        MENUITEM    "Scroll Screen",        IDM_SCROLL_SCREEN
        MENUITEM    "Scroll Window",        IDM_SCROLL_WINDOW,
                                                CHECKED
    END
END
```

Miscellaneous Topics 10

The Include File: TEN.H

```
/************************************************************
    Include file for the program from Chapter 10.  Contains
    typedefs, constants, and external declarations.
*************************************************************/



extern int PASCAL WinMain();
extern int register_window();
extern long FAR PASCAL MsgServer();
extern long process_menu_cmds();
extern draw_all_lines();
extern add_point();
extern set_up_coords();
extern int process_scroll_cmds();



extern POINT    *pt_list_glbl;
extern int      cur_pt_glbl;
extern int      show_coords_glbl;
extern int      scroll_pos_glbl;
extern int      scroll_amt_glbl;
extern int      scroll_chg_glbl;
extern int      scroll_method_glbl;


#define MAX_POINTS      100

/* constants for menus   */

#define IDM_NULL            0
#define IDM_CLEAR           100
#define IDM_COORDS_SHOW     210
#define IDM_COORDS_NOSHOW   220
#define IDM_SCROLL_SCREEN   310
#define IDM_SCROLL_WINDOW   320
```

10 Miscellaneous Topics

The Code: TEN.C

```
/************************************************************
        File:      ten.c
        Program:   ten

        This is the Windows program from Chapter 10.  It shows
        how to draw on the icon box and how to use scroll bars.
        It is based on the program from Chapter 7.

        Two methods of scrolling are shown.  The first uses a
        system call that the moves the screen display area.
        The second changes the window/viewport mapping.  As
        the window is scrolled, the drawing moves.  New points
        that are added appear at lower y coordinates.

        When the program is made iconic, the icon is a
        miniaturized picture of the drawing from the screen.

        Note that this application uses a different Window
        style than the previous ones, so that it can include
        a scroll bar.
************************************************************/


#include "windows.h"
#include "string.h"
#include "stdio.h"
#include "stdlib.h"
#include "ten.h"
```

continued...

Miscellaneous Topics 10

...from previous page

```
/*-----------------------------------------------------
   global variables
   ---------------------------------------------------*/

POINT    pt_list_glbl[MAX_POINTS];
int      cur_pt_glbl;
int      show_coords_glbl;
int      scroll_pos_glbl;
int      scroll_amt_glbl;
int      scroll_chg_glbl;
int      scroll_method_glbl;




/*-----------------------------------------------------
   This is the Start Up procedure and message relayer
   ---------------------------------------------------*/

int PASCAL
WinMain(hInstance, hPrevInstance, lpszCmdLine, cmdShow)
HANDLE   hInstance, hPrevInstance;
LPSTR    lpszCmdLine;
int      cmdShow;
{
    HWND      hWnd;
    MSG       msg;

    /* If this is the first instance, register the
       window class
    */
    if (!hPrevInstance)
        register_window(hInstance);

    /* Create a tiled window with a vertical scroll
       bar.  Note the use of WS_VSCROLL.
```

continued...

10 Miscellaneous Topics

...from previous page

```
    */
    hWnd = CreateWindow( (LPSTR) "Chap10WIN",
                (LPSTR) "Scrolls and Changes Icon",
                WS_TILEDWINDOW | WS_VSCROLL,
                0, 0, 0, 0,
                (HWND) NULL,
                (HMENU) NULL,
                (HANDLE) hInstance,
                (LPSTR) NULL );

    /* display the window */
    ShowWindow(hWnd,cmdShow);
    UpdateWindow(hWnd);


    /* initialize global variables */
    cur_pt_glbl = 0;
    show_coords_glbl = IDM_COORDS_SHOW;
    scroll_pos_glbl = 0;
    scroll_chg_glbl = FALSE;
    scroll_method_glbl = IDM_SCROLL_WINDOW;


    /* relay all messages to the message server */
    while (GetMessage( (LPMSG) &msg, NULL, 0, 0) ) {
        TranslateMessage( (LPMSG) &msg);
        DispatchMessage( (LPMSG) &msg);
    }

    exit(msg.wParam);
}




/*-------------------------------------------------------------
   This procedure registers the window.  Note that the icon
   parameter is set to NULL.  This allows us to write to the
   icon using any of the standard GDI calls.
   -----------------------------------------------------------*/
```

continued...

...from previous page

```
int
register_window( hInstance )
HANDLE   hInstance;
{
    PWNDCLASS       pClass;

    pClass = (PWNDCLASS) LocalAlloc(LPTR, sizeof(WNDCLASS));
    pClass->hCursor = LoadCursor(hInstance, (LPSTR) "face");

    /* set the icon to NULL, so that we can draw to it using
       GDI calls
    */
    pClass->hIcon = NULL;

    pClass->lpszMenuName = (LPSTR) "ten";
    pClass->lpszClassName = (LPSTR) "Chap10WIN";
    pClass->hbrBackground = GetStockObject(WHITE_BRUSH);
    pClass->hInstance = hInstance;
    pClass->style = CS_HREDRAW | CS_VREDRAW;
    pClass->lpfnWndProc = MsgServer;

    RegisterClass( (LPWNDCLASS) pClass);
    LocalFree( (HANDLE) pClass);
}




/*-----------------------------------------------------------
    This procedure receives the messages and decides how to
    process them.
-------------------------------------------------------------*/

long FAR PASCAL
MsgServer( hWnd, message, wParam, lParam )
HWND      hWnd;
unsigned  message;
WORD      wParam;
LONG      lParam;
```

continued...

10 Miscellaneous Topics

...from previous page

```
{
    switch (message) {
    case WM_COMMAND:
        return( process_menu_cmds(hWnd, wParam) );
    case WM_PAINT:
        DefWindowProc(hWnd,message,wParam,lParam);

        /* A WM_PAINT message will be sent each time the
           screen is scrolled.  Only redraw the lines the
           scroll method is WINDOW or the scroll position
           didn't change.
        */
        if ((scroll_method_glbl == IDM_SCROLL_WINDOW) ||
            (scroll_chg_glbl == FALSE))
            draw_all_lines(hWnd);

        /* indicate that have updated for the scroll */
        scroll_chg_glbl = FALSE;
        break;

    case WM_LBUTTONUP:
        /* add a point at the mouse position */
        if (cur_pt_glbl < MAX_POINTS)
            add_point(hWnd,MAKEPOINT(lParam));
        break;

    case WM_VSCROLL:
        /* This is the message that there has been activity
           on the scroll bar.  The message can be that a
           new position has arrived, or that the thumb is
           in motion.  We are only interested in new
           positions.  process_scroll_cmds will return
           TRUE if a new position has been chosen.  If not,
           we just use the default scroll bar adjustment
           routines.
        */
        if (process_scroll_cmds(wParam,lParam) != TRUE)
```

continued...

...from previous page

```
                return( DefWindowProc( hWnd, message, wParam,
                    lParam) );

        /* the new position is in scroll_pos_glbl.  Thus,
           we need to update the thumb position on the
           scroll bar.
        */
        SetScrollPos(hWnd, SB_VERT, scroll_pos_glbl, TRUE);
        scroll_chg_glbl = TRUE;

        /* if we use the screen scrolling method, scroll
           the screen.  If not, post a message that the
           current window display is invalid.
        */
        if (scroll_method_glbl == IDM_SCROLL_SCREEN)
            ScrollWindow(hWnd, 0, scroll_amt_glbl,
                (LPRECT) NULL, (LPRECT) NULL);
        else
            InvalidateRect(hWnd, (LPRECT) NULL, TRUE);

        break;

    default:
        return( DefWindowProc( hWnd, message, wParam,
            lParam) );
    }
    return(0L);
}


/*-----------------------------------------------------------
    This procedure processes the scroll commands.  It only
    deals with commands that give a new scroll thumb
    position.  It returns TRUE if the command was processed,
    and FALSE if it wasn't.
-----------------------------------------------------------*/
```

continued...

10 Miscellaneous Topics

...from previous page

```
int
process_scroll_cmds( command, pos)
WORD      command;
LONG      pos;
{
    int       retval;

    /* set defaults.  use scroll_amt_glbl = 0 in case try
       to move more than can.  That way, the screen won't
       change because of a thumb adjust position that was
       invalid.
    */
    retval = TRUE;
    scroll_amt_glbl = 0;


    /* scroll_pos_glbl stores the location of the scroll
       thumb.  This value will range between 0 and 100.
       scroll_amt_glbl stores the amount that the screen
       was scrolled.  scroll_amt_glbl is only needed for
       the SCREEN scrolling method.
    */

    switch (command) {
    case SB_LINEUP:
        /* move up one unit */
        if (scroll_pos_glbl > 0) {
            scroll_pos_glbl -= 1;
            scroll_amt_glbl = 1;
        }
        break;
    case SB_PAGEUP:
        /* move up one (arbitrarily sized) page */
        if (scroll_pos_glbl > 20) {
            scroll_pos_glbl -= 20;
            scroll_amt_glbl = 20;
```

continued...

...from previous page

```
        }
        break;
    case SB_LINEDOWN:
        /* move down one line */
        if (scroll_pos_glbl < 100) {
            scroll_pos_glbl += 1;
            scroll_amt_glbl = -1;
        }
        break;
    case SB_PAGEDOWN:
        /* move down one page */
        if (scroll_pos_glbl < 80) {
            scroll_pos_glbl += 20;
            scroll_amt_glbl = -20;
        }
        break;
    case SB_TOP:
        /* move to the top of the page */
        scroll_amt_glbl = scroll_pos_glbl;
        scroll_pos_glbl = 0;
        break;
    case SB_BOTTOM:
        /* move to the bottom of the page */
        scroll_amt_glbl = scroll_pos_glbl - 100;
        scroll_pos_glbl = 100;
        break;
    case SB_THUMBPOSITION:
        /* move to the position passed in pos */
        scroll_amt_glbl = scroll_pos_glbl - LOWORD(pos) ;
        scroll_pos_glbl = LOWORD(pos);
        break;
    default:
        retval = FALSE;
    }

    return (retval);
}
```

continued...

10 Miscellaneous Topics

...from previous page

```
/*-----------------------------------------------------------
    This routine processes commands from the menu
-------------------------------------------------------*/
long
process_menu_cmds( hWnd, command )
HWND     hWnd;
WORD     command;
{
    HDC      hDC;
    HBRUSH   hBr,hBrOld;
    RECT     rect;
    HMENU    hMenu;

    switch (command) {
    case IDM_CLEAR:
        /* because of scrolling, changed this so that it
           clears the client rect.  It is no longer
           guaranteed that the area on the screen is
           (0,0) - (100,100).
        */
        cur_pt_glbl = 0;
        hDC = GetDC(hWnd);
        GetClientRect(hWnd, (LPRECT) &rect);
        hBr = CreateSolidBrush(GetBkColor(hDC));
        hBrOld = SelectObject(hDC, hBr);
        FillRect(hDC, (LPRECT) &rect, hBr);
        SelectObject(hDC, hBrOld);
        DeleteObject(hBr);
        ReleaseDC(hWnd, hDC);
        break;

    case IDM_COORDS_NOSHOW:
    case IDM_COORDS_SHOW:
        hMenu = GetMenu(hWnd);
        CheckMenuItem(hMenu,show_coords_glbl,MF_UNCHECKED
            | MF_BYCOMMAND);
        CheckMenuItem(hMenu,command,MF_CHECKED |
            MF_BYCOMMAND);
        show_coords_glbl = command;
        break;
```

continued...

Miscellaneous Topics 10

...from previous page

```
    case IDM_SCROLL_SCREEN:
    case IDM_SCROLL_WINDOW:
        /* set the scrolling method */
        hMenu = GetMenu(hWnd);
        CheckMenuItem(hMenu,scroll_method_glbl,MF_UNCHECKED
            | MF_BYCOMMAND);
        CheckMenuItem(hMenu,command,MF_CHECKED |
            MF_BYCOMMAND);
        scroll_method_glbl = command;
        break;
    }
    return(0L);

}
```

```
/*-----------------------------------------------------------
   Sets up the coordinate system.  If the scrolling method
   is IDM_SCROLL_SCREEN, it is just as in Chapter 7.  But
   if the method is IDM_SCROLL_WINDOW, something very
   different happens.  The point mapped to the viewport
   origin is no longer (0,0).  Instead, the y value is
   shifted down.  This means that the window coordinates
   that will be displayed on the screen are those with
   lower y values.  For example, if the screen is scrolled
   10 units, the coordinates that appear on the screen will
   be those between (0, -10) and (100, 90).

   The scrolling amount was taken directly from the scroll
   position.  The range of values this has is controlled
   by the user.  Thus, it is very easy to scroll over a
   much larger or smaller range.
-----------------------------------------------------------*/
```

continued...

10 Miscellaneous Topics

...from previous page

```
set_up_coords( hWnd, hDC )
HWND    hWnd;
HDC     hDC;
{
    RECT        client_rect;

    /* sets mapping mode */
    GetClientRect(hWnd,(LPRECT)&client_rect);
    SetMapMode(hDC,MM_ANISOTROPIC);

    /* if scrolling by adjusting the window, move the
       screen up if the THUMB moves down.  Moving to the
       bottom moves one whole screen full (100 units).
       The window is moved in the opposite direction of
       the thumb to give the effect of moving down (the
       direction of the thumb) the page.  That is, the
       "paper" moves in an equal but opposite direction
       of the thumb.
    */
    if (scroll_method_glbl == IDM_SCROLL_WINDOW)
        SetWindowOrg(hDC, 0, -scroll_pos_glbl);
    else
        SetWindowOrg(hDC,0,0);

    /* the rest is unchanged */
    SetWindowExt( hDC, 100, 100);
    SetViewportOrg( hDC, client_rect.left,
        client_rect.bottom);
    SetViewportExt(hDC, client_rect.right -
        client_rect.left, client_rect.top -
        client_rect.bottom);

}
```

continued...

...from previous page

```c
/*-----------------------------------------------------------
    This routine adds a point to the list structure.  It is
    the same as in Chapter 7.
-------------------------------------------------------------*/
add_point( hWnd, pt )
HWND    hWnd;
POINT   pt;
{
    HDC     hDC;
    char    coords[35],temp[10];

    /* set up coordinates */
    hDC = GetDC(hWnd);
    set_up_coords( hWnd, hDC );

    /* convert to the logical coordinate system */
    DPtoLP(hDC, (LPPOINT) &pt, 1);

    /* add the point and draw if possible */
    pt_list_glbl[cur_pt_glbl] = pt;
    if (cur_pt_glbl >= 1) {
        MoveTo(hDC, pt_list_glbl[cur_pt_glbl - 1].x,
            pt_list_glbl[cur_pt_glbl - 1].y);
        LineTo(hDC, pt_list_glbl[cur_pt_glbl].x,
            pt_list_glbl[cur_pt_glbl].y);
    }
    cur_pt_glbl++;

    /* print the coordinates if desired */
    if (show_coords_glbl == IDM_COORDS_SHOW) {
        itoa(pt.x,coords,10);
        itoa(pt.y,temp,10);
        strcat(coords," ");
        strcat(coords,temp);
        TextOut(hDC, pt.x,pt.y, (LPSTR) coords,
            strlen(coords));
    }
    ReleaseDC(hWnd,hDC);
}
```

continued...

10 Miscellaneous Topics

...from previous page

```
/*-------------------------------------------------------
    This procedure draws all the lines.  It is the same as in
    Chapter 7.
---------------------------------------------------------*/
draw_all_lines( hWnd )
HWND     hWnd;
{
    HDC      hDC;

    hDC = GetDC(hWnd);
    set_up_coords( hWnd, hDC );
    if (cur_pt_glbl >= 2)
        Polyline(hDC, (LPPOINT) pt_list_glbl, cur_pt_glbl);
    ReleaseDC(hWnd,hDC);
}
```

The Module Definition File: TEN.DEF

```
NAME        Ten
DESCRIPTION     'Tenth Window Program'
STUB        'winstub.exe'
CODE        MOVEABLE
DATA        MOVEABLE MULTIPLE
HEAPSIZE  4096
STACKSIZE 4096
EXPORTS
            MsgServer @1
```

ADVANCED CONCEPTS: USING THE WIN.INI FILE AND PRINTING

The WIN.INI file describes the system configuration. It tells what programs to run or load when Windows starts, the colors to use for the screen, and, more importantly, what devices are attached. It also tells the default device to use for printing.

Miscellaneous Topics 10

In this section, you will learn how to read the WIN.INI file. By reading the WIN.INI file, you, through your program, can present the user with a list of output devices from which to choose.

There are several sections in the WIN.INI file, each with a title appearing in square brackets. The default printing device is listed in the [windows] section. Its format is as follows:

Device = output_device_name, device_driver_name, port_name

All of the devices available are listed in the [devices] section. Their format is as follows:

device_name = driver_name, port_name

For example, following is an excerpt from a WIN.INI file:

```
[windows]
spooler=yes
DoubleClickSpeed=500
CursorBlinkRate=550
programs=com exe bat
NullPort=None
load=
run=
device=Epson LQ-1500,LQ1500,LPT1:

[extensions]
cal=calendar.exe ^.cal
crd=cardfile.exe ^.crd
trm=terminal.exe ^.trm
txt=notepad.exe ^.txt
ini=notepad.exe ^.ini
msp=paint.exe ^.msp
wri=write.exe ^.wri
doc=write.exe ^.doc
```

continued...

10 Miscellaneous Topics

...from previous page

[colors]

[ports]
LPT1:=
LPT2:=
LPT3:=
COM1:=1200,n,8,1
COM2:=1200,n,8,1

[devices]
Epson LQ-1500=LQ1500,LPT1:

To read the settings from WIN.INI, use the **GetProfileString** function. Its format is as follows:

```
int
GetProfileString( lpSection, lpKey, lpDefault, lpBuffer, Count )
```

lpSection   is a long pointer to an ASCIIZ string naming the WIN.INI section to examine. Set this value to the title of the section. For example, to read the default device, use "windows". To read from the list of available devices, use "devices".

lpKey   is a long pointer to an ASCIIZ string naming the key word to search for. The key word is the word to the left of the equal sign. If it is NULL, the function will return all of the listings in the section. For example, to read the default device, use "device". To get a list of all available devices, use NULL.

lpDefault   is a long pointer to an ASCIIZ string that will be returned in the buffer if the key wasn't found.

Miscellaneous Topics 10

lpBuffer is a long pointer to a character buffer into which the string from the WIN.INI file will be read. Make sure that the buffer is fairly large. Allow at least 80 characters when searching for single responses. If you set lpKey to NULL, allocate room for at least 10 strings.

If the NULL option is specified, all of the strings from the section will be stored in the buffer. Each string will be null terminated. The last string will have two nulls after it.

Count is the maximum number of characters to read. Set this value to the size of the buffer.

The return value is the actual number of characters read.

If you want to let the user choose the output device, read all of the available devices by setting **lpSection** to "devices" and **lpKey** to NULL. Read through the resulting buffer, and copy the device name section of each string into a list box. After the user selects an item from the list box, read the rest of the parameters for that device.

To write to a device, you need only create a display context for the device. Do so with the following:

```
HDC
CreateDC( lpDriverName, lpDeviceName, lpPort, lpInit )
```

lpDriverName is a long pointer to the ASCIIZ name of the device driver.

lpDeviceName is a long pointer to the ASCIIZ name of the device.

lpPort is a long pointer to the ASCIIZ name of the port.

lpInit is a long pointer to initialization data for the device driver. Use NULL if there is no initialization.

The return value is a handle to a display context for the device. If there was an error, the return value is NULL.

10 Miscellaneous Topics

You can use any GDI or text functions to print to the output device.

When you are finished with the display context for a device, remove it with the following:

```
DeleteDC( hDC )
```

hDC is the display context to delete.

PRINTING

This section covers the fundamentals of printing. It will show you how to set up a bare-bones routine for printing. After you read it, you should read Chapter 12, which covers printing in depth and includes an example that you should use as a model for your printing routines.

To print an image, first get a display context for the output device, as discussed earlier. Either use the default printer device or let the user select from the available devices.

All printing goes through the *print spooler*. The print spooler organizes and queues documents sent to the printer from various applications. When you print a document, the spooler is automatically loaded in iconic form. You can bring up this icon if you want to examine the spooler's contents.

There are several commands to communicate with the driver for a device; these commands are used for printing. The commands are sent with the **Escape** command.

Before you start printing, inform the printer that a new job is starting with the following command:

```
Escape( hPr, STARTDOC, TitleLen, lpTitle, NULL )
```

hPr   is a display context for the printer.

STARTDOC   is the constant STARTDOC, which indicates that a document is starting.

TitleLen   is the length of the title for the document. Use **strlen(lpTitle)**

lpTitle   is a long pointer to the ASCIIZ name of the document. This name will be listed by the print spooler.

Now, set up the coordinate system using **SetMapMode**, **SetWindowOrg**, **SetViewportOrg**, and so forth. Execute all GDI and text commands to create the page.

When you are finished creating the page, send the **NEWFRAME** message. This message indicates that a page has finished; all further information will start on a new page:

```
int
Escape( hPr, NEWFRAME, NULL, NULL, NULL)
```

hPr is the display context for the printer. The return value will be less than zero if there was an error.

When you send the NEWFRAME message, the printer's display context will be reset to MM_TEXT. Set your own coordinate system after each NEWFRAME call. If you have an image that covers several pages, you can change the printer display context's window origin so that the graphics from the next page you want to draw appear on the next page on the printer.

Continue setting the coordinate system, making GDI calls, and sending the NEWFRAME message for every page that you want to print.

When you are finished printing, send the **ENDDOC** message:

```
Escape( hPr, ENDDOC, NULL, NULL, NULL )
```

10 Miscellaneous Topics

hPr is a display context handle for the printer.

Then, delete the display context for the printer.

You may want to get information about the display size of the printer. This information tells the size or number of dots on a page. You can use this information when you set up the coordinate system. For example, you could map the coordinate system so that an image uses a whole page. Get the device characteristics with the following:

```
int
GetDeviceCaps( hDC, Param )
```

> **hDC** is a display context handle for the device.
>
> **Param** indicates what information to return. It can be one of the following:
>
>> HORZSIZE — width of the display in millimeters
>> VERTSIZE — height of the display in millimeters
>> HORZRES — width of the display in dots
>> VERTRES — height of the display in dots
>> RASTERCAPS — gets raster display characteristics of the device. The value will be a combination of the following:
>>
>>> RC_BITBLT — supports bit maps
>>> RC_BANDING — supports banding
>>> RC_SCALING — supports scaling
>>
>> For example, to determine if a device supports banding, set **Param** to RASTERCAPS and & the result with RC_BANDING.
>
> There are many additional parameters besides these, but they are not particularly useful for most applications. For a complete listing, refer to the Windows Toolkit reference manual.

Miscellaneous Topics 10

The function returns the value requested by **Param**.

A PRINTING EXAMPLE

The following procedure prints a graphics image. It first gets the default printing device from WIN.INI. It parses this string and creates a display context for the printer. It then sends an image to the printer.

This procedure was created to be added to TEN. To adapt it for a different application, just change the calls that set the coordinate system and display the image.

Note: this procedure is a bare-bones routine. Chapter 12's printing routine includes thorough error coverage and has the ability to abort a document in the middle of printing.

```
/------------------------------------------\
|                                          |
| A version of TEN with the printing routine |
| installed is in the TEN\PRINT directory. |
| TENPRINT.C is the code.  TENPRINT.RC is  |
| the resource file.  TENPRINT.H is the    |
| include file.  TENPRINT is the make file.|
| TENPRINT.EXE is the executable.          |
|                                          |
\------------------------------------------/
```

```
/*-----------------------------------------------------
    This procedure prints a document.  It reads the default
    printer from WIN.INI.  It parses the profile string and
    creates a display context for the printer.  It then
    prints the screen.

    This procedure does not use banding.  It also does not
    trap printing errors.
```
continued...

10 Miscellaneous Topics

...from previous page

```
    The file is sent to the print spooler.  The spooler can
    be used to terminate the job.

    Note that the viewport and window are set after each
    NEWFRAME.  The display size is gotten from the printer
    device characteristics.

    This procedure is written to display the picture from
    TEN.  You can easily substitute other graphics routines
    to use it with a different program.

    Also look over the printing routine in TWELVE.C
------------------------------------------------------------*/
print_it( hWnd )
HWND     hWnd;
{
    HDC      hPr;
    char     devicestring[100];

    /* pointer to device name string */
    char     *device;

    /* pointer to device driver string */
    char     *driver;

    /* pointer to port string */
    char     *port;
    int      width, height;


    GetProfileString( (LPSTR) "windows", (LPSTR) "device",
       (LPSTR) NULL, (LPSTR) devicestring, 100);

    if (*devicestring == NULL)
        /* print a message if there was no printing
            device
        */
        MessageBox( hWnd, (LPSTR) "No device", NULL,
           MB_OK);
```

continued...

Miscellaneous Topics 10

...from previous page

```
else {
    /* skip leading spaces to get the device name.
       Make the device name ASCIIZ.  Note:  the device
       name can contain spaces in it.
    */
    device = strtok( devicestring, ",");

    /* find the driver name -- cannot contain spaces */
    driver = strtok( NULL, ", ");

    /* find the port name -- cannot contain spaces */
    port = strtok( NULL, ", ");

    /* create a display context for the device */
    hPr = CreateDC( (LPSTR) driver, (LPSTR) device,
        (LPSTR) port, (LPSTR) NULL);

    /* print an error message if couldn't create
       the DC
    */
    if (hPr == NULL) {
        MessageBox( hWnd, (LPSTR) "Couldn't create DC",
            NULL, MB_OK);
        return(NULL);
    }

    /* find the size of the display device.  This is
       used to set the window and viewport.  Depending
       upon your application, you may or may not want
       to find the device size.
    */
    width = GetDeviceCaps( hPr, HORZRES );
    height = GetDeviceCaps( hPr, VERTRES );


    /* tell the spooler that a document is coming.  For
       demonstration purposes, it is called "test".
    */
    Escape( hPr, STARTDOC, strlen("test"), (LPSTR)
        "test", NULL);
```

continued...

10 Miscellaneous Topics

...from previous page

```
            /* set the coordinate system.  This must be done
               every NEWFRAME.  This coordinate system is for
               the program TEN.
            */
            SetMapMode(hPr,MM_ANISOTROPIC);
            SetWindowOrg(hPr, 0, -scroll_pos_glbl);
            SetWindowExt(hPr,100,100);
            SetViewportOrg(hPr, 0, height);
            SetViewportExt(hPr, width, -height);


            /* draw the image for the page.  Again, this is for
               TEN.
            */
            if (cur_pt_glbl >= 2)
                Polyline(hPr, (LPPOINT) pt_list_glbl,
                    cur_pt_glbl);

            /* tell the spooler that the page image has been
               sent.  The spooler will print it.
            */
            Escape( hPr, NEWFRAME, NULL, NULL, NULL);

            /* print any other pages here */

            /* tell the spooler that we're finished printing */
            Escape( hPr, ENDDOC, NULL, NULL, NULL );

            /* delete the printer display context */
            DeleteDC( hPr );
        }
}
```

ADVANCED PRINTING FEATURES

There are many additional features you might want to add to the printing routine. These features are used in Chapter 12. When a file is spooling, other programs will not be able to run. Further, if the print spooler is temporarily out of memory, it will abort your print job. You can get around these problems by setting up a procedure to process error messages from the print spooler. Do so with the following:

Miscellaneous Topics 10

```
Escape( hPr, SETABORTPROC, NULL, lpprocAbortProc, NULL )
```

hPr   is a display context for the printer.

lpprocAbortProc

is a long pointer to the procedure that will handle error messages from the print spooler. This pointer should be one returned from a **MakeProcInstance** call. The procedure must be of the following format:

```
BOOL far PASCAL
proc_name( hPr, Code )
HDC      hPR;
short    Code;
```

Code is SP_OUTOFDISK if the spooler is temporarily out of disk space. The return value should be set to TRUE to continue the job; the return value should be set to FALSE to cancel it.

In addition, set up a modeless dialog box that allows the user to cancel the printing at any time and a procedure to process errors when sending data.

The ABORTPROC routine will be periodically called during spooling. You can use it to pass messages to the abort dialog box and to other procedures, which will allow you to work with other procedures while a program is printing. Refer to Chapter 12 for more information and an example of these techniques.

Banding

Some printing devices support a technique called *banding*. Banding allows the display area to be broken into bands, each of which is printed one at a time. This technique reduces the memory requirements. At best, banding is quirky. Avoid it if possible.

Use **GetDeviceCaps** to determine if a printer supports banding.

10 Miscellaneous Topics

The **NEXTBAND** message is used for banding instead of the **NEWFRAME** message. The NEXTBAND message returns the device coordinates for the band. If you can, save time by only drawing items that fall within the band. Use **DPtoLP** to convert the band coordinates to logical coordinates. Send NEXTBAND again to move on to the next band.

```
int
Escape( hPr, NEXTBAND, NULL, NULL, lpRect )
```

hPr is a display context handle for the printer.

lpRect is a long pointer to a RECT structure. The coordinates for the next band will be returned in this structure. If it is the last band for the page, all coordinates will be set to zero.

The return value will be less than zero if there was an error.

Unfortunately, as said previously, banding is quirky. The bands returned by NEXTBAND might not be directly related to the size of the page. Some areas of the page might be covered more than once. The procedure given with the ABORTPROC is not consistently called.

SUMMARY

- Message boxes are a convenient way to send a message to the user. They can contain several buttons, and return the value of the button pressed. The program will not continue until a button is pressed. As an option, no programs will continue until a button is pressed.

- If you set the class icon to NULL, all graphics commands sent when processing the WM_PAINT message will appear in the icon box.

Miscellaneous Topics 10

- Change the window style in the **CreateWindow** command to add vertical and horizontal scroll bars. Process the scroll commands to update the thumb position. Move the window origin to scroll the screen image.

- You can create separate windows within a program by creating child or pop-up windows. These windows can ease and enhance input and output.

- The timer provides a way to send a message to a program after a certain amount of time has elapsed. Up to 16 timers can be active at once. Before a program terminates, it must kill any timers that it is using.

- You can see how variables were set in a previous instance.

- You can change the system menu just as you can any other menu.

- If you have procedures that will take a long time to execute, such as heavy computation loops, use the **PeekMessage** command to let other applications get a share of processing time.

- To let users without a mouse operate programs, you must trap and process all keystrokes yourself.

- Adding an option that will print out variable status can help during debugging.

- The WIN.INI file describes the Windows setup. It includes information on the default printer and on all available display devices.

- To print an image, you must create a display context for the output device. Find the device from the WIN.INI file. You can get information about the device, such as its display size, using **GetDeviceCaps**.

- Printing is done through the print spooler.

10 Miscellaneous Topics

- Start and end documents with the STARTDOC and ENDDOC messages. Send images to print one page at a time. Separate each page with a NEWFRAME message. Set the coordinate system each time you send the NEWFRAME message.

- As an option, set up a modeless dialog box that allows the user to cancel a print operation. Also, set up a procedure to handle error messages from the print spooler.

CHAPTER 11

THE CLIPBOARD

11 The Clipboard

In this chapter, you will learn to transfer data between programs by using the clipboard.

USING THE CLIPBOARD

The clipboard is a way to pass information back and forth between programs. You can copy information from your application to the clipboard or copy information from the clipboard to your application.

Clipboard data can be in several formats. The standard formats are text, bit maps, metafiles, SYLK, and DIF. If the data is in this format, it can be viewed using the CLIPBRD program. You can also create your own data format.

For example, if you have a drawing program and a word processor, you can transfer text from the word processor into the drawing program (using the text format). Also, you can transfer a picture to the word processor (using the metafile format). If you have some scientific applications, you can transfer information between them, possibly with your own format.

Using the clipboard is simple. To retrieve data from the clipboard, you open the clipboard, ask for the data, then close the clipboard. If you want to place data in the clipboard, you open it, clear it, send the data, and then close it.

Information is always transferred to and from the clipboard through global memory blocks. When you send data, you pass a handle to a block of global memory. When you read data, you receive a handle to global memory.

Your application is responsible for formatting and interpreting the data. The clipboard maintains a list of the formats in the clipboard. The application indicates the format it wants to receive. If the clipboard has data in that format, the data is sent. If there isn't any such information, the clipboard reports this condition.

Use the following command to open the clipboard:

```
BOOL
OpenClipboard( hWnd )
```

hWnd is a handle for the window. If the clipboard was opened, the function returns a non-zero number. If the clipboard couldn't be opened, the result is zero.

Because only one program can access the clipboard at a time, be sure to check the return value of **OpenClipboard**. Display a message if you cannot open the clipboard.

Once you have opened the clipboard, clear it using the following:

```
EmptyClipboard()
```

To send data to the clipboard, secure a block of global memory large enough for the formatted data. Lock the block and format the data. Then unlock the block. Do not free or lock the block after you have sent it to the clipboard. Transfer the data using the following:

```
SetClipboardData( Format, GlobHandle )
```

Format	is a WORD that indicates the format of the data that is being sent. It can be one of the following:

    CF_TEXT   ASCIIZ text

11 The Clipboard

CF_METAFILEPICT An image in metafile format. **GlobHandle** points to a structure of METAFILEPICT type. This structure has the following fields:

mm the mapping mode in which the picture was drawn.

xExt, yExt

the size of the picture. If the mode is MM_ISOTROPIC, put a suggested size in MM_HIMETRIC units. The ratio should be the aspect ratio of the original. For MM_ANISOTROPIC, put a suggested size in MM_HIMETRIC units or zeros if the size doesn't matter.

hMF a handle to the metafile

CF_SYLK the data is in Microsoft's Symbolic Link format

CF_DIF the data is in Software Arts' Data Interchange Format

private format number

if you have created a private format, place its number here. Creating private formats is discussed shortly.

There are several other less important formats.

GlobHandle is a handle to a block of unlocked global data. The data in this block is transferred to the clipboard.

To read data from the clipboard, call the following function; it returns a handle to a block of global memory containing the data:

```
GLOBALHANDLE
GetClipboardData( Format )
```

Format is a word indicating the desired format. It can be any of the formats specified in **SetClipboardData**.

If the clipboard contains information in the requested format, the function returns a handle to a block of global memory containing the formatted data. If there was no information in the requested format, the result is NULL.

When you attempt to read from the clipboard, be sure to check the return result. If it is NULL, display a message indicating that no data was available.

If data was available, close the clipboard, lock the memory, and copy the data or process it immediately. Then unlock the handle. Do not free the data. The handle belongs to the clipboard and will be freed at the clipboard's convenience.

Indicate that you are finished with the clipboard by calling the following:

```
CloseClipboard()
```

Because clipboard data is transferred in global memory, you cannot use C functions in a small model program to process it. For example, if you plan to use **memcpy** or **strcpy** to process the information, you must use a model that supports multiple data segments or write your own copy routines that use long pointers. The compact model, used by the program in this chapter, is probably the best model to use. You can also use the large and huge models. If you are unfamiliar with the different memory models, refer to the "Advanced Concepts" section of Chapter 9.

11 The Clipboard

MAKING YOUR OWN FORMAT

For many applications, the built-in formats are not convenient. For example, the program in this chapter is based on the drawing program from Chapter 10; it uses the clipboard to paste an image from one program to another. Both programs keep data in an array of POINTs. Transferring this data with one of the standard formats requires much processing on the sending and receiving ends. Further, the formatted copy would occupy much more memory than the original. A better method is to copy the whole point array—in its binary format—into the clipboard. The receiving application can transfer this block of binary data as is to the end of its point array.

If you have several applications that might benefit from clipboard capabilities that store data in a special format, you should probably make your own clipboard format.

Create a format by registering the format's name with Windows. Windows returns a number to use for the format. This number is passed to **GetClipboardData** and **SetClipboardData**.

All programs that register the same format name get the same format number; thus, any program that knows how to process the particular format can register the format name and transfer data in tnat format through the clipboard.

Use the following command to register a special format:

```
WORD
RegisterClipboardFormat( lpFormatName )
```

lpFormatName   is a long pointer to the ASCIIZ string name of the
format. You can use anything here, for example, "Binary Point Format".

The return value is the format number.

GETTING A LIST OF AVAILABLE FORMATS

Use the **EnumClipboardFormats** command to get a list of formats currently available in the clipboard. Its format is as follows:

```
WORD
EnumClipboardFormats( CurFormat )
```

CurFormat is the number of a format in the clipboard. The function returns the number of the next available format or 0 if there are no other formats.

Set **CurFormat** to 0 the first time you call this function. Feed back the result until there are no more available formats or until you have found a format for which you are looking. For example, you can examine all formats using the following:

```
/* this procedure lists all available clipboard formats */
find_formats()
{
    int        format;
    format = 0;     /* initialize it */
    while (format = EnumClipboardFormats( format ) ) {
        /* format will be sequentially set to all formats
            in the list. Check its value here.
        */
    }
}
```

If your program allows users to paste information from the clipboard, you may want to enable or disable the paste command, depending on whether valid formats are available in the clipboard. Each time WM__INITMENU is received, open the clipboard and check for formats the program can process. If any such formats are found, enable the paste command. If no such formats are found, gray the paste command. Examine the routine **update__menu** in the program at the end of this chapter to see an example.

11 The Clipboard

FORMATTING ON DEMAND

If your program is able to send data to the clipboard in several formats, it should send the data in all the formats it recognizes. This way, the widest variety of applications can receive the data. Transferring data in so many formats can take much time and memory; instead, the application can use the *format on demand* protocol.

With the format on demand protocol, the application doesn't send a handle to data when it issues a **SetClipboardData** call; instead, it calls **SetClipboardData** for all the formats that it recognizes but sets **GlobHandle** to NULL. This procedure informs the clipboard that the program is capable of sending data in that format. The program keeps an unformatted copy of the data that would be sent.

When another application requests data in one of the available formats, the program that sent the data receives a WM_RENDERFORMAT message. The desired format number is passed in **wParam**. The program must format the copy of data that was saved and transfer it with **SetClipboardData**.

If another user empties the clipboard, the program will receive a WM_DESTROYCLIPBOARD message. After receiving this message, you can delete information saved for formatting on demand.

When an application that used the format on demand protocol terminates, it will receive the WM_RENDERALLFORMATS message. At this point, the application should format and send the selected data in all the formats it recognizes.

STYLISTIC CONSIDERATIONS

Most Windows programs that use the clipboard for transferring data do so in a pop-up menu called Edit. This menu usually occurs immediately after the File pop-up menu, and contains at least the following:

```
MENUITEM      "Cut",   ....
MENUITEM      "Copy",  ....
MENUITEM      "Paste", ....
```

The program in this chapter uses such a menu.

A PROGRAM: ELEVEN

The following program uses the clipboard; it is based on the program from Chapter 7. By using the clipboard, the user can transfer a drawing from one instance of the program to another. The image in the clipboard is appended to the end of the receiving program's drawing (see Figure 11.1).

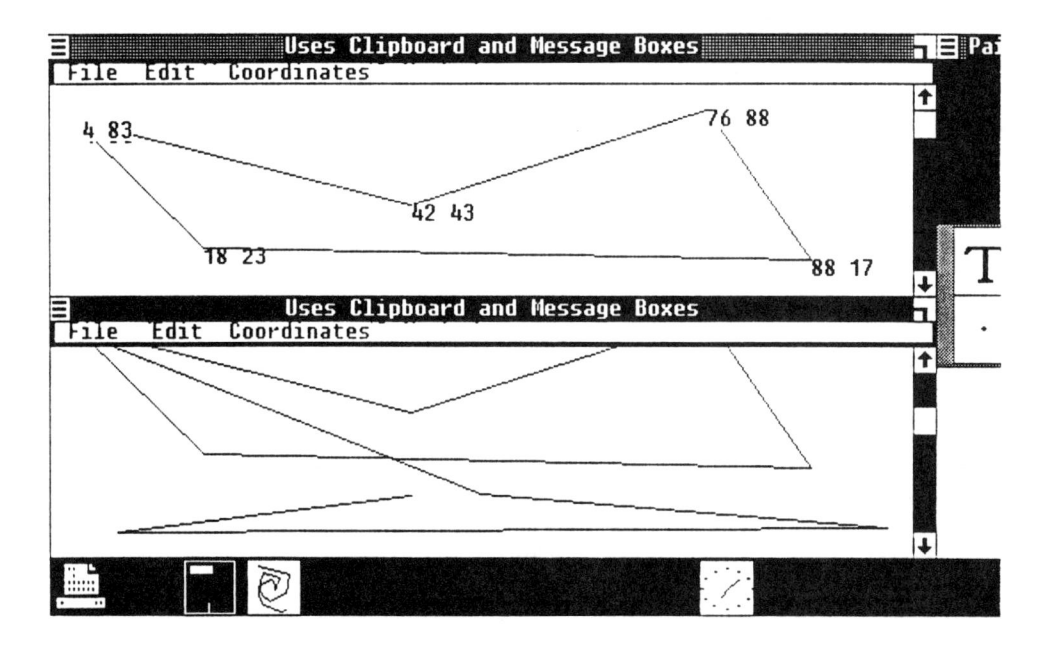

Figure 11.1 The program ELEVEN. The lines from the upper drawing have been pasted to the lower. Also note the line icon at the bottom of the screen.

The program registers its own clipboard format, which is done in **WinMain**. This format is used for efficiently transferring arrays of points. The data is transferred as an array of endpoints. The x coordinate of the first point indicates the number of points in the array. The rest of the array contains this number of points.

11 The Clipboard

The routines **copy_to_clipboard** and **copy_from_clipboard** access the clipboard. Note how they use message boxes if there is an error in accessing the clipboard.

copy_to_clipboard sets up a block of global memory containing enough room for the program's point array, plus an extra entry for the length. It stores the length in the first entry and then uses **memcpy** to copy the list of points. It then transfers the data to the clipboard.

copy_from_clipboard gets a handle to a block of point data using **GetClipboardData**, determines the number of points in the array, and copies them to the end of its point array. If there is not enough room in the point array to add all of the new points, as many points as possible are added. After the points are added, the procedure calls **InvalidateRect** to indicate that the window needs repainting because there are new points to draw in the window.

Because ELEVEN uses **memcpy** to access global memory, it is compiled using the compact memory model. Note the changes to the make file and to the module definition file. Because data pointers are always long in the compact model, using the LPTR option with **LocalAlloc** is no longer valid; thus, **register_window** is changed also.[1]

Run several copies of the program at the same time. Copy data back and forth between them. Be sure to note the effects of scrolling. Also load the CLIPBRD program and the calculator. Note also what happens when you copy a number from the calculator to the clipboard. Try opening the clipboard from two applications at the same time.

This program uses the standard Edit menu style.

---

[1] It would be simpler to create a routine, lmemcpy, that used long pointers to copy one block of memory to another. This program uses the compact model for demonstration purposes.

The Clipboard 11

```
/--------------------------------------------------\
|                                                  |
| The files for this program are in the ELEVEN     |
| directory.  The make file is ELEVEN.  The        |
| resource file is ELEVEN.RC.  ELEVEN.H is the     |
| include file. ELEVEN.C is the code.  The         |
| module definition file is ELEVEN.DEF.  The       |
| cursor, MIKE.CUR, is in the root directory.      |
| ELEVEN.EXE is the executable.                    |
|                                                  |
\--------------------------------------------------/
```

The Make File: ELEVEN

```
#
#  Make file for the program from Chapter 11
#
#  Note that this program uses the compact memory model.
#  Thus, it is able to use long pointers with all of the
#  standard C functions.  This does require some changes
#  to the way it is compiled, in particular, the cc flags
#  and the link4 library.
#

cc=cl -d -c -AC -Gsw -Os -Zpe

.c.obj:
    $(cc) $*.c


eleven.obj: eleven.c  eleven.h

eleven.res: eleven.rc eleven.h mike.cur
    rc -r eleven.rc

eleven.exe: eleven.obj eleven.res eleven.def
    link4 eleven, /align:16, NUL, clibw, eleven.def
    rc eleven.res
```

345

11 The Clipboard

The Resource File: ELEVEN.RC

```
/************************************************************
    This is the resource file for the program from Chapter
    11.
*************************************************************/

#include "windows.h"
#include "eleven.h"


face        CURSOR      mike.cur

eleven      MENU
BEGIN
    POPUP       "File"
    BEGIN
        MENUITEM    "New",          IDM_CLEAR
        MENUITEM    "Open...",      IDM_NULL, GRAYED
        MENUITEM    "Save",         IDM_NULL, GRAYED
        MENUITEM    "Save As...",   IDM_NULL, GRAYED
        MENUITEM    "Print",        IDM_NULL, GRAYED
    END
    POPUP       "Edit"
    BEGIN
        MENUITEM    "Cut",          IDM_NULL, GRAYED
        MENUITEM    "Copy",         IDM_CLIP_COPY
        MENUITEM    "Paste",        IDM_CLIP_PASTE
    END
    POPUP       "Coordinates"
    BEGIN
        MENUITEM    "Print Values",     IDM_COORDS_SHOW,
                                            CHECKED
        MENUITEM    "Don't Print Values", IDM_COORDS_NOSHOW
    END
END
```

The Include File: ELEVEN.H

```
/***********************************************************
    This is the include file for the program from Chapter
    11.  Contains typedefs, constants, and external
    declarations.
***********************************************************/



extern int PASCAL WinMain();
extern int register_window();
extern long FAR PASCAL MsgServer();
extern long process_menu_cmds();
extern set_up_coords();
extern int process_scroll_cmds();
extern draw_all_lines();
extern add_point();
extern copy_to_clipboard();
extern copy_from_clipboard();




extern POINT     *pt_list_glbl;
extern int       cur_pt_glbl;
extern int       show_coords_glbl;
extern int       scroll_pos_glbl;
extern int       scroll_amt_glbl;
extern int       scroll_chg_glbl;
extern WORD      clipboard_style_glbl;

#define  MAX_POINTS      100


/* constant definitions for menus */

#define    IDM_NULL            0
#define    IDM_CLEAR           110
#define    IDM_CLIP_COPY       410
#define    IDM_CLIP_PASTE      420
#define    IDM_COORDS_SHOW     310
#define    IDM_COORDS_NOSHOW   320
```

11 The Clipboard

The Code: ELEVEN.C

```
/************************************************************
        File:       eleven.c
        Program:    eleven

        This is the Windows program from Chapter 11. It
        demonstrates using the clipboard. In particular, it
        shows how to register and use a private format for
        efficient transfer of information between programs.  The
        WM_INITMENU message is used to determine if there is
        data in a valid format in the clipboard.

        This program also demonstrates using the compact memory
        model.  This model was chosen so that the memcpy command
        would work with long pointers.  Because of the change of
        model, eleven, eleven.def, and the procedure
        register_window had to be changed.

        This program also demonstrates using message boxes, and
        LocalLock and Unlock.

        You might like to run this program with CLIPBRD active.

************************************************************/


#include "windows.h"
#include "string.h"
#include "memory.h"
#include "stdio.h"
#include "stdlib.h"
#include "eleven.h"
```

continued...

...from previous page

```
/*-------------------------------------------------
   global variables
-------------------------------------------------*/

POINT    pt_list_glbl[MAX_POINTS];
int      cur_pt_glbl;
int      show_coords_glbl;
int      scroll_pos_glbl;
int      scroll_amt_glbl;
int      scroll_chg_glbl;
int      scroll_method_glbl;
WORD     clipboard_style_glbl;




/*-------------------------------------------------
   This is the Start Up procedure and message relayer
-------------------------------------------------*/

int PASCAL
WinMain(hInstance, hPrevInstance, lpszCmdLine, cmdShow)
HANDLE   hInstance, hPrevInstance;
LPSTR    lpszCmdLine;
int      cmdShow;
{
    HWND     hWnd;
    MSG      msg;

    /* If this is the first instance, register the
       window class
    */
    if (hPrevInstance == NULL)
        register_window(hInstance);
```

continued...

11 The Clipboard

...from previous page

```
    /* Create a tiled window with a scroll bar */
    hWnd = CreateWindow( (LPSTR) "Chap11WIN",
                (LPSTR) "Uses Clipboard and Message Boxes",
                WS_TILEDWINDOW | WS_VSCROLL,
                0, 0, 0, 0,
                (HWND) NULL,
                (HMENU) NULL,
                (HANDLE) hInstance,
                (LPSTR) NULL );

    /* display the window */
    ShowWindow(hWnd,cmdShow);
    UpdateWindow(hWnd);


    /* Register the special clipboard format.  We must save
       this value so that we can use it later.  Every window
       that registers the same format name will get the same
       format number.  Thus, windows that recognize the
       format can transfer information.  We use a special
       format to allow for efficient transfer of numbers.
       In particular, the format will read and write arrays
       of points directly from memory.  The style name will
       appear in the CLIPBRD window if you run that program
       and clip points
    */
    clipboard_style_glbl = RegisterClipboardFormat(
        (LPSTR) "Binary Point Array" );


    /* initialize global variables */
    cur_pt_glbl = 0;
    show_coords_glbl = IDM_COORDS_SHOW;
    scroll_pos_glbl = 0;
    scroll_chg_glbl = FALSE;
```

continued...

...from previous page

```
    /* relay all messages to the message server */
    while (GetMessage( (LPMSG) &msg, NULL, 0, 0) ) {
        TranslateMessage( (LPMSG) &msg);
        DispatchMessage( (LPMSG) &msg);
    }

    exit(msg.wParam);
}
```

```
/*----------------------------------------------------------
    This procedure registers the window.  Because we are
    using the compact model, we can not use the shortcut of
    accessing local memory that we previously used.  Instead,
    we must use the usual routine of locking and unlocking
    memory.
-----------------------------------------------------------*/


int
register_window( hInstance )
HANDLE   hInstance;
{
    PWNDCLASS      pClass;
    LOCALHANDLE    hCl;

    /* allocate the memory.  We can use the fixed class,
       because we will be freeing it immediately.
    */
    hCl = LocalAlloc(LMEM_FIXED | LMEM_ZEROINIT,
        sizeof(WNDCLASS));

    /* lock it and go through the normal registration */
    pClass = (PWNDCLASS) LocalLock(hCl);
```

continued...

11 The Clipboard

...from previous page

```
    pClass->hCursor = LoadCursor(hInstance, (LPSTR) "face");
    pClass->hIcon = NULL;
    pClass->lpszMenuName = (LPSTR) "eleven";
    pClass->lpszClassName = (LPSTR) "Chap11WIN";
    pClass->hbrBackground = GetStockObject(WHITE_BRUSH);
    pClass->hInstance = hInstance;
    pClass->style = CS_HREDRAW | CS_VREDRAW;
    pClass->lpfnWndProc = MsgServer;

    RegisterClass( (LPWNDCLASS) pClass);

    /* now unlock and free the memory */
    LocalUnlock(hCl);
    LocalFree(hCl);
}




/*-------------------------------------------------------
    This procedure receives the messages and decides what to
    do with them.  It is the same as in Chapter 10.
  -------------------------------------------------------*/
long FAR PASCAL
MsgServer( hWnd, message, wParam, lParam)
HWND        hWnd;
unsigned    message;
WORD        wParam;
LONG        lParam;
{
    switch (message) {
    case WM_COMMAND:
        return( process_menu_cmds(hWnd, wParam) );

    case WM_PAINT:
        DefWindowProc(hWnd,message,wParam,lParam);
        draw_all_lines(hWnd);
        break;
```

continued...

...from previous page

```
    case WM_INITMENU:
        update_menu( hWnd );
        break;

    case WM_LBUTTONUP:
        /* add a point at the mouse position */
        if (cur_pt_glbl < MAX_POINTS)
            add_point(hWnd,MAKEPOINT(lParam));
        break;

    case WM_VSCROLL:
        /* process_scroll_cmds is TRUE if the thumb has
           been moved to a new position.
        */
        if (process_scroll_cmds(wParam,lParam) != TRUE)
            return( DefWindowProc( hWnd, message, wParam,
                lParam) );

        /* update the thumb position */
        SetScrollPos(hWnd, SB_VERT, scroll_pos_glbl, TRUE);

        /* update the window */
        InvalidateRect(hWnd, (LPRECT) NULL, TRUE);
        break;

    default:
        return(DefWindowProc(hWnd,message,wParam,lParam));

    }
    return(0L);
}
```

continued...

11 The Clipboard

...from previous page

```
/*-----------------------------------------------------------
    This procedure is called every time the user clicks on a
    menu item.  It checks if there is point data in the
    clipboard.  If there is, the Paste command is enabled.
    If there isn't, the Paste command is grayed.
-------------------------------------------------------------*/
update_menu( hWnd )
HWND      hWnd;
{
    HMENU     hMenu;
    int       clip_format;
    int       paste;

    /* assume that there is no data available */
    paste = MF_GRAYED;

    /* get a handle to the window's menu */
    hMenu = GetMenu( hWnd );

    /* open the clipboard */
    if (OpenClipboard( hWnd )) {

        /* go through the list of available formats.
           If the special point data format is
           available, set paste to MF_ENABLED.
        */
        clip_format = 0;
        while (clip_format = EnumClipboardFormats(
           clip_format ))
               if (clip_format == clipboard_style_glbl)
                   paste = MF_ENABLED;

        /* close the clipboard */
        CloseClipboard();
    }

    /* either enable or gray the Paste menu option,
       depending upon whether the special format
       was available.
    */
    EnableMenuItem( hMenu, IDM_CLIP_PASTE, paste);
}
```

continued...

...from previous page

```
/*-----------------------------------------------------------
    This procedure processes the scroll commands.  It is the
    same as for Chapter 10.  It returns TRUE if the thumb has
    been moved to a new position.
-----------------------------------------------------------*/

int
process_scroll_cmds( command, pos)
WORD      command;
LONG      pos;
{
    int       retval;

    /* set defaults */
    retval = TRUE;
    scroll_amt_glbl = 0;

    switch (command) {
    case SB_LINEUP:
        if (scroll_pos_glbl > 0) {
            scroll_pos_glbl -= 1;
            scroll_amt_glbl = 1;
        }
        break;
    case SB_PAGEUP:
        if (scroll_pos_glbl > 20) {
            scroll_pos_glbl -= 20;
            scroll_amt_glbl = 20;
        }
        break;
    case SB_LINEDOWN:
        if (scroll_pos_glbl < 100) {
            scroll_pos_glbl += 1;
            scroll_amt_glbl = -1;
        }
        break;
    case SB_PAGEDOWN:
        if (scroll_pos_glbl < 80) {
            scroll_pos_glbl += 20;
            scroll_amt_glbl = -20;
        }
        break;
```
continued...

11 The Clipboard

...from previous page

```
    case SB_TOP:
        scroll_amt_glbl = scroll_pos_glbl;
        scroll_pos_glbl = 0;
        break;
    case SB_BOTTOM:
        scroll_amt_glbl = scroll_pos_glbl - 100;
        scroll_pos_glbl = 100;
        break;
    case SB_THUMBPOSITION:
        scroll_amt_glbl = scroll_pos_glbl - LOWORD(pos) ;
        scroll_pos_glbl = LOWORD(pos);
        break;
    default:
        retval = FALSE;
    }

    return (retval);
}




/*-------------------------------------------------------------
    This routine processes commands from the menu.  Note the
    addition of the cut and paste commands.
-------------------------------------------------------------*/
long
process_menu_cmds( hWnd, command )
HWND    hWnd;
WORD    command;
{
    HDC     hDC;
    HBRUSH  hBr, hBrOld;
    RECT    rect;
    HMENU   hMenu;
```

continued...

...from previous page

```
    switch (command) {
    case IDM_CLEAR:
        cur_pt_glbl = 0;
        hDC = GetDC(hWnd);
        GetClientRect(hWnd, (LPRECT) &rect);
        hBr = CreateSolidBrush(GetBkColor(hDC));
        hBrOld = SelectObject(hDC, hBr);
        FillRect(hDC, (LPRECT) &rect, hBr);
        SelectObject(hDC, hBrOld);
        DeleteObject(hBr);
        ReleaseDC(hWnd, hDC);
        break;

    case IDM_COORDS_NOSHOW:
    case IDM_COORDS_SHOW:
        hMenu = GetMenu(hWnd);
        CheckMenuItem(hMenu,show_coords_glbl,MF_UNCHECKED
            | MF_BYCOMMAND);
        CheckMenuItem(hMenu,command,MF_CHECKED |
            MF_BYCOMMAND);
        show_coords_glbl = command;
        break;

    case IDM_CLIP_COPY:
        copy_to_clipboard(hWnd);
        break;

    case IDM_CLIP_PASTE:
        copy_from_clipboard(hWnd);
        break;
    }
    return(0L);
}
```

continued...

11 The Clipboard

...from previous page

```
/*----------------------------------------------------------
    This procedure sets up the coordinate system.  It is the
    same as in Chapter 10
------------------------------------------------------------*/
set_up_coords( hDC, hWnd )
HDC     hDC;
HWND    hWnd;
{
    RECT        client_rect;

    /* sets mapping mode */
    GetClientRect(hWnd,(LPRECT)&client_rect);
    SetMapMode(hDC,MM_ANISOTROPIC);

    /* move the screen up if the THUMB moves down.  Moving
       to the bottom moves one whole screen full (100 units)
    */
    SetWindowOrg( hDC, 0, -scroll_pos_glbl);

    SetWindowExt( hDC, 100, 100);
    SetViewportOrg( hDC, client_rect.left,
        client_rect.bottom);
    SetViewportExt( hDC, client_rect.right -
        client_rect.left, client_rect.top -
        client_rect.bottom);

}




/*----------------------------------------------------------
    This procedure adds a point to the point structure.  It
    is the same as in Chapter 10.
------------------------------------------------------------*/
add_point( hWnd, pt )
HWND    hWnd;
POINT   pt;
{
    HDC         hDC;
    char        coords[35],temp[10];
```
continued...

...from previous page
```
    hDC = GetDC(hWnd);
    set_up_coords(hDC,hWnd);
    DPtoLP(hDC, (LPPOINT) &pt, 1);

    pt_list_glbl[cur_pt_glbl] = pt;
    if (cur_pt_glbl >= 1) {
        MoveTo(hDC, pt_list_glbl[cur_pt_glbl - 1].x,
            pt_list_glbl[cur_pt_glbl - 1].y);
        LineTo(hDC, pt_list_glbl[cur_pt_glbl].x,
            pt_list_glbl[cur_pt_glbl].y);
    }
    cur_pt_glbl++;

    if (show_coords_glbl == IDM_COORDS_SHOW) {
        itoa(pt.x,coords,10);
        itoa(pt.y,temp,10);
        strcat(coords," ");
        strcat(coords,temp);
        TextOut(hDC, pt.x,pt.y, (LPSTR) coords,
            strlen(coords));
    }

    ReleaseDC(hWnd,hDC);
}


/*-----------------------------------------------------------
    This procedure draws all the lines.  It is the same as in
    Chapter 10.
------------------------------------------------------------*/

draw_all_lines( hWnd )
HWND     hWnd;
{
```
continued...

11 The Clipboard

...from previous page
```
    HDC        hDC;

    hDC = GetDC(hWnd);
    set_up_coords(hDC,hWnd);
    if (cur_pt_glbl >= 2)
        Polyline(hDC, (LPPOINT) pt_list_glbl, cur_pt_glbl);
    ReleaseDC(hWnd,hDC);
}
```

```
/*-------------------------------------------------------
    This routine copies the endpoints of all of the points
    to the clipboard.  Could transfer the image by a
    metafile, but we want to add the points to the other
    point list.  To make things quicker and use less memory,
    we will transfer the whole array in binary format, using
    our specially declared format.  Then, we can read it in
    as a block of memory as well.

    In other words, we will copy the whole array, as a chunk
    of memory, to the clipboard.  To add the array to
    another array, we only need to copy the chunk of memory
    to the end of another array and update its point
    pointer.
---------------------------------------------------------*/
copy_to_clipboard( hWnd )
HWND      hWnd;
{
    GLOBALHANDLE    hlist;
    POINT           FAR *mem_pts;
```

continued...

The Clipboard 11

...from previous page
```
    /* Start by opening the clipboard.  If we couldn't open
       it, display a message box.
    */
    if ( !OpenClipboard(hWnd) )
        MessageBox(hWnd, (LPSTR)
            "Could not access clipboard", (LPSTR) NULL,
            MB_OK);

    else {
        /* was able to open it.  First clean it out. */
        EmptyClipboard();

        /* now allocate enough global memory for the copy
           of the data.  We will add an array element and
           store the number of points in the x coordinate
           of this first entry.  We allocate a little more
           memory than necessary, for good luck.
        */
        hlist = GlobalAlloc(GMEM_MOVEABLE, (long)
            (cur_pt_glbl + 2) * sizeof(POINT) + 1);
        mem_pts = (POINT FAR *) GlobalLock( hlist );

        /* Now we store the number of points we are
           transferring
        */
        mem_pts[0].x = cur_pt_glbl;

        /* now we copy the data from the point array to the
           global block.  Note that we copy it to the area
           after the zeroth entry, so that we don't write
           over mem_pts[0].x
        */
        memcpy( (char FAR *) &mem_pts[1], (char FAR *)
            pt_list_glbl, cur_pt_glbl * sizeof(POINT) );

        /* Now we unlock the memory block */
        GlobalUnlock( hlist );

        /* now transfer it.  Note the use of
           clipboard_style_glbl
        */
        SetClipboardData(clipboard_style_glbl, hlist);
```
continued...

11 The Clipboard

...from previous page

```
        /* close the clipboard */
        CloseClipboard();
    }

}



/*-----------------------------------------------------------
   This routine copies data from the clipboard.  It opens
   the clipboard and tries to get data in the special Binary
   Points Array format.  If it couldn't open the clipboard
   or there wasn't any points data in it, it prints and
   error message through a message box.

   If there was data, it finds how many points there were,
   adjusts the number so as not to overflow the pt_list
   array, and then memcpy's the new points to the end of the
   current point list array.
-------------------------------------------------------------*/

copy_from_clipboard( hWnd )
HWND      hWnd;
{
    GLOBALHANDLE   hNewlist;
    POINT          FAR *newlist;
    int            num_pts;


    /* Try to open the clipboard */
    if ( !OpenClipboard(hWnd) )
        /* if we couldn't open up the clipboard, print a
            message.  This message really should be loaded
            in from a string table
        */
        MessageBox(hWnd, (LPSTR)
            "Could not access clipboard", (LPSTR) NULL,
            MB_OK);
```

continued...

...from previous page
```
    else {
        /* was able to open it.  Try to read in
           point data
        */
        hNewlist = GetClipboardData(clipboard_style_glbl);

        /* hNewlist will be a global memory handle if the
           read was successful
        */
        if ( !hNewlist )
            /* we couldn't find any point data in the
               clipboard.  This shouldn't occur, because
               the paste option is disabled if no point
               data is available.
            */
            MessageBox(hWnd, (LPSTR)
                "No point data in clipboard",
                (LPSTR) NULL, MB_OK);

        else {
            /* data was available.  lock the memory */
            newlist = (POINT FAR *) GlobalLock(hNewlist);

            /* find the number of points */
            num_pts = newlist[0].x;

            /* make sure that there aren't too many
               new points
            */
            if (num_pts + cur_pt_glbl >= MAX_POINTS)
                num_pts = MAX_POINTS - cur_pt_glbl;

            /* now copy the data and update the number
               of points
            */
            memcpy( (char FAR *)
                &pt_list_glbl[ cur_pt_glbl ],
                (char FAR *) &newlist[1],
                num_pts * sizeof(POINT) );

            cur_pt_glbl += num_pts;
```
continued...

11 The Clipboard

...from previous page

```
            /* unlock the global memory */
            GlobalUnlock( hNewlist );

            /* because new points have been added, we want
                to redraw the screen
            */
            InvalidateRect(hWnd, (LPRECT) NULL, TRUE);
        }
        /* close the clipboard */
        CloseClipboard();
    }
}
```

The Module Definition File: ELEVEN.DEF

```
NAME        Eleventh
DESCRIPTION 'Eleventh Window Program - FIXED data'
STUB        'winstub.exe'
CODE        MOVEABLE
DATA        FIXED
HEAPSIZE  4096
STACKSIZE 4096
EXPORTS
        MsgServer @1
```

SUMMARY

- You can use the clipboard to transfer information between programs.

- There are several formats for transferring data. In addition, you can make your own format.

- To put data in the clipboard, open the clipboard, empty it, transfer the information, and close it. To get data from the clipboard, open it, get the information, and close it.

The Clipboard 11

- You can use **EnumClipboardFormats** to see if data is available in the clipboard in a format your program can use. Disable or enable the paste option, depending on the result.

- Clipboard data is transferred using global memory. If you plan to use C functions to process this memory, you must use the compact, large, or huge memory model. You can also write your own routines to access the data through long pointers.

- A program should transfer data in all the formats it knows. It can also format by demand.

- A program that uses the format by demand protocol needs to keep a copy of the data to put in the clipboard. When another application reads the clipboard, it will request this data.

- Before a program that uses the format by demand protocol terminates, it should transfer the data in all the formats that it knows.

CHAPTER 12

BIT MAPS AND ADVANCED PRINTING

12 Bit Maps and Advanced Printing

Bit maps are a powerful graphics feature; they allow you to quickly transfer and replicate complex images. This chapter discusses creating, displaying, and transferring bit maps. In addition, this chapter covers printer error routines and concludes with a program demonstrating how to print bit maps.

WHAT ARE BIT MAPS?

Graphics screens are composed of row after row of tiny dots called *pixels*. The value of each pixel is stored in the graphics screen's display memory. Depending on the type of screen, it may take part of a byte or many bytes to represent each pixel.

When you draw on the screen, for example, using GDI, the resulting picture is just a pattern formed by many separate dots; thus, a picture that starts out as a continuous image—a collection of curves—becomes a discrete image—a collection of dots.

Bit maps are graphics images in their dot-by-dot form. Rather than containing information on how an image was drawn, bit maps are a direct memory image of the drawing. Bit maps are always rectangular.

For example, suppose you are in MM_TEXT mode. You draw an ellipse in the box (0,0) - (10,10), which turns a set of the dots on the screen on or off. If you were to cut out the memory used for the 121 dots between (0,0) and (10,10), you would have a bit map picture of the ellipse.

WHY USE BIT MAPS?

Bit maps allow fast and compact transfer of images. Unlike metafiles, they do not store a series of commands used to make an image; they store the result of the commands. If you copied an image several times using a metafile, you would redraw it each time. If you used a bit map, you would simply copy a block of memory from one part of the screen to another, and the process would be very fast.

Bit Maps and Advanced Printing 12

Depending on an image's size, bit maps are a very compact way to represent an image. For example, suppose it takes one bit to represent each dot in a bit map. An 8 by 8 bit map would use 8 bytes. Suppose you drew a freehand picture in the bit map's portion of the screen. You would need to store the end points of each dot, line, or circle drawn, color selections, and much other data. This process would easily use more than 8 bytes.

While bit maps are fast and compact, they do not preserve the full information of a picture. For example, when you stretch a bit map to fill a screen, the edges appear more jagged. An expanded bit map of a circle has large squares where each pixel gets blown up. If you stretch a metafile or a circle command, the edges do not appear more jagged. The mathematical formula behind the drawing command is continuous.

Bit maps are useful for cutting, moving, and replicating portions of an image. They are also useful for transferring images initially drawn dot by dot or images that won't expand. For example, if you wanted to make a freehand drawing of a mountain and then cut and move the scenery, you would use bit maps. If you wanted to draw a line graph in different parts of the screen, you wouldn't use bit maps. Icons are bit maps.

A BIT MAP'S STRUCTURE

As mentioned, bit maps are a collection of bits that represent dots on a screen. Depending on the display device, these bits may take different formats. Some displays have separate *planes* for each color. Some use an indexing scheme. Fortunately, you do not need to worry about the actual memory format. Windows is set up to copy bit maps from all the devices it supports and transfer them to any other device.

Bit maps are always accessed through bit-map handles. These are of type HBITMAP. Among other things, these handles contain a pointer to a BITMAP structure. This structure indicates the size and format of the bit map and contains a pointer to the actual bit map data. Its form is as follows:

12 Bit Maps and Advanced Printing

Bit Map Structure:

Variable	Content
bmWidth	width of bit map in pixels
bmHeight	height of bit map in pixels
bmWidthBytes	bytes per row of pixels. The bit map uses bmHeight * bmWidthBytes of storage.
bmPlanes	number of color planes
bmBitsPixel	number of bits per pixel per plane
bmBits	a long pointer to an array containing the pixel values

DISPLAYING BIT MAPS

You will start by learning how to display a bit map, which will introduce you to the basic terminology. Then, you will learn how to make bit maps.

For a bit map to be displayed, it must first be associated with a display context. The bit map becomes the display memory used for this display context; the display context is useful for creating bit maps, as you will see shortly. Because the bit map becomes the display memory, however, you can't associate bit maps with the display context for a device. Instead, you must create a memory display context. You do so with the **CreateCompatibleDC** function.

The **CreateCompatibleDC** function creates a display context structure that has the same characteristics as another DC, only it is not associated with a physical device; thus, you can use it to convert logical to physical coordinates or for drawing objects and so forth. Instead of the results appearing on a printer or on the screen, the results are written to the bit map associated with the DC.

Bit Maps and Advanced Printing 12

CreateCompatibleDC's format is as follows:

```
HDC
CreateCompatibleDC( hDC )
```

The resulting handle will be a memory display context with the same display features as the DC passed through hDC, which means that any calls to **GetDeviceCaps** and so forth will have the same results with the memory display context as with the physical display context. Note, however, that coordinate system settings and other parameters are not copied. The new DC has the default attribute settings.

Once you have created a memory DC for device, associate the bit map with it by using **SelectObject**. Be sure to save the returned value so that you can restore the original value later.

Then, use the **BitBlt** and **StretchBlt** functions, discussed shortly, to display the bit map.

When you are finished with the memory display context, free it with **DeleteDC**.

BITBLT AND STRETCHBLT

BitBlt and **StretchBlt** are the two commands used to transfer bit maps. They stand for bit block transfer and stretched bit block transfer. Both of these commands move a bit map from one display context to another, converting the bit format as necessary. **BitBlt** preserves the size of the bit map; **StretchBlt** allows it to be stretched.

12 Bit Maps and Advanced Printing

Following is the format of the two commands:

```
BitBlt( hDestDC, xdest, ydest, width, height, hSrcDC, xsrc,
ysrc, CombineStyle)
```

hDestDC is the display context to which the bit map will be copied or displayed.

xdest is the x location, in logical coordinates, to which the bit map will be copied.

ydest is the y location, in logical coordinates, to which the bit map will be copied.

width is the width, in the logical coordinates of **hDestDC**, of the location to which the bit map will be copied. This width will be used to determine how many columns of pixels to copy from the bit map.

height is the height, in the logical coordinates of **hDestDC**, of the location to which the bit map will be copied. This height will be used to determine how many rows of pixels to copy from the bit map.

hSrcDC is the display context with which the bit map is associated.

xsrc is the x coordinate, in the logical units of **hSrcDC**, from which to start copying pixels.

ysrc is the y coordinate, in the logical units of **hSrcDC**, from which to start copying pixels.

CombineStyle indicates how to combine the pixels of the bit map with any pixels already drawn on **hDestDC**. See the table of Combine Styles. You will typically use SRCCOPY.

Note that the **xsrc** and **ysrc** parameters allow you to define what portion of the bit map to copy. Typically, you will set these parameters both to 0.

Bit Maps and Advanced Printing 12

```
StretchBlt( hDestDC, xdest, ydest, destwidth, destheight,
    hSrcDC, xsrc, ysrc, srcwidth, srcheight, CombineStyle)
```

hDestDC is the display context to which the bit map will be copied or displayed.

xdest is the x location, in the logical coordinates of **hDestDC**, to which the bit map will be copied.

ydest is the y location, in the logical coordinates of **hDestDC**, to which the bit map will be copied.

destwidth is the width, in logical coordinates, of the location to which the bit map will be copied.

destheight is the height, in logical coordinates, of the location to which the bit map will be copied.

hSrcDC is the display context with which the bit map is associated.

xsrc is the x coordinate, in the logical units of **hSrcDC**, from which to start copying pixels.

ysrc is the y coordinate, in the logical units of **hSrcDC**, from which to start copying pixels.

srcwidth is the width, in the logical coordinates of **hSrcDC**, of the bit map to copy.

srcheight is the height, in the logical coordinates of **hSrcDC**, of the bit map to copy.

CombineStyle indicates how to combine the pixels of the bit map with any pixels already drawn on **hDestDC**. See the table of Combine Styles. You will typically use SRCCOPY.

StretchBlt will take all the pixels from the rectangle (**srcx, srcy**)−(**srcx + srcwidth, srcy + srcheight**)−and stretch them to fit in the rectangle (**destx, desty**)−(**destx + destwidth, desty + destheight**). Typically, **srcx** and **srcy** will be 0, and **srcwidth** and **srcheight** will be the size of the whole bit map.

12 Bit Maps and Advanced Printing

For example, suppose you have a handle to a bit map, **hBit**. It is 10 pixels wide and 15 pixels high. You want to draw on your display screen. You already have a display context handle, **hDC**, for the display screen.

Start by creating a compatible display context for **hDC**:

```
hMemDC = CreateCompatibleDC( hDC );
```

Now, associate the bit map with this display context:

```
hOldBM = SelectObject( hMemDC, hBit );
```

You want to display this bit map on the screen starting at the coordinate (120, 23). The mapping mode for the screen is also MM_TEXT:

```
BitBlt( hDC, 120, 23, 10, 15, hMemDC, 0, 0, SRCCOPY );
```

Now you want to make a copy of the bit map that is 22 by 34 dots, and place it at (200, 50). You could do the following:

```
StretchBlt( hDC, 200, 50, 22, 34, hMemDC, 0, 0, 10, 15, SRCCOPY );
```

Having finished, restore the original bit map to the memory display context, then delete the DC:

```
SelectObject( hMemDC, hOldBM );
DeleteDC( hMemDC );
```

This example moved the bit map between two display contexts that used the MM_TEXT mapping mode. As you will see in the sections on creating and copying bit maps, the display context holding the bit map should always be in MM_TEXT mode. If you want to copy the bit map to a display context not using MM_TEXT, use the **StretchBlt** command. The **BitBlt** command will determine the number of pixels to transfer based on the number of pixels in the destination rectangle. Depending on the resolution of the destination device, this process could result in different numbers of pixels; thus, the amount of the bit map that is transferred will vary. If the size is too big, garbage will be transferred.

For example, suppose you have the same 10 by 15 bit map from the previous example. This time, you want to transfer it to a one-inch by one-and-a-half-inch section of the screen. The destination screen is in MM_LOENGLISH. You would do the following:

```
StretchBlt( hDC, 300, 300, 100, 150, hMemDC, 0, 0, 10, 15,
    SRCCOPY);
```

which will work fine, no matter if the destination DC is for a 60-pixel-per-inch display screen or a 300-pixel-per-inch laser printer.

THE COMBINE STYLE OPTIONS

When you copy a bit map to a display, there may already be a pattern in the area where the bit map will be copied. The **CombineStyle** parameter of **BitBlt** and **StretchBlt** allows you to specify how the new bit map and the old pattern will be combined. There are many different options:

Bit Map Copy Styles:

CombineStyle	Meaning
SRCCOPY	The bit maps from the source are copied directly to the destination. All destination bits are overwritten.
NOTSRCCOPY	The bit maps from the source are inverted (logical not) and then copied directly to the destination. All destination bits are overwritten.

12 Bit Maps and Advanced Printing

SRCPAINT
: The destination bits are ORed with the source bits; thus, the pictures are merged together, which is useful for pasting bit maps without having the blank areas of the source rectangle overwrite what is underneath in the destination rectangle.

SRCAND
: The destination and source bits are ANDed together. Only bits set in both maps are displayed.

SRCERASE
: The destination bits are inverted then ANDed with the source bits—dest = source AND !dest. Any areas of the destination that are blank will be overwritten. Areas that aren't blank will be cleared.

SRCINVERT
: The two bit maps are XORed together, which allows a bit map to be moved across a screen without disturbing the background. If you SRCINVERT the same bit map twice, the original background is fully restored, which is useful for letting a user see how a bit map will look on the screen before actually copying it.

NOTSRCERASE
: The result is (not source) AND (not dest). Only bits that were blank in both the source and destination areas will be set. All pixels that were set in either map will be blank.

DSTINVERT
: All pixels in the destination rectangle will be inverted.

MERGECOPY
: The destination bits will be set to the source bit map ANDed with the currently selected brush, which "brushes" over the source bit map, blanking any pixels not set in the corresponding position in the brush.

MERGEPAINT
: The destination bits will be ORed with the source bit map ANDed with the currently selected brush.

PATINVERT
: The destination is XORed with the currently selected brush.

The most useful options are SRCCOPY, SRCPAINT, and SRCINVERT.

Bit Maps and Advanced Printing 12

MAKING A BIT MAP

You can create a bit map using GDI calls or by copying a section of an already created image. To make a bit map using GDI calls, you need to create a memory display context, create a blank bit map for that display context, and then execute a series of GDI calls. The calls will write into the bit map. Delete the display context when you are finished.

Make the memory display context using **CreateCompatibleDC**. Make the blank bit map using the **CreateCompatibleBitmap** function. This function creates a bit map that has a format compatible with the display structure of a particular display context. You can use that bit map as the "screen memory" for a memory display context.

CreateCompatibleBitmap's format is as follows:

```
BOOL
CreateCompatibleBitmap( hDC, width, height )
```

hDC is the display context with which the bit map will be compatible.

width is the width of the bit map in pixels.

height is the height of the bit map in pixels.

The result is FALSE if the bit map couldn't be made. Note that the units are in pixels. Bit maps cannot use more than 64K memory.

Make sure that the bit map that you create is large enough to contain all the GDI calls you will send to it. You can change the mapping mode of the memory display context if it is convenient.

For example, suppose you want to make a bit map that is a pie chart. Create a bit map that is large enough to hold the chart. If you make the chart in MM_TEXT mode, make the bit map big enough to hold the extents of the ellipse. If you use a different mapping mode, use **LPtoDP** to determine the size in pixels. Draw the pie chart using GDI functions, such as **Pie**. You can then use the bit map.

The following example creates a bit map with a few lines in it:

```
hMemDC = CreateCompatibleDC( hDC );
hBitmap = CreateCompatibleBitmap( hDC, 10, 10 );
SelectObject( hMemDC, hBitmap );
MoveTo( hMemDC, 0, 0 );
LineTo( hMemDC, 6, 2 );
LineTo( hMemDC, 3, 9 );
/* now draw it */
StretchBlt( hDC, 10, 10, 40, 40, hMemDC, 0, 0, 10, 10, SRCCOPY );
DeleteDC( hMemDC );
/* you can still use the hBitmap handle */
```

CREATING A BIT MAP FROM AN EXISTING IMAGE

You can also copy an already existing image into a bit map, which is useful for cutting and pasting sections of a screen or moving part of an image from one program to another.

To copy an existing image, create a compatible DC and a bit map for the DC, using **CreateCompatibleDC**, **CreateCompatibleBitmap**, and **SelectObject**, just as you did when drawing into a bit map with GDI. Then, use the **StretchBlt** or **BitBlt** command to move a section of the screen to the compatible DC.

For example, suppose you want to copy the rectangle (10, 10) - (45, 60) to a bit map that has the same size. You could do the following:

```
hMemDC = CreateCompatibleDC( hDC );
hBitmap = CreateCompatibleBitmap( hMemDC, 35, 50 );
BitBlt( hMemDC, 0, 0, 35, 50, hDC, 10, 10, SRCCOPY );
DeleteDC( hMemDC );
```

TIPS ON SUCCESSFULLY USING BIT MAPS

There are several problems that can occur when copying a bit map from a memory DC to a screen DC. If the source size that you specify with **BitBlt** or **StretchBlt** is larger than the actual source bit map size, you will get garbage on your screen. You may also have strange results if you specify the source size in non-MM_TEXT coordinates; therefore, you should always use the MM_TEXT mode for the source DC if it is a memory DC. Keep a record of the size of the bit map in pixels. Use these numbers when specifying the source size of the bit map.

If you want to keep the bit map size constant—for example, if you always want it to be 3 inches by 1.3 inches—keep these measurements also. You might want to determine the measurement when you first create the bit map. If you are copying it from an MM_TEXT mode screen, you can convert the size to inches, meters, or twips by setting up a display context with MM_LOENGLISH, MM_LOMETRIC, or so forth, and using **DPtoLP**.

For example, you might use the following data structure for storing bit maps:

```
typedef struct bitstruc {
POINT    bitsize;
POINT    inchsize;
HBITMAP  hMap;
} bitstruct;
```

COPYING A BIT MAP USING THE CLIPBOARD

You can easily pass bit maps between programs using the clipboard. Bit maps are indicated by the CF_BITMAP format. To pass a bit map to the clipboard, select the CF_BITMAP format and send a handle to the bit map to the clipboard.

When you get a bit map from the clipboard, you get a handle to the bit map. This handle, however, belongs to the clipboard, so you need to make a copy of the data. To do so, you need to copy the bit map.

12 Bit Maps and Advanced Printing

The first step is to determine the size and format of the bit map data. Do so using the **GetObject** command. This command copies all of the information associated with a particular handle. In this case, it copies all of the information about the bit map, except for the pixels. Next, create a compatible DC and a compatible bit map. **BitBlt** the clipboard bit map into this bit map.

The format of **GetObject** is as follows:

```
int
GetObject( hObject, size, lpBuffer )
```

hObject is a handle to the object to be copied. It can be a HPEN, HBRUSH, HFONT, or HBITMAP.

size is the number of bytes to copy. It should be **sizeof(LOGPEN)**, **sizeof(LOGBRUSH)**, **sizeof(LOGFONT)**, or **sizeof(BITMAP)**.

lpBuffer is a long pointer to the buffer that will receive the copied data. It should be of type LOGPEN, LOGBRUSH, LOGFONT, or BITMAP.

The information of **hObject** will be copied to the indicated buffer. With bit maps, only the description, not the actual bits, will be copied. The function returns the number of bytes copied.

For example, the following routine gets passed a handle to a bit map and a handle to a display context, and then returns a handle to a copy of the bit map, in a format compatible with the display context:

Bit Maps and Advanced Printing 12

```c
/* this routine makes a copy of a bitmap.  You may want to
   have it return the dimensions of the bitmap as well.
*/

HBITMAP
copy_bitmap( hDestDC, hSrcBitmap )
HDC      hDC;
HBITMAP  hSrcBitmap;
{
    HDC      hMemDC, hSrcDC;
    HBITMAP  hCopyBitmap;
    BITMAP   mapinfo;

    /* create compatible display contexts */
    hMemDC = CreateCompatibleDC( hDestDC );
    hSrcDC = CreateCompatibleDC( hDestDC );

    /* copy the information describing the bitmap format */
    GetObject(hSrcBitmap, sizeof(BITMAP), (LPSTR)&mapinfo);

    /* create an empty bitmap into which the info. will
       be copied.  Make it the same size as the original
       bitmap, but compatible with hDestDC.
    */
    hCopyBitmap = CreateCompatibleBitmap( hMemDC,
        mapinfo.bmWidth, mapinfo.bmHeight);

    /* associate the source and target bitmaps with DC's */
    SelectObject( hMemDC, hCopyBitmap );
    SelectObject( hSrcDC, hSrcBitmap );

    /* copy the pixels from the source bitmap to the copy
       bitmap
    */
    BitBlt(hMemDC, 0, 0, mapinfo.bmWidth, mapinfo.bmHeight,
        hSrcDC, 0, 0, SRCCOPY);

    /* delete the memory display contexts */
    DeleteDC( hSrcDC );
    DeleteDC( hMemDC );

    /* return a handle to the copied bitmap */
    return( hCopyBitmap );
}
```

12 Bit Maps and Advanced Printing

SAVING AND LOADING BIT MAPS

You can also save and load bit maps to disk. To save a bit map, use **GetObject** to copy the bit map description to a BITMAP structure. Save this structure to disk. Then use the **GetBitmapBits** command to copy all the bit map pixel data to an array. Save this array to disk.

To load a bit map from disk, read in the bit map description data and read the bit map pixel data into an array. Then, use the **CreateBitmap** function to create the bit map.

The format of **GetBitmapBits** is as follows:

```
LONG
GetBitmapsBits( hBitmap, count, lpBits )
```

hBitmap	is the handle of the bit map containing the pixels to be read.
count	is an unsigned long integer telling the number of bytes to be copied.
lpBits	is a long pointer to the buffer into which the bit map bits will be copied.

Note that **count** specifies the number of bytes, not pixels, to copy. The return value is the number of bytes copied.

The format of **CreateBitmap** is as follows:

```
HBITMAP
CreateBitmap( width, height, planes, bits_per_pixel, lpBits )
```

width	is the width of the bit map in pixels.
height	is the height of the bit map in pixels.
planes	is the number of color planes.
bits_per_pixel	is the number of bits per pixel.

Bit Maps and Advanced Printing 12

lpBits   is a long pointer to an array containing the pixels to be placed in the bit map. Use the same array passed to **GetBitmapBits.**

ADDITIONAL COMMENTS

Remember that to display a bit map on a device, you must first associate the bit map with a compatible DC, then **BitBlt** it or **StretchBlt** it to the display context for the device. You cannot associate the bit map with the display context of the device, and you cannot **BitBlt** or **StretchBlt** between display contexts of two devices.

Before you attempt to **BitBlt** or **StretchBlt** to a device, you might want to use **GetDeviceCaps** to make sure that the device can handle bit maps, which is particularly important before transferring bit maps to printers.

Remember that bit maps are limited to 64K bytes. If you want to use a larger bit map, break it into several smaller ones.

The program at the end of this chapter copies bit maps from the clipboard and prints them on the screen and a printer. Examine the program.

PRINTER ERROR ROUTINES

In Chapter 10, the elements of printing were covered. In this section, the basic topics from Chapter 10 will be built on to create a robust printing routine.

To make the printing routine complete, it needs to handle error conditions, give processor time to concurrent applications, and give the user the option of canceling the printing.

Set up a global variable, say, **print_abort_glbl**, that indicates if a printing error occurred. Check this variable in the printing loops. Terminate the loop if **print_abort_glbl** is set.

12 Bit Maps and Advanced Printing

To start, you should check the return code of NEWFRAME and NEXTBAND **Escape**s. If the return code is less than 0, an error occurred. Possible errors are as follows:

Error	Code Meaning
SP_ERROR	general error
SP_APPABORT	the job was aborted
SP_USERABORT	the job was aborted
SP_OUTOFDISK	not enough disk space for spooling
SP_OUTOFMEMORY	not enough memory for spooling

AND the error code with SP_NOTREPORTED. If the result is nonzero, then the user has not yet been notified of the error. Display an appropriate error message box and set **print_abort_glbl**.

Before you start spooling, disable the main window with **EnableWindow**. Reenable the window when spooling is finished, which will prevent the queue from being clogged by unnecessary messages and prevent other program options from being selected once you let concurrent processes run.

When you send information to the spooler, it can take a long time for it to be processed and sent to the printer. With the rudimentary routine of Chapter 10, no other applications could run during spooling. You can get around this problem with the SETABORTPROC **Escape**. It passes a pointer to a function to the spooler. While the spooler is spooling a document, it periodically calls this function. The function should use **PeekMessage** to check the global message queue and pass along any messages that are waiting. This allows other applications to run, as was discussed in the beginning of Chapter 10. If the function passed to the spooler returns 0, then the print job will be aborted, so return the inverted value of **print_abort_glbl**.

Also, set up a modeless dialog box with a Cancel option. When this button is pressed, set **print_abort_glbl**. Be sure to reenable the main window and close the dialog box if the print job is terminated.

The program in this chapter contains a robust printer routine. Be sure to look over it carefully.

Bit Maps and Advanced Printing 12

A PROGRAM: TWELVE

The following program illustrates all of the techniques from this chapter. It reads bit maps from the clipboard, and lets the user place them on a document. The document is composed of several pages, which are indicated by page break lines. The MM_LOENGLISH mode is used, so the bit map's size is the same on the screen and on the printer. Two scroll bars are used to let the user move around the whole document. Constants define the size and number of pages (see Figure 12.1).

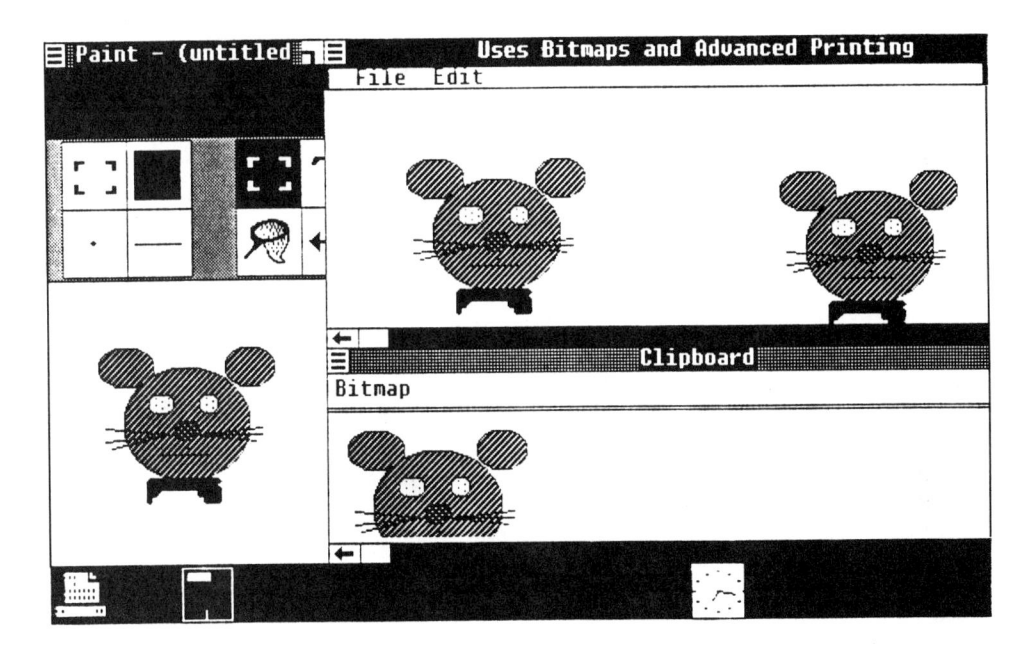

Figure 12.1 The program TWELVE. A picture was drawn with PAINT, as is seen in the left side of the screen. This picture was copied to the clipboard, as is demonstrated in the CLIPBRD window, and pasted twice into the program TWELVE.

385

12 Bit Maps and Advanced Printing

The WM_INITMENU message is trapped to determine when there are bit maps waiting in the clipboard. The cursor is changed whenever the user copies a new bit map from the clipboard. When the user presses the left mouse button, the bit map is added to the page.

There is a general routine to display all bit maps. It is passed a display context for the screen or the printer. Review how it operates.

The printer routine sets up a modeless cancel dialog box. It also checks for printer errors and lets concurrent processes operate.

Be sure to carefully look over all the routines in this program. Note how they check for error conditions. Note how the printer routine allows other applications to operate through the use of **PeekMessage** in **PrintAbort**. Also note how bit maps are used and how their bit and screen size are stored.

The menus for this program use the standard File and Edit style.

```
/------------------------------------------\
|                                          |
| The files for this program are found in  |
| the TWELVE directory.  TWELVE is the make|
| file.  TWELVE.H is the include file.     |
| TWELVE.RC and TWELVE.DLG are the resource|
| files.  TWELVE.C is the code.  TWELVE.DEF|
| is the module definition file.  TWELVE.EXE|
| is the executable.                       |
|                                          |
\------------------------------------------/
```

The Make File: TWELVE

```
#
#   Make file for the program from Chapter 12
#

cc=cl -d -c -AS -Gsw -Os -Zpe

.c.obj:
    $(cc) $*.c


twelve.obj: twelve.c  twelve.h

twelve.res: twelve.rc twelve.h twelve.dlg
    rc -r twelve.rc

twelve.exe: twelve.obj twelve.res twelve.def
    link4 twelve, /align:16, NUL, slibw, twelve.def
    rc twelve.res
```

The Resource File: TWELVE.RC

```
/*******************************************************
    Resource file for TWELVE
*******************************************************/

#include "windows.h"
#include "twelve.h"


rcinclude twelve.dlg


twelve    ICON twelve.ico
```

continued...

12 Bit Maps and Advanced Printing

...from previous page

```
twelve MENU
BEGIN
    POPUP      "File"
    BEGIN
        MENUITEM   "New",           IDM_CLEAR
        MENUITEM   "Open...",       IDM_NULL, GRAYED
        MENUITEM   "Save",          IDM_NULL, GRAYED
        MENUITEM   "Save As...",    IDM_NULL, GRAYED
        MENUITEM   "Print",         IDM_PRINT
    END

    POPUP      "Edit"
    BEGIN
        MENUITEM   "Cut",           IDM_NULL, GRAYED
        MENUITEM   "Copy",          IDM_NULL, GRAYED
        MENUITEM   "Paste",         IDM_PASTE, GRAYED
    END
END
```

The Dialog Description File: TWELVE.DLG

```
abort DIALOG LOADONCALL MOVEABLE DISCARDABLE
      61, 45, 113, 57
STYLE WS_DLGFRAME | WS_VISIBLE | WS_POPUP
BEGIN
    CONTROL     "CANCEL"  0,                "button",
                BS_DEFPUSHBUTTON | WS_TABSTOP | WS_CHILD,
                36, 39, 36, 14
    CONTROL     "Spooling Document" 1,  "static",
                SS_CENTER | WS_CHILD, 10, 7, 93, 15
END
```

12 Bit Maps and Advanced Printing

The Include File: TWELVE.H

```
/************************************************************
    This is the include file for the program from Chapter
    12.  Contains typedefs, constants, and external
    declarations.
************************************************************/


/* this structure stores information about a bitmap.
        loc      is the screen position of the bitmaps's
                 location
        scrnsize is the size of the bitmap in logical
                 coordinates
        bitsize  is the size of the bitmap in device
                 coordinates (pixels)
        map      is the bitmap's handle
*/

typedef struct bitstruc {
    POINT    loc;
    POINT    scrnsize;
    POINT    bitsize;
    HBITMAP  map;
} bitstruct;


/* constants */

#define   MAX_MAPS        30
#define   PAGES_DOWN       2
#define   PAGES_ACROSS     1
#define   PAGE_WIDTH     850     /* 8.5" */
#define   PAGE_HEIGHT   1100     /* 11"  */
```

continued...

12 Bit Maps and Advanced Printing

...from previous page

```
/* constant definitions for menus */

#define   IDM_NULL        0
#define   IDM_CLEAR       110
#define   IDM_PRINT       120
#define   IDM_PASTE       210


/* external declarations */

bitstruct     bitmaps_glbl[MAX_MAPS];
int           cur_map_glbl;
bitstruct     clipped_map_glbl;
int           map_used_glbl;
int           scroll_pos_glbl;
HANDLE        hInstance_glbl;
HWND          hAbortDlg_glbl;
int           abort_print_glbl;


extern int PASCAL WinMain();
extern int register_window();
extern long FAR PASCAL MsgServer();
extern long process_menu_cmds();
bitstruct copy_bitmap();
extern int FAR PASCAL DlgPrintAbort();
extern int FAR PASCAL PrintAbort();
extern HDC get_printerDC();
extern init_bars(), set_up_coords(), set_unscrolled();
extern add_map(), copy_from_clipboard(), print_it();
extern set_page_scroll(), process_print_error();
extern draw_page_break();
extern draw_all_maps(), free_all_maps();
```

12 Bit Maps and Advanced Printing

The Code: TWELVE.C

```
/************************************************************
    File:     twelve.c
    Program:  twelve

    This is the Windows program from Chapter 12.  It
    demonstrates using bitmaps.  It also demonstrates
    creating compatible DC's, creating compatible bit maps,
    transferring bit maps to the printer (that is, between
    devices), and copying bitmaps (from the clipboard).

    This program uses the clipboard CF_BITMAP format and the
    LOENGLISH mapping mode.  It has a vertical and
    horizontal scroll bar.

    It includes printer abort and error procedures.

    It uses the standard style menu entries for cutting,
    pasting, clearing, and printing.  It traps the
    WM_INITMENU message to determine if bitmap data is
    available in the clipboard.

************************************************************/


#include "windows.h"
#include "string.h"
#include "memory.h"
#include "stdio.h"
#include "stdlib.h"
#include "twelve.h"
```

continued...

12 Bit Maps and Advanced Printing

...from previous page

```
/*-------------------------------------------------
    global variables
---------------------------------------------------*/

bitstruct    bitmaps_glbl[MAX_MAPS];
int          cur_map_glbl;
bitstruct    clipped_map_glbl;
int          map_used_glbl;
int          scroll_pos_glbl;
HANDLE       hInstance_glbl;
HWND         hAbortDlg_glbl;
int          abort_print_glbl;




/*-------------------------------------------------
    This is the Start Up procedure and message relayer
---------------------------------------------------*/

int PASCAL
WinMain(hInstance, hPrevInstance, lpszCmdLine, cmdShow)
HANDLE   hInstance, hPrevInstance;
LPSTR    lpszCmdLine;
int      cmdShow;
{
    HWND     hWnd;
    MSG      msg;

    /* If this is the first instance, register the
       window class
    */
    if (!hPrevInstance)
        register_window(hInstance);
```

continued...

Bit Maps and Advanced Printing 12

...from previous page

```
/* Create a tiled window with two scroll bars */
hWnd = CreateWindow( (LPSTR) "Chap12WIN",
          (LPSTR) "Uses Bitmaps and Advanced Printing",
          WS_TILEDWINDOW | WS_VSCROLL | WS_HSCROLL,
          0, 0, 0, 0,
          (HWND) NULL,
          (HMENU) NULL,
          (HANDLE) hInstance,
          (LPSTR) NULL );

/* display the window */
ShowWindow(hWnd,cmdShow);
UpdateWindow(hWnd);


/* initialize scroll bars */
init_bars( hWnd );

/* initialize global variables */
cur_map_glbl = 0;
clipped_map_glbl.map = NULL;
map_used_glbl = FALSE;
hInstance_glbl = hInstance;



/* relay all messages to the message server */
while (GetMessage( (LPMSG) &msg, NULL, 0, 0) ) {
    TranslateMessage( (LPMSG) &msg);
    DispatchMessage( (LPMSG) &msg);
}

    exit(msg.wParam);
}
```

continued...

12 Bit Maps and Advanced Printing

...from previous page

```
/*-------------------------------------------------------
    This procedure registers the window.
-------------------------------------------------------*/

int
register_window( hInstance )
HANDLE   hInstance;
{
    PWNDCLASS      pClass;

    pClass = (PWNDCLASS) LocalAlloc(LPTR, sizeof(WNDCLASS));
    pClass->hCursor = LoadCursor(NULL, IDC_ARROW);
    pClass->hIcon = LoadIcon( hInstance, (LPSTR) "twelve");
    pClass->lpszMenuName = (LPSTR) "twelve";
    pClass->lpszClassName = (LPSTR) "Chap12WIN";
    pClass->hbrBackground = GetStockObject(WHITE_BRUSH);
    pClass->hInstance = hInstance;
    pClass->style = CS_HREDRAW | CS_VREDRAW;
    pClass->lpfnWndProc = MsgServer;
    RegisterClass( (LPWNDCLASS) pClass);
    LocalFree( (HANDLE) pClass);
}




/*-------------------------------------------------------
    This procedure receives the messages and decides what to
    do with them.
-------------------------------------------------------*/

long FAR PASCAL
MsgServer( hWnd, message, wParam, lParam)
HWND      hWnd;
unsigned message;
WORD      wParam;
LONG      lParam;
{
    HDC  hDC;
```

continued...

...from previous page

```
    switch (message) {
    case WM_COMMAND:
        return( process_menu_cmds(hWnd, wParam) );

    case WM_PAINT:
        /* clear the screen */
        DefWindowProc( hWnd, message, wParam, lParam);

        /* draw the page breaks */
        hDC = GetDC( hWnd );
        set_up_coords( hWnd, hDC );
        draw_page_break( hWnd, hDC );

        /* draw the bitmaps */
        draw_all_maps( hDC );
        ReleaseDC( hWnd, hDC );
        break;

    case WM_LBUTTONUP:
        /* add a bitmap if there is a bitmap ready to
           paste.  Change the cursor back to an arrow to
           indicate that the new bitmap has been used.
        */
        if (clipped_map_glbl.map) {
            add_map( hWnd, MAKEPOINT( lParam ) );
            SetClassWord( hWnd, GCW_HCURSOR,
                LoadCursor( NULL, IDC_ARROW ));
        }
        break;


    case WM_INITMENU:
        /* before the user selects a menu item, see if
           there is a bitmap in the clipboard.  Disable the
           Paste command if there isn't one.
        */
        update_menu( hWnd );
        break;
```

continued...

12 Bit Maps and Advanced Printing

...from previous page

```
        case WM_VSCROLL:
            /* process_scroll_cmds is TRUE if the thumb has
               been moved to a new position.
            */
            if (process_scroll_cmds(wParam,lParam) != TRUE)
                return( DefWindowProc( hWnd, message, wParam,
                    lParam) );

            /* update the thumb position */
            SetScrollPos(hWnd, SB_VERT, scroll_pos_glbl, TRUE);

            /* update the window */
            InvalidateRect(hWnd, (LPRECT) NULL, TRUE);
            break;

        case WM_HSCROLL:
            /* process_scroll_cmds is TRUE if the thumb has
               been moved to a new position.
            */
            if (process_scroll_cmds(wParam,lParam) != TRUE)
                return( DefWindowProc( hWnd, message, wParam,
                    lParam) );

            /* update the thumb position */
            SetScrollPos(hWnd, SB_HORZ, scroll_pos_glbl, TRUE);

            /* update the window */
            InvalidateRect(hWnd, (LPRECT) NULL, TRUE);
            break;

        case WM_DESTROY:
            /* free up resources */
            free_all_maps();
            break;

        default:
            return( DefWindowProc( hWnd, message, wParam,
                lParam ) );

    }
    return(0L);
}
```

continued...

...from previous page

```
/*------------------------------------------------------------
    This procedure is called each time the user hits a
    button on the menu.  It checks the clipboard to see if a
    bitmap is available.  If so, it enables the Paste
    command.  If not, it grays the Paste command.
------------------------------------------------------------*/

update_menu( hWnd )
HWND    hWnd;
{
    HMENU   hMenu;
    int     clip_format;
    int     paste;


    /* assume no bit maps are available */
    paste = MF_GRAYED;

    /* get a handle for the window's menu */
    hMenu = GetMenu( hWnd );

    /* open the clipboard */
    if (OpenClipboard( hWnd )) {

        /* go through the list of available clipboard
           formats.  Check for the CF_BITMAP format.
        */
        clip_format = 0;
        while (clip_format = EnumClipboardFormats(
           clip_format ))
                if (clip_format == CF_BITMAP)
                    paste = MF_ENABLED;

        /* close the clipboard */
        CloseClipboard();
    }

    /* enable or gray the Paste command */
    EnableMenuItem( hMenu, IDM_PASTE, paste);
}
```

continued...

12 Bit Maps and Advanced Printing

...from previous page

```
/*----------------------------------------------------------
    This procedure processes the scroll commands.  It returns
    TRUE if the thumb has been moved to a new position.  All
    other scrolling commands are ignored
------------------------------------------------------------*/
int
process_scroll_cmds( command, pos)
WORD     command;
LONG     pos;
{
    if (command == SB_THUMBPOSITION) {
        scroll_pos_glbl = LOWORD( pos );
        return( TRUE );
    }
    else
        return( FALSE );
}




/*----------------------------------------------------------
    This routine processes commands from the menu.
------------------------------------------------------------*/
long
process_menu_cmds( hWnd, command )
HWND     hWnd;
WORD     command;
{
    HDC       hDC;
    HBRUSH    hBr, hBrOld;
    RECT      rect;
    HMENU     hMenu;
```

continued...

...from previous page

```
    switch (command) {
    case IDM_CLEAR:
        /* free up all the bitmaps */
        free_all_maps();

        /* clear the screen */
        hDC = GetDC(hWnd);
        GetClientRect(hWnd, (LPRECT) &rect);
        hBr = CreateSolidBrush(GetBkColor(hDC));
        hBrOld = SelectObject(hDC, hBr);
        FillRect(hDC, (LPRECT) &rect, hBr);
        SelectObject(hDC, hBrOld);
        DeleteObject(hBr);

        /* draw the page breaks */
        set_up_coords( hWnd, hDC );
        draw_page_break( hDC );

        ReleaseDC(hWnd, hDC);
        break;


    case IDM_PASTE:
        /* switch to the cross cursor */
        SetClassWord( hWnd, GCW_HCURSOR, LoadCursor(NULL,
            IDC_CROSS));

        /* get the clipboard data */
        copy_from_clipboard(hWnd);
        break;

    case IDM_PRINT:
        /* reset the abort flag and print the file */
        abort_print_glbl = FALSE;
        print_it(hWnd);
    }
    return(0L);

}
```

continued...

12 Bit Maps and Advanced Printing

...from previous page

```
/*--------------------------------------------------------
   This procedure sets up the scroll bar values.  The scroll
   bars move from 0 to the end of the pages vertically and
   horizontally.  PAGE_WIDTH and PAGE_HEIGHT are constants
   defining the page size.  PAGES_ACROSS and PAGES_DOWN
   define the number of pages.
----------------------------------------------------------*/

init_bars( hWnd )
HWND     hWnd;
{
    SetScrollRange( hWnd, SB_HORZ, 0, PAGE_WIDTH *
       PAGES_ACROSS, FALSE );
    SetScrollRange( hWnd, SB_VERT, 0, PAGE_HEIGHT *
       PAGES_DOWN, FALSE );
}




/*--------------------------------------------------------
   This procedure sets up the coordinate system.  It uses a
   LOENGLISH system.  Thus all logical coordinates are in
   terms of hundredths of inches.
----------------------------------------------------------*/

set_up_coords( hWnd, hDC )
HWND     hWnd;
HDC      hDC;
{
    int  scroll_x, scroll_y;

    /* set MM_LOENGLISH mapping mode */
    SetMapMode(hDC,MM_LOENGLISH);

    /* move the screen up if the THUMB moves down.  Move the
       screen right if the thumb moves left.  Determine the
       thumb position by reading it from the scroll bar.
```

continued...

400

...from previous page

```
    */
    scroll_x = GetScrollPos( hWnd, SB_HORZ );
    scroll_y = GetScrollPos( hWnd, SB_VERT );
    SetWindowOrg(hDC, scroll_x, -scroll_y);
}




/*-----------------------------------------------------------
    This procedure sets up the coordinate system, but doesn't
    account for scrolling.  This is used for the memory
    display contexts.
-------------------------------------------------------------*/

set_unscrolled( hDC )
HDC     hDC;
{
    SetMapMode(hDC, MM_LOENGLISH);
}




/*-----------------------------------------------------------
    This procedure sets up the coordinate system and scrolls
    page  pages down.  This is useful for printing.
-------------------------------------------------------------*/

set_page_scroll( hDC, page )
HDC     hDC;
int     page;
{
    SetMapMode( hDC, MM_LOENGLISH );
    SetWindowOrg( hDC, 0, -page*PAGE_HEIGHT);
}
```

continued...

12 Bit Maps and Advanced Printing

...from previous page

```
/*-----------------------------------------------------------
   This procedure draws lines that indicate where pages end.
   It determines the page size from the page size constants.
   Typically, these could be 850 for 8.5 inches and 1100 for
   11 inches.  It draws a line at the end of each page.
-------------------------------------------------------------*/
draw_page_break( hWnd, hDC )
HWND    hWnd;
HDC     hDC;
{
    int i;

    /* for each page going down, draw a line going across
       all pages.  Note that the negative signs are used
       because in MM_LOENGLISH mode, the y coordinates
       increase going up, and the origin starts at the upper
       left corner of the screen.
    */
    for (i = 1; i <= PAGES_DOWN; i++) {
        MoveTo(hDC,0,-i*PAGE_HEIGHT);
        LineTo(hDC,PAGE_WIDTH,-i*PAGE_HEIGHT);
    }

    /* for each page going across, draw a line going down
       all pages
    */

    for (i = 1; i <= PAGES_ACROSS; i++) {
        MoveTo(hDC, i*PAGE_WIDTH, 0);
        LineTo(hDC, i*PAGE_WIDTH, -PAGE_HEIGHT*PAGES_DOWN);
    }

}
```

continued...

...from previous page

```
/*-------------------------------------------------------------
    This procedure adds a map to the map list.  If a bitmap
    has been cut from the clipboard, this procedure adds it
    to the list of bitmaps.  It determines the bitmaps screen
    position, and then displays it on the screen.  Note that
    the size information -- both device and logical size --
    are gotten from the global bitstruct structure that is
    set when the bitmap is clipped.

    This procedure also sets a flag that indicates the
    clipped map has been used.  This prevents the clipped map
    from being erased when the next map is read in.
-------------------------------------------------------------*/
add_map( hWnd, pt )
HWND    hWnd;
POINT   pt;
{
    HDC     hDC, hMemDC;
    char    msg[40];
    POINT   size, dispsize;


    /* check if a bitmap has been cut from the clipboard */
    if (!clipped_map_glbl.map) {
        MessageBox( hWnd, (LPSTR) "Nothing Clipped Yet",
            (LPSTR) NULL, MB_OK);
        return(NULL);
    }

    /* see if have room for the new bitmap */
    if (cur_map_glbl == MAX_MAPS) {
        sprintf(msg, "Can only have %d bitmaps", MAX_MAPS);
        MessageBox( hWnd, (LPSTR) msg, (LPSTR) "Sorry!",
            MB_OK);
        return( NULL );
```

continued...

...from previous page
```
    }

    /* find the bitmap's position in the logical coordinate
       system.  Get the display context for the screen and
       create a memory display context for use later on.
    */

    hDC = GetDC(hWnd);
    hMemDC = CreateCompatibleDC( hDC );
    set_up_coords(hWnd, hDC);
    DPtoLP(hDC, (LPPOINT) &pt, 1);


    /* copy the pixel and logical size from the global
       bitstruct structure into variables with smaller
       names.  This isn't necessary, but it makes the Blt
       command easier to read.
    */
    size = clipped_map_glbl.bitsize;
    dispsize = clipped_map_glbl.scrnsize;


    /* add the clipped bitmap to the bitmap list.  First
       copy all of the size information and the handle, then
       set its screen location
    */
    bitmaps_glbl[cur_map_glbl] = clipped_map_glbl;
    bitmaps_glbl[cur_map_glbl].loc = pt;

    /* increment the count of bitmaps in the list */
    cur_map_glbl++;


    /* associate the bitmap with the memory display
       context
    */
    SelectObject( hMemDC, clipped_map_glbl.map);

    /* copy the bitmap to the display screen */
    StretchBlt( hDC, pt.x, pt.y, dispsize.x, dispsize.y,
        hMemDC, 0, 0, size.x, size.y, SRCCOPY);
```
continued...

...from previous page

```
    /* free up the display contexts */
    DeleteDC( hMemDC );
    ReleaseDC(hWnd,hDC);

    /* indicate that the bitmap has been used */
    map_used_glbl = TRUE;
}
```

```
/*-------------------------------------------------------------
    This procedure draws all of the bitmaps to the
    destination display context, which is passed in hDestDC.
    Note that it does not know, or even care, what device
    this is for.  The routine works fine if you give it a
    printer DC, a screen DC, or the DC for some other device.

    The routine creates a compatible DC to the destination
    DC, associates each bitmap with this DC, and then copies
    it to the destination DC.

    Note that the compatible DC is in MM_TEXT mode, and that
    the measurements of the source bitmap are given in actual
    pixel size.  This ensures that the bitmap size won't be
    translated improperly.
-------------------------------------------------------------*/
draw_all_maps( hDestDC )
HDC     hDestDC;
{
    int   i;
    HDC   hMemDC;
    POINT    loc,size,dstsize;
```

continued...

12 Bit Maps and Advanced Printing

...from previous page

```
    /* get a compatible display context.  Make sure that it
       uses the MM_TEXT mode.
    */

    hMemDC = CreateCompatibleDC( hDestDC );
    SetMapMode( hMemDC, MM_TEXT);


    /* go through a loop for each bitmap in the list of
       bitmaps.
    */
    for (i = 0; i < cur_map_glbl; i++) {

        /* associate the bitmap with the memory display
           context
        */
        SelectObject( hMemDC, bitmaps_glbl[i].map);

        /* put its size and location into variables with
           small names.  This isn't necessary, but it makes
           the StretchBlt command easier to read.
        */
        size = bitmaps_glbl[i].bitsize;
        loc = bitmaps_glbl[i].loc;
        dstsize = bitmaps_glbl[i].scrnsize;

        /* move the bitmap to the destination DC */
        StretchBlt(hDestDC, loc.x, loc.y, dstsize.x,
            dstsize.y, hMemDC, 0, 0, size.x, size.y,
            SRCCOPY);
    }

    /* free up the memory display context */
    DeleteDC( hMemDC );

}
```

continued...

...from previous page

```
/*-----------------------------------------------------------
    This procedures frees up the memory used by all of the
    bitmaps.  It frees the bitmap that is the copy of the
    clipboard data, and all of the bitmaps in the bitmap
    list.
-------------------------------------------------------------*/

free_all_maps()
{
    int  i;

    /* free the clipboard copy */
    DeleteObject( clipped_map_glbl.map );
    clipped_map_glbl.map = NULL;

    /* free all bitmaps in the bitmap list */
    for (i = 0; i < cur_map_glbl; i++)
        DeleteObject( bitmaps_glbl[i].map );

    /* clear the bitmap counter */
    cur_map_glbl = 0;

}




/*-----------------------------------------------------------
    This routine copies a bitmap from the clipboard.  It tries
    to read a bitmap from the clipboard.  It should always be
    able to do this, because the Paste command is disabled if
    there isn't any bitmap data, but it doesn't hurt to check
    again, in case the status has changed.  If a bitmap is
    found, it is copied by calling the copy_bitmap procedure.
-------------------------------------------------------------*/

copy_from_clipboard( hWnd )
HWND     hWnd;
{
    int          num_pts;
    HBITMAP      hNewmap;
```

continued...

...from previous page

```
    /* Try to open the clipboard */
    if (!OpenClipboard(hWnd))
        MessageBox(hWnd,
            (LPSTR) "Could not access clipboard",
            (LPSTR) NULL, MB_OK);
    else {
        /* was able to open it.  Read in a bitmap */
        hNewmap =  (HBITMAP) GetClipboardData(CF_BITMAP);
        if (!hNewmap)
            /* we couldn't find any bitmap data in the
               clipboard.
            */
            MessageBox(hWnd,
                (LPSTR) "No bitmap in clipboard",
                (LPSTR) NULL, MB_OK);
        else {
            /* copy the bitmap */
            clipped_map_glbl = copy_bitmap(hWnd,
                clipped_map_glbl.map, hNewmap);
        }

        /* close the clipboard */
        CloseClipboard();
    }

}
```

continued...

...from previous page

```
/*----------------------------------------------------------
    This routine makes a copy of a bitmap.  It returns a
    handle to a bitstruct structure, which contains a handle
    to the copied bitmap and information about the copied
    bitmaps size.

    This procedures takes a handle to the window, a handle to
    the destination bitmap, which may or may not have a
    bitmap in it, and a handle to the source bitmap.

    This routine first copies format information about the
    bitmap.  It creates an empty bitmap of the same size, and
    BitBlts the pixel data.  It determines the logical size
    of the bitmap, and stores all of the information in the
    returned bitstruct structure.

    Be sure to note the use of CreateCompatibleDC,
    CreateCompatibleBitmap, and BitBlt.
-----------------------------------------------------------*/
bitstruct
copy_bitmap( hWnd, hDestBM, hSrcBM )
HWND     hWnd;
HBITMAP  hDestBM;
HBITMAP  hSrcBM;
{
    HDC  hSrcDC, hDestDC, hDC;
    bitstruct copied_map;
    POINT      scrnsize;
    BITMAP     mapinfo;


    /* get a display context for the screen, and make two
       memory display contexts that are compatible with it.
       This will make the bitmap copy compatible with the
       display screen, since presumable it was copied from
       the display screen originally.
    */
    hDC = GetDC( hWnd );
    hSrcDC = CreateCompatibleDC( hDC );
    hDestDC = CreateCompatibleDC( hDC );
    ReleaseDC( hWnd, hDC );
```

continued...

12 Bit Maps and Advanced Printing

...from previous page

```
/* if there was already a bitmap in the clipped bitmap
   structure, but it was never added to the list of used
   bitmaps, then delete it to save space.
*/
if (hDestBM && !map_used_glbl)
    DeleteObject( hDestBM );


/* get the information about the bitmap's format */
GetObject(hSrcBM, sizeof(BITMAP), (LPSTR)&mapinfo);

/* create an empty bitmap that is compatible with the
   display screen and has the same size as the source
   bitmap
*/
hDestBM = CreateCompatibleBitmap( hDestDC,
    mapinfo.bmWidth, mapinfo.bmHeight);

/* associate the bitmaps with memory display contexts */
SelectObject( hDestDC, hDestBM );
SelectObject( hSrcDC, hSrcBM );

/* now copy all of the pixel information from the source
   to the copy bitmap
*/
BitBlt(hDestDC, 0, 0, mapinfo.bmWidth, mapinfo.bmHeight,
    hSrcDC, 0, 0, SRCCOPY);


/* set the bit size and bitmap handle */
scrnsize.x = mapinfo.bmWidth;
scrnsize.y = mapinfo.bmHeight;
copied_map.map = hDestBM;
copied_map.bitsize = scrnsize;
```

continued...

...from previous page

```
    /* determine the logical size of the bitmap, by
       converting its pixel size to LOENGLISH values.  Note
       that the unscrolled coordinate system is used to
       insure that the origin is at the upper left corner of
       the screen.  This means that the width and height
       values, when converted to logical units, represent
       the logical width and height.
    */
    set_unscrolled( hDestDC );
    DPtoLP( hDestDC, (LPPOINT) &scrnsize, 1 );
    copied_map.scrnsize = scrnsize;
    DeleteDC( hSrcDC );
    DeleteDC( hDestDC );

    map_used_glbl = FALSE;
    return( copied_map );
}




/*-----------------------------------------------------------
    This procedure returns a display context handle for the
    printer.  It reads the WIN.INI file to determine the
    default printer.  It checks that the printer can handle
    bitmaps.  It returns NULL if a printer could not be
    found.
-----------------------------------------------------------*/

HDC
get_printerDC( hWnd )
HWND    hWnd;
{
```

continued...

12 Bit Maps and Advanced Printing

...from previous page

```
    char    devicestring[100];
    /* pointer to device name string */
    char    *device;
    /* pointer to device driver string */
    char    *driver;
    /* pointer to port string */
    char    *port;
    HDC     hPr;

    /* read the WIN.INI file for the printer string */
    GetProfileString( (LPSTR) "windows", (LPSTR) "device",
       (LPSTR) NULL, (LPSTR) devicestring, 100);

    /* parse the string */
    if (*devicestring == NULL) {
        /* print a message if there was no
           printing device
        */
        MessageBox( hWnd, (LPSTR) "No device", NULL,
           MB_OK);
        return( NULL );
    }

                            ---

    /* Skip leading spaces to get the device name.  Make the
       device name ASCIIZ.  Note:  the device name can
       contain spaces in it.
    */
    device = strtok( devicestring, ",");

    /* find the driver name -- cannot contain spaces */
    driver = strtok( NULL, ", ");

    /* find the port name -- cannot contain spaces */
    port = strtok( NULL, ", ");
```

continued...

...from previous page

```
    /* create a display context for the device */
    hPr = CreateDC( (LPSTR) driver, (LPSTR) device,
       (LPSTR) port, (LPSTR) NULL);

    /* print an error message if couldn't create the DC */
    if (hPr == NULL) {
       MessageBox( hWnd, (LPSTR) "Couldn't create DC",
          NULL, MB_OK);
       return(NULL);
    }

    /* see if supports bitmaps
    */
    if (!(GetDeviceCaps( hPr, RASTERCAPS) & RC_BITBLT)) {
       MessageBox( hWnd, (LPSTR) "Can't use this printer",
          (LPSTR) NULL, MB_OK);
       return( NULL );
    }

    return( hPr );
}



/*-------------------------------------------------------
    This routine prints out the bitmaps.  Because LOENGLISH
    mode is used, the bitmaps appear as the same size and the
    same position on the printer as they do on the screen.

    Note the use of the error checking routines.  Note how
    the window is disabled and reenabled, how a cancel
    dialog box is set up, and how the print_abort_glbl
    variable is checked to halt the printing loop.
    -------------------------------------------------------*/
```

continued...

12 Bit Maps and Advanced Printing

...from previous page

```
print_it( hWnd )
HWND    hWnd;
{
    HDC         hPr;
    FARPROC     lpfnDlgPrintAbort;
    FARPROC     lpfnPrintAbort;
    int         prnt_err;
    int         cur_page;


    /* get a display context for the printer */
    hPr = get_printerDC( hWnd );
    if (!hPr)
        return( NULL );


    /* avoid cluttering up the queue: ignore all mouse and
       keyboard activity in the main window.
    */
    EnableWindow(hWnd, FALSE);


    /* bind the data segment to routines that will be called
       by the Windows system.  These are the printer abort
       routine that is passed to the spooler, and the
       modeless dialog box with the cancel button.
    */
    lpfnDlgPrintAbort = MakeProcInstance( (FARPROC)
        DlgPrintAbort, hInstance_glbl );
    lpfnPrintAbort = MakeProcInstance( (FARPROC) PrintAbort,
        hInstance_glbl );


    /* set up the modeless dialog box.  Store its handle in
       a global variable so that it can receive messages and
       be canceled from other routines.
    */
    hAbortDlg_glbl = CreateDialog(hInstance_glbl,
        (LPSTR) "abort", hWnd, lpfnDlgPrintAbort);
```

continued...

Bit Maps and Advanced Printing 12

...from previous page

```
   /* give the spooler a routine to periodically call */
   Escape( hPr, SETABORTPROC, NULL, lpfnPrintAbort, NULL );


   /* Now continue with the printing: */


   /* tell the spooler that a document is coming.
   */
   Escape( hPr, STARTDOC, strlen("twelve"),
      (LPSTR) "twelve", NULL);


   /* go through this loop for each page.  Before doing
      each page, check that the printing hasn't been
      aborted.  Then, set up the display context for each
      page, and draw all the bitmaps on the printer.  Note
      that each time a new page is drawn, the printer
      screen is "scrolled" to the next page with
      set_page_scroll.  This insures that the proper page
      portion appears on the printer.  One word of caution:
      if the printer page size doesn't correspond to the
      page size defined in the include file (PAGE_WIDTH and
      PAGE_HEIGHT) then parts of the page may be cut off.
   */

   cur_page = 0;
   while ((cur_page < PAGES_DOWN) && !abort_print_glbl) {
       set_page_scroll( hPr, cur_page);
       cur_page++;
       draw_all_maps( hPr );

       /* tell the spooler that the page image has been
          sent.  The spooler will print it.
       */
       if ( (prnt_err = Escape( hPr, NEWFRAME, NULL, NULL,
          NULL)) < 0)
             /* call an error routine if there was a
                problem
             */
             process_print_error( hWnd, prnt_err );
   }
```

continued...

12 Bit Maps and Advanced Printing

...from previous page

```
    /* if the printing wasn't aborted, tell the spooler that
       printing is finished, and clear out the modeless
       dialog box.
    */
    if (!abort_print_glbl) {
        /* tell the spooler that we're finished printing */
        Escape( hPr, ENDDOC, NULL, NULL, NULL );

        /* reenable the main window, then kill the dialog
           box.
        */
        EnableWindow( hWnd, TRUE );
        DestroyWindow( hAbortDlg_glbl );
    }


    /* delete the printer display context */
    DeleteDC( hPr );

    /* unbind the procedures */
    FreeProcInstance( lpfnDlgPrintAbort );
    FreeProcInstance( lpfnPrintAbort );
}




/*-----------------------------------------------------------
    This procedure handles any errors that the spooler
    reports
-----------------------------------------------------------*/

process_print_error( hWnd, error )
HWND    hWnd;
int     error;
{
    HDC hDC;
```

continued...

...from previous page

```
    /* indicate that an error occurred */
    abort_print_glbl = TRUE;


    /* if the modeless dialog box is still up, get rid of it
       and reenable the main window
    */
    if (hAbortDlg_glbl) {
        EnableWindow( GetParent(hAbortDlg_glbl), TRUE);
        DestroyWindow(hAbortDlg_glbl );
        hAbortDlg_glbl = NULL;
    }


    /* see if user already knows about the error */
    if (error & SP_NOTREPORTED)
        switch (error) {
        case SP_OUTOFMEMORY:
        case SP_OUTOFDISK:
            hDC = GetDC( hWnd );
            MessageBox(hDC,
                (LPSTR) "Out of Printing Resources",
                (LPSTR) NULL, MB_OK | MB_ICONEXCLAMATION );
            ReleaseDC( hWnd, hDC );
            break;
        default:
            break;
        }
}
```

continued...

12 Bit Maps and Advanced Printing

...from previous page

```
/*-----------------------------------------------------------
    This procedure is periodically called by the spooler.
    When it is called, it checks the message queue (allowing
    other programs to get time).  If there is a message for
    the abort dialog box it passes it on.  If not, it
    translates and dispatches the message.

    Note how the routine checks abort_print_glbl.

    If this routine returns 0, then the spooler will cancel
    printing.  Because we want to cancel printing if and only
    if print_abort_glbl is TRUE, we return !print_abort_glbl.
-------------------------------------------------------------*/

int FAR PASCAL
PrintAbort( hPr, code )
HDC     hPr;
int     code;
{
    MSG   msg;

    /* check the message queue */
    while (!abort_print_glbl && PeekMessage( (LPMSG)&msg,
       NULL, NULL, NULL, TRUE ))
          /* pass on messages to the modeless dialog box */
          if (!hAbortDlg_glbl || !IsDialogMessage(
             hAbortDlg_glbl, (LPMSG)&msg)) {
                /* pass on any other messages */
                TranslateMessage( (LPMSG)&msg );
                DispatchMessage((LPMSG) &msg);
          }

    return( !abort_print_glbl );
}
```

continued...

...from previous page

```
/*----------------------------------------------------------
   This is the modeless dialog box for aborting print
   operations.  As it only has one option, any WM_COMMAND
   messages must be requests to cancel printing.  Note that
   because it is a dialog box, it returns TRUE if it
   processed the message.  Also note the use of SetFocus.
----------------------------------------------------------*/

int FAR PASCAL
DlgPrintAbort( hDlg, message, wParam, lParam )
HWND       hDlg;
unsigned message;
WORD       wParam;
LONG       lParam;
{
    switch (message) {
    case WM_COMMAND:
        /* must be the abort command, so abort */
        abort_print_glbl = TRUE;
        EnableWindow( GetParent(hDlg), TRUE);
        DestroyWindow(hDlg );
        hAbortDlg_glbl = NULL;
        return( TRUE );

    case WM_INITDIALOG:
        /* get keyboard input, so can cancel through
           keyboard
        */
        SetFocus( hDlg );
        return( TRUE );
    default:
        return( FALSE );
    }
}
```

12 Bit Maps and Advanced Printing

The Module Definition File: TWELVE.DEF

```
NAME       Twelve
DESCRIPTION    'Twelth Window Program'
STUB       'winstub.exe'
CODE       MOVEABLE
DATA       MOVEABLE MULTIPLE
HEAPSIZE 4096
STACKSIZE 4096
EXPORTS
        MsgServer @1
        DlgPrintAbort @2
        PrintAbort @3
```

SUMMARY

- Bit maps let you quickly and compactly transfer images. Bit maps are copies of the memory values that turn screen dots on or off.

- Bit maps are referred to by a HBITMAP handle. The BITMAP structure describes the format of the bit map. It also contains a pointer to the pixel data.

- To display a bit map, associate it with a memory display context. Create the memory display context with **CreateCompatibleDC**, and associate the bit map with **SelectObject**. Then, use **BitBlt** or **StretchBlt** to copy the bit map to the display.

- **BitBlt** and **StretchBlt** copy a bit map from one display context to another. Windows will adjust the data as it is being transferred so that it is compatible with the format of the destination display context.

- The Combine Style determines how dots on the information display area will be combined with those from a bit map being copied. There are many options, involving the source pixels, destination pixels, and brush pixels.

Bit Maps and Advanced Printing 12

- To make a bit map with GDI calls, create a memory display context and a blank bit map. Execute GDI calls using the memory display context. All of the graphics calls will write to the bit map.

- To copy an existing screen image to a bit map, create a memory display context and a blank bit map. Use **BitBlt** or **StretchBlt** to copy the screen image to the bit map.

- When you copy a bit map from a memory display context, be sure to use the MM_TEXT mode, and specify the bit map size in pixels. This will prevent conversion errors. You can specify the destination size in any coordinate system.

- Use a data structure that stores the bit map handle, the number of pixel rows and columns, and a suggested height and width for the bit map. You can compute the height and the width in device-independent units so that the bit map's size will not depend on the pixel size of the display.

- Use the CF_BITMAP format when copying bit maps to or from the clipboard. If you get a bit map handle from the clipboard, be sure to copy the bit map information. Do so using **GetObject** and **BitBlt**.

- You can save and load bit maps from disk by saving, or loading, the format description and the pixel data.

- Use **GetDeviceCaps** to determine if a device can handle bit maps.

- Bit maps can only use 64K of memory. You can break large bit maps into a group of smaller ones.

- Have a global variable that indicates if a printing error occurred. Stop your printing operations if it is set.

- Check the return value of NEWFRAME and NEXTBAND calls. Pass any error messages to an error routine.

- Disable the main window before you begin printing. Enable it when you finish.

12 Bit Maps and Advanced Printing

- Set up a modeless dialog box with a cancel button. If this button is pressed, stop printing.

- Use the SETABORTPROC escape command to set up a procedure that is called by the spooler. Use this procedure to give other applications and the modeless dialog box a chance to run.

BIBLIOGRAPHY

Hyman, Michael I. *Advanced IBM PC Graphics.* New York: Brady Communications Co., Inc., 1985.

Hyman, Michael I. *Memory Resident Utilities, Interrupts, and Disk Management with MS and PC DOS.* Portland, OR: MIS:Press, Inc., 1987.

Microsoft C Run-Time Library Reference. Microsoft Corp., 1986.

Microsoft C User's Guide. Microsoft Corp., 1986.

Microsoft Windows Software Development Kit 1.03:

> *Update*
> *Programmer's Utility Guide*
> *Programmer's Reference*
> *Quick Reference*
> *Programming Guide*
> *Application Style Guide*

Microsoft Corp., 1986.

INDEX

SUBJECT INDEX

[devices] 321
[windows] 321

A

Accelerator keys 81 - 85
    Loading 83
    Using 84 - 85
Assembly Language 261 - 273
    Creating module 261
    Language protocal 262
    Memory model 262
    Parameters 264 - 265
    Procedures 263 - 267
    Return values 267
    Segments 263
    Variables 266
    Windows protocol 263

B

Background brush 22
Background color 116 - 117
Bit maps 368 - 383
    Associating with display context 371
    Bit block transfer 371 - 375
    Characteristics 380
    Clipboard 379 - 381
    Combine style 375 - 376
    Compared to metafiles 369
    Copying 380 - 381
    Copying description 380
    Copying pixel data 382
    Creating 377 - 378, 382 - 383
    Creating compatible 377
    Cutting 378
    Deleting 111
    Displaying 370 - 375
    Handle 369
    Loading 382 - 383
    Pasting 378
    Printing 370 - 375
    Saving 382

Size limitations 383
　　　Stretched bit block transfer 371 - 375
　　　Structure 369 - 370
　　　Tips 379, 383
　　　Transferring 371 - 375
　　　Transferring to non-MM_TEXT 375
　　　What they are 368
　　　Why use them 368 - 369
　Brush 22
　　　Creating 169 - 170
　　　Deleting 111

C

Cancelling
　　　Long process 302
Check boxes 206
Child windows 293 - 296
　　　Creating 294
　　　Destroying 296
　　　Sending messages 296
Class 53
　　　Changing values 59 - 60
　　　Cursor 59
Clearing the screen 182
Clipboard 336 - 344
　　　Bit maps 379 - 381
　　　Clearing 337
　　　Closing 339
　　　Copying data 336, 339
　　　Disabling commands 341
　　　Enabling commands 341
　　　Formatting on demand 342
　　　Inserting data 336 - 339
　　　Listing available formats 341
　　　Making own format 340
　　　Opening 337
　　　Registering format 340
　　　Style 342 - 343
Closing window 135
Code 7
Color 116
　　　Background 22, 116 - 117
　　　Of point 171

Text 116 - 117
   Compiling
      With resources 45 - 46
Converting
   Between coordinate systems 182 - 183
   Numbers to text 100
   Text to numbers 216
Cooperation 300 - 303
   When printing 330 - 331, 384
Coordinate system 159, 162, 182 - 183, 325
Cursor 20
   Changing 58 - 60
   Making own 43

D

Devices
   Available 321
   Characteristics 326
   Choosing 323
   Communicating with 324
   Default printing 321
   Size 326
Dialog box 204 - 221
   Adding to a program 210 - 212
   Creating 207 - 208, 210 - 212
   Disk directory 216
   Displaying 211 - 212
   Declaring 204
   Features 206 - 207
   Format 208 - 210
   Initialization 137, 213
   List boxes 216 - 220
   Messages 137, 206
   Modal 206
   Modeless 206
   Reading values 213 - 220
   Setting values 213 - 220
   Style 212
   Unprocessed messages 206
   Why use 204
Disk files 240 - 246
   Assigning unique name 244
   Checking for existence 244

Closing 245
　　　Listing 216, 219
　　　Low-level access 241, 245, 269 - 273
　　　Opening 242
　　　Prompting for 243
　　　Reading 245
　　　Reopening 244
　　　Style 246
　　　Using 240 - 241
　　　Writing 245
Display context 98
　　　And bit maps 370
　　　Compatible 370 - 371
　　　Coordinates of compatible 371
　　　Creating 323
　　　Deleting 324, 371
　　　Getting 98
　　　Releasing 98

E

Ending session 136

F

Fonts 108 - 115
　　　Selecting 111
　　　Deleting 111
　　　Metrics 113 - 114
Freeing resources 136

G

Global Variables 60 - 61
Graphics 158 - 200
　　　Application area 158
　　　Arcs 175
　　　Axis direction 165
　　　Bit maps (see Bit maps)
　　　Brushes 169 - 170
　　　Centered screen 165
　　　Clearing screen 182
　　　Clipping region 183
　　　Converting coordinate systems 182 - 183
　　　Coordinate system 162

Coordinate system for printing 325
Curves 175 - 177
Displaying 159
Displaying a whole object 163
Displaying several graphs 165, 293
Ellipses 175
Filling 177
GDI 158
Keeping position and size constant 165
Line commands 171 - 172
Making icons 282
Mapping modes 159 - 162
Metafiles 198 - 200
Pens 168 - 169
Pie charts 176
Point commands 170 - 171
Polygons 175
Printing 325
Rectangles 173 - 174
Regions 177 - 181
Scrolling 165, 283 - 293
System area 158
Viewport 162 - 168
Window 162 - 168
Zooming 165

I

Initialization routine 17 - 22
    register_window 18
Icon 21
    Making own 69 - 70
    Making with GDI 282 - 283
Input 214 - 215, see also Dialog box, Mouse
    Capturing 138
    Disabling 302
    Enabling 302
Instance 13, 33 - 34
    Binding 210
    Getting data 83 - 84
    Multiple 299
Invalidating screen 293

K

Keyboard
    And menu commands 42
    And menu commands, Windows 2.0 42 - 43
    Messages 141 - 142
    Style 303

L

Linked lists 239
List boxes 207, 216 - 220
    Adding object 218
    Directory listing 216 - 217, 219
    Getting object 218 - 219
    Messages 218 - 220
    Removing object 218 - 219
    Sending messages 217 - 220
    Size 220
    Text length 219

M

Make file 8
Mapping modes 159 - 162
    MM_ANISOTROPIC 162
    MM_HIENGLISH 161
    MM_HIMETRIC 161
    MM_ISOTROPIC 162
    MM_LOENGLISH 161
    MM_LOMETRIC 161
    MM_TEXT 161, 379
    MM_TWIPS 161
    Setting 162
Memory 234 - 240
    Allocating 235 - 236
    Freeing 237
    Global 234
    Handle 234
    Linked lists 239
    Local 234
    Locking 236
    Pointers 239 - 240
    Reallocating 237 - 238
    Unlocking 236 - 237
    Using 234

Memory models 273 - 275, 344
Menus 38 - 43, 56 - 69
    Accelerators 81 - 85
    Adding pop up 68
    Altering item 66 - 67
    Altering top level 67
    Check marks 62 - 65
    Choosing names 42
    Creating new 68
    Deleting item 66 - 67
    Describing 39 - 41
    Disabling 65, 136, 341
    Enabling 65, 136, 341
    Example 42
    Getting commands 56 - 57
    Getting text 68
    Graying 65, 136
    Including in a program 43
    Initializing 136
    Inserting item 66 - 67
    Messages 56 - 57
    Modifying 61 - 67
    Mutually exclusive choices 63 - 65
    Numbers 57 - 58
    Options 41
    Redrawing 67
    Replacing 69
    Resource file 39 - 41
    Sending 217
    System 299 - 300
    What they are 38
Message boxes 278 - 280
Messages 4, 10, 134 - 144
    Activation 136
    Checking for 301
    Close window 135
    Default processing 135
    Destroying window 136
    Dialog box 137
    Ending session 136
    Initialize window 136
    Keyboard 141 - 142
    List boxes 217 - 220

Menu 56 - 57
Menu activity 136
Mouse 138 - 141
Processing routine 23 - 24
Scroll bar 143
Scrolling 142 - 144
Sending 217, 296
Sending periodically 297
Sending WM_PAINT 293
System menu 144
System messages 134 - 144
Timer 142
Update window 135
Why use 134
Window related 135 - 137
Window size 137
WM_ACTIVATE 136
WM_CHAR 142
WM_CLOSE 135
WM_COMMAND 56
WM_CREATE 136
WM_DESTROY 136, 237, 298
WM_DESTROYCLIPBOARD 342
WM_ERASEBKGND 137
WM_HSCROLL 143, 284
WM_INITDIALOG 137, 213
WM_INITMENU 136, 341
WM_LBUTTONDBLCLK 141
WM_LBUTTONDOWN 139
WM_LBUTTONUP 140
WM_MBUTTONDBLCLK 141
WM_MBUTTONDOWN 140
WM_MBUTTONUP 141
WM_MOUSEMOVE 139
WM_PAINT 135, 293
WM_QUERYENDSESSION 136
WM_RBUTTONDBLCLK 141
WM_RBUTTONDOWN 140
WM_RBUTTONUP 140
WM_RENDERALLFORMATS 342
WM_RENDERFORMAT 342
WM_SIZE 137
WM_SYSCHAR 142

    WM_SYSCOMMAND 144, 300
    WM_TIMECHANGE 142, 298
    WM_TIMER 142, 297
    WM_VSCROLL 143, 284
Message processing routine 23 - 24
Metafiles 198 - 200
    Compared to bit maps 369
    Copying 199
    Creating 198
    Displaying 200
    Drawing to 199
    Freeing 200
    Opening 199
Module definition file 7, 32 - 33
Mouse 138 - 141
    Buttons 139 - 141
    Capturing all positions 138
    Converting position 182
    Double clicks 141
    Messages 138 - 141
    Movement 139
    Position 138, 182

O

Overlapping windows 30

P

Parts of a Windows program 7 - 8
PASCAL keyword 13
Pen
    Creating 168 - 169
    Deleting 111
Pointers 239 - 240, 303
Points 138, 170 - 171
Printing 320 - 332
    Abort procedure 331, 383 - 384
    Advanced features 330 - 332, 383 - 384
    Banding 331 - 332
    Bit maps 370 - 375
    Capabilities 326
    Cooperating 330 - 331, 384
    Creating image 325
    Ending document 325

Ending page 325
　　　Error messages 330, 383
　　　Example 327 - 330, 387 - 420
　　　New document 324 - 325
　　　Page size 326
　　　Setting up coordinate system 325
　　　Spooler 324
　　　Text on screen 98 - 115
Push buttons 206, 213

R

Radio buttons 206, 213
Region 177 - 181
　　　Clipping 183
　　　Deleting 111
register__window 18
Resource compiler 38, 45 - 46
Resource file 7, 38
　　　Accelarator table 82
　　　Cursor 44
　　　Dialog boxes 208 - 210
　　　Icon 69
　　　Menus 39 - 41, 69 - 70
　　　String table 281 - 282

S

Screen size 115
Scrolling 115, 165, 283 - 293
　　　Adding scroll bars 283 - 284
　　　Messages 142 - 144
　　　Thumb 283
　　　Thumb position 285 - 286
　　　Thumb range 284 - 285
　　　Window 286 - 287
String resource table 281 - 282
System configuration 320 - 323
　　　Default printing device 321
　　　Devices 321
　　　Reading 322
System menu
　　　Changing 299 - 300
　　　Messages 144

System resources 234 - 248
System time 142

T

Text 98 - 118, 129 - 130
    Accounting for screen size 115
    Character size 113 - 114
    Color 116 - 117
    Determining length 112
    Formatting 100, 129 - 130
    Metrics 113 - 115
    Tracking location 99, 112, 115
Text control boxes 206
Text entry boxes 206, 214 - 215
Timer 297 - 298
    Messages 142
    Starting 297
    Stopping 298

V

Variable types 30 - 32
Viewport 162 - 168

W

WIN.INI 320 - 323, see also WIN.INI
Window 162 - 168
Windows
    Application area 158
    Child 293 - 296
    Clearing 182
    Closing 135
    Destroying 136
    Disabling 302
    Enabling 302
    Initializing 136
    Messages 135 - 137
    Overlapping 30
    System area 158
    Updating 135
Windows.h 24
WinMain 10, 11 - 17

Y

Yielding 300 - 303

COMMAND INDEX

& (Menus) 42
?PLM 262
?WIN 263
ACCELERATORS 82
Arc 175
assumes 263
BitBlt 372
cBegin 265
cCall 266
cEnd 265
ChangeMenu 66
CheckDlgButton 213
CheckMenuItem 62
CheckRadioButton 213
CloseClipboard 339
CloseMetaFile 199
CombineRgn 179
CopyMetaFile 199
cProc 263
CreateBitmap 382
CreateCompatibleBitmap 377
CreateCompatibleDC 371
CreateDC 323
CreateDialogBox 211
CreateEllipticRgn 179
CreateEllipticRgnIndirect 179
CreateFontIndirect 110
CreateHatchBrush 169
CreateMenu 68
CreateMetaFile 198
CreatePen 168
CreatePolygonRgn 178
CreateRectRgn 177
CreateRectRgnIndirect 178
CreateSolidBrush 169
CreateWindow 14
CURSOR 44

DefWindowProc 23
DeleteDC 323
DeleteMetaFile 200
DeleteObject 111
DestroyWindow 296
DIALOG 208
DialogBox 212
DispatchMessage 17
DlgDirList 216
DlgDirSelect 217
DPtoLP 182
DrawMenuBar 67
DrawText 129
Ellipse 175
EmptyClipboard 337
EnableMenuItem 65
EnableWindow 302
end 266
EndDialog 212
EnumClipboardFormats 341
Escape(ENDDOC) 325
Escape(NEWFRAME) 325
Escape(NEXTBAND) 332
Escape(SETABORTPROC) 331
Escape(STARTDOC) 324
fileclose 245
fileread 245
filewrite 245
FillRect 174
FillRgn 181
FloodFill 177
FrameRect 174
FrameRgn 181
GetBitmapBits 382
GetBkColor 117
GetClientRect 115
GetClipboardData 339
GetDC 98
GetDeviceCaps 326
GetDlgItemInt 214
GetDlgItemText 215
GetInstanceData 83
GetMenu 61

GetMenuString 68
GetMessage 16
GetMetaFile 199
GetObject 380
GetPixel 171
GetProfileString 322
GetScrollPos 286
GetScrollRange 284
GetStockObject 22
GetSystemMenu 300
GetTempFileName 244
GetTextColor 117
GetTextExtent 112
GetTextMetrics 113
GetViewportExt 167
GetViewportOrg 167
GetWindowExt 167
GetWindowOrg 167
GlobalAlloc 235
GlobalFree 237
GlobalLock 236
GlobalRealloc 238
GlobalUnlock 237
HIWORD 112
ICON 69
InvalidateRect 293
IsDlgButtonChecked 214
KillTimer 298
LineTo 172
lmemcpy 274
LoadAccelerators 83
LoadCursor 20
LoadIcon 21
LoadString 282
LocalAlloc 235
LocalB 266
LocalCP 266
LocalD 266
LocalDP 266
LocalFree 237
LocalLock 236
LocalQ 266
LocalRealloc 237

LocalT 266
LocalUnlock 236
LocalW 266
LOWORD 112
LPtoDP 183
MAKEPOINT 138
MakeProcInstance 210
memC 262
memH 262
memL 262
memM 262
memS 262
MENU 39
MENUBARBREAK 41
MENUITEM 39
MENUITEM SEPARATOR 41
MessageBox 278
MoveTo 171
OFF_ 265
OpenClipboard 337
OpenFile 242
PaintRgn 181
parmB 264
parmCP 264
parmD 264
parmDP 264
parmQ 264
parmT 264
parmW 264
PeekMessage 302
Pie 176
PlayMetaFile 200
Polygon 175
Polyline 172
POPUP 39
PostMessage 296
PtInRegion 180
rcinclude 207
Rectangle 173
RegisterClass 20
RegisterClipboardFormat 340
ReleaseCapture 138
ReleaseDC 98

RoundRect 174
sBegin 263
ScrollWindow 286
SEG__ 265
SelectClipRgn 183
SelectObject 111
sEnd 266
SendDlgItemMessage 217
SendMessage 296
SetBkColor 116
SetCapture 138
SetClassWord 59
SetClipboardData 337
SetCursor 58
SetDlgItemInt 214
SetDlgItemText 215
SetMapMode 162
SetMenu 69
SetPixel 170
SetScrollPos 285
SetScrollRange 285
SetTextColor 116
SetTimer 297
SetViewportExt 166
SetViewportOrg 166
SetWindowExt 167
SetWindowOrg 166
ShowWindow 16
StretchBlt 373
STRINGTABLE 281
TextOut 99
TranslateAccelerator 84
TranslateMessage 17
UpdateWindow 16

TYPE AND TABLE INDEX

Clipboard formats 337 - 338
Combine styles 375 - 376
Coordinate systems 159
Cursors 20
Debugging 303 - 304
Dialog box features 209
File open options 242 - 243
Icons 21
List box commands 218 - 220
LOGFONT 108 - 110
Mapping modes 159
Memory models 274 - 275
Menu options 41
Menu edit options 67
POINT 138
Printer errors 384
RECT 115
RGB 116
TEXTMETRIC 113 - 114
Scroll bar commands 143
System menu messages 144
Types 31 - 32
    Font 32
    General 31
    Graphics 31
    Prefixes 32
    System 31
Window types 294 - 295
WNDCLASS 19

Windows Guide Diskette

by Michael I. Hyman

Save yourself hours of development time and get complete code listings with: **the Windows Guide Diskette**. Contains all the programs in this book, in source and ready to run form. A two-disk set.

TWO DISKS: ONLY $25.00 !!

The Advanced DOS Guide Diskette

Contains valuable disk utilities with complete source code! You can: PROTECT your hard disk from accidental reformatting, EXPLORE disks and get back erased files, DIRECTLY examine and edit all sectors on disks, RENAME DOS commands, and much much more!!!

ONLY $20.00

FAILSAFE

An extremely powerful utility for DOS program developers. You can: BREAK programs out of endless loops, RECOVER text files lost in RAM, get back NEWed BASIC files, and EXAMINE and EDIT any part of RAM at any time. Saves hours of debugging time.

ONLY $49.95

☐ YES! I want to master WINDOWS PROGRAMMING with the WINDOWS GUIDE DISKETTE!

☐ YES! I want POWERFUL DISK utilities, with the ADVANCED DOS GUIDE DISKETTE!

☐ YES! I want to save hours of development time, with FAILSAFE!

ENCLOSED IS A CHECK OR MONEY ORDER. PLEASE MAKE ALL CHECKS PAYABLE TO: MICHAEL I. HYMAN.

NAME: _____
COMPANY: _____
ADDRESS: _____
CITY_____ STATE_____ ZIP_____

SEND TO:
Princeton Software Group
11500 Homewood Road
Ellicott City, MD 21043
Attn: Michael Hyman

Outside USA and CANADA: Add $5 for air mail shipping.
INVOICES and COD: Add $5 for handling.

RELATED TITLES IN THE MIS: PRESS PROGRAMMER SERIES

MEMORY RESIDENT UTILITIES, INTERRUPTS, AND DISK MANAGEMENT WITH MS AND PC DOS
An indispensable resource for serious DOS programmers. Includes chapters on disk data storage, BIOS and DOS interrupts, utility programming, and memory-resident utilities.
Michael Hyman 0-943518-73-3 $22.95 Book/Disk: $44.95

ASSEMBLY LANGUAGE INTERFACING IN TURBO PASCAL
Allows Turbo Pascal programmers to bring the power and speed of assembly language code to their programs. Includes an assembly language primer and reference section, communications and graphics routines, Turbo Pascal inline machine code, and several ready-to-use routines.
Sanjiva Nath 0-943518-25-3 $20.95 Book/Disk: $40.95

LINEAR AND DYNAMIC PROGRAMMING WITH LOTUS 1-2-3 RELEASE 2
Explains and illustrates the basic concepts of Linear and Dynamic Programming within the Lotus 1-2-3 spreadsheet environment, with numerous examples from business and industry.
James Ho 0-943518-72-5 $19.95 Book/Disk: $39.95

TURBO PROLOG FEATURES FOR PROGRAMMERS
Explores the limits of Turbo Prolog's possibilities and provides programmers with numerous ready-to-use routines.
Sanjiva Nath 0-943518-68-7 $22.95

dBASE III PLUS NETWORKING AND MULTI-USER SYSTEMS
Includes a discussion of the benefits and limitations of networking, accessing mainframe data through a network, and step-by-step programming instructions for developing applications and installing the dBASE III Plus network.
Joseph-David Carrabis 0-943518-26-1 $20.95 Book/Disk: $40.95

dBASE III PLUS POWER TOOLS
Outlines integrating data into spreadsheets and documents, accessing mainframe data, installing memory resident utilities, debugging and compiling the program, and expanding dBASE III Plus into a comprehensive computing system.
Rob Krumm 0-943518-66-0 $21.95

SCREEN I/O PROGRAMMING TECHNIQUES USING TURBO PASCAL
Explains how students and professionals alike can write customized applications programs, saving hours of programming time and lending visual appeal and professionalism to programming efforts.
Andy Stuart 0-943518-28-8 $24.95 Book/Disk: $44.95

TURBO C: MEMORY RESIDENT UTILITIES, SCREEN I/O AND PROGRAMMING TECHNIQUES
Covers topics and techniques including memory management, ROM BIOS functions, programming screen input/output, and writing memory-resident utility programs in Turbo C.
Al Stevens 0-943518-35-0 $24.95

C DATA BASE DEVELOPMENT
All the tools programmers need for writing C data base programs—with complete, detailed instructions on how to use them.
Al Stevens 0-943518-33-4 $23.95 Book/Disk: $43.95

*A*vailable where fine books are sold.

MANAGEMENT INFORMATION SOURCE, INC.
P.O. Box 5277 • Portland, OR 97208-5277
(503) 222-2399

*C*all free
1-800-MANUALS

MIS: PRESS

M A N A G E M E N T   I N F O R M A T I O N   S O U R C E ,   I N C .